Science Fiction and Postmodern Fiction

American University Studies

Series XIX
General Literature
Vol. 29

PETER LANG
New York • San Francisco • Bern
Frankfurt am Main • Berlin • Wien • Paris

Barbara Puschmann–Nalenz

Science Fiction and Postmodern Fiction

A Genre Study

PETER LANG
New York • San Francisco • Bern
Frankfurt am Main • Berlin • Wien • Paris

Library of Congress Cataloging-in-Publication Data

Puschmann–Nalenz, Barbara.
    [Science Fiction und ihre Grenzbereiche. English]
    Science fiction and postmodern fiction : a genre
study / Barbara Puschmann–Nalenz.
       p. cm. — (American university studies. Series XIX,
General literature ; vol. 29)
    Translation of: Science Fiction und ihre
Grenzbereiche.
    Includes bibliographical references and index.
    1. Science fiction, American—History and
criticism.   2. American fiction—20th century—
History and criticism.   3. English fiction—20th
century—History and criticism.   4. Science fiction,
English—History and criticism.   5. Postmodernism
(Literature)—United States.   6. Postmodernism
(Literature)—Great Britain. 7. Literary form.
I. Title. II. Series.
PS374.S35P8713   1992   91-21112
ISBN 0-8204-1670-3   CIP
ISSN 0743-6645

Die Deutsche Bibliothek-CIP-Einheitsaufnahme

Puschmann–Nalenz, Barbara:
Science fiction and postmodern fiction : a genre study /
Barbara Puschmann–Nalenz.—New York; Berlin;
Bern; Frankfurt/M.; Paris; Wien: Lang, 1992
  (American university studies : Ser. 19, General
literature ; Vol. 29)
  ISBN 0-8204-1670-3
NE: American university studies / 19

The paper in this book meets the guidelines for permanence and
durability of the Committee on Production Guidelines for
Book Longevity of the Council on Library Resources.

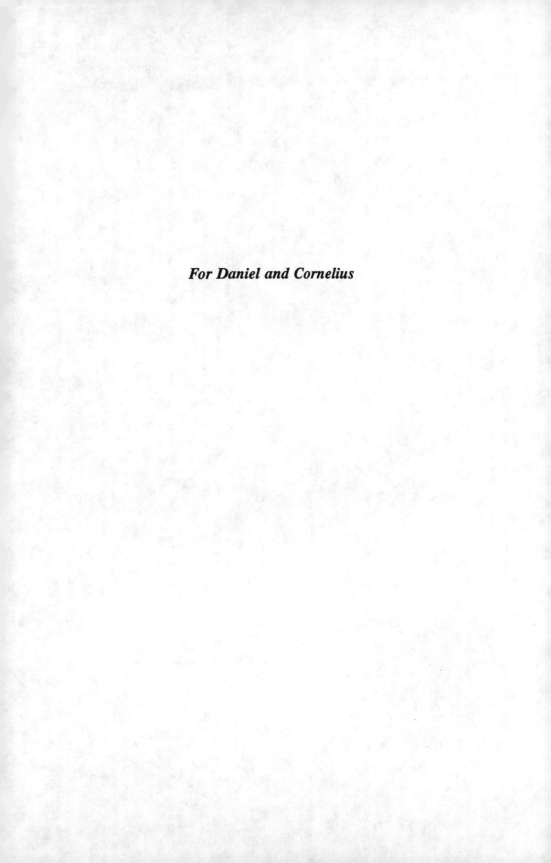

For Daniel and Cornelius

Acknowledgements

I thank Professors U. Broich (Munich) and U. Suerbaum (Bochum) for accompanying the growth of this study by their knowledge and encouragement. Furthermore I wish to express my gratitude to those who by their criticism and advice contributed to its progress, in particular Professors G. Ahrends, H.-J. Diller, W.A. Koch, R. Schiffer, and G. Stratmann of the English Department at Ruhr-Universität Bochum, Professor H.-U. Seeber (Stuttgart), Professor H.J. Schrimpf of the German Department, Professors K. Maurer and J. Schulze of the Department of Romance Philology, and Professor F. Rodi of the Philosophy Department.

I am grateful to my colleague, Dr. James Bean, for accomplishing my translation of the book into English. Finally, I would like to thank Ruhr-Universität Bochum for their support.

For giving permission for the publication in English I wish to thank Dr. Heinrich Wimmer of Corian Verlag Meitingen.

Contents

Preface

This book was translated from the original German by the author. The German title was *Science Fiction und ihre Grenzbereiche. Ein Beitrag zur Gattungsproblematik zeitgenössischer angloamerikanischer Erzählliteratur.* It was published in 1986 by Corian-Verlag Meitingen (Federal Republic of Germany).

Science Fiction and Postmodern Fiction

1. SCIENCE FICTION AND RESEARCH

Introduction

The history of Science Fiction (SF) as an area of academic research and teaching is still a brief one. In a period of not even fifteen years (1965-1980) the landscape of SF-criticism changed completely. This rapid change and the ensuing lack of distance in time form a major difficulty in dealing with this field.

The development in the United States can be considered paradigmatic for the breakthrough of SF in university teaching and research at German universities. As late as 1967 Mark Hillegas published an article entitled "The Course in Science Fiction: a Hope deferred", where he wrote about the difficulties and disappointments involved in his attempt to introduce SF as a teaching subject at the college level.[1] In 1975, however, one could rightly say that "Science Fiction is finding its way into the college curriculum as a new and exciting genre for people to study and enjoy".[2]

The introduction of SF into academic teaching proves that the field has reached a stage of considerable stability. This is even more surprising as only two decades have passed since literary criticism first showed any interest in SF - at first only sporadically, then at a rapidly increasing pace and finally in a real explosion of publications. In 1960 the first comprehensive study of the genre was published, with a survey of its history and a description of its types and forms, written by an author both famous and popular: Kingsley Amis. For several years his book with the promising title *New Maps of Hell*, remained the only critical book-length study on SF. In the meantime it has come to be considered a "classic" of SF-criticism. Amis' definition of SF as the "literature of change" has been varied innumerable times, disputed frequently, and occasionally replaced by something allegedly better; but so far nobody can ignore it who wants to explore and describe this genre and define its distinctive characteristics.[3]

Twelve years later Eike Barmeyer published a widely read collection of critical essays on the theory and history of SF in the FRG. This book was highly significant for the German reading audience and initiated the serious interest of professional literary scholars and critics.[4]

In the meantime the research on SF has made progress. Book-length studies, collections of critical essays, a great number of articles, the foundation of a new journal in the US (*Science Fiction Studies*), and the often-mentioned increase of interest in a periodical that had been founded during the frontier years of SF-criticism (*Extrapolation*) - these and other similar phenomena showed the growing popularity of a field recently discovered for literary scholarship; and in turn they themselves initiated new publications. The themes and subjects of investigation of these studies were problems of the history of the genre, its theory, reception and promotion. Diverse, variegated to the point of anarchy, and very disparate in regard to quality the research on SF presents itself now to the reader as an attractive but also a difficult field. In contrast to the fields of literature written in English which are sanctified by a long tradition SF is an area where there is no consensus on appropriate methods of analysis, on the evaluation of studies already published or on a canon of particularly significant texts.

The published criticism on SF shows a more diversified typology than most areas of research on fiction do and hence it cannot be easily systematized. At present it is correct to say that SF is primarily, but not exclusively, the object of literary criticism and analysis.[5] The scope of publications reaches beyond literary scholarship into the fields of sociology and psychology, and includes a traditional but often tense or ambivalent affinity to futurology;[6] simultaneously, however, there is also a vivid self-presentation of SF and a discussion among authors, editors and readers, which reveals itself in more popular publications for a less academically inclined audience and proves that there are currents between literary scholarship on popular literature in general and SF in particular.

The increasing number of publications on SF testifies to a tendency which also becomes evident in their extending scope: from the periphery SF has been constantly moving to a central position in the interest of a broad readership. At the same time the concept of "literature" has been enlarging, so that serious academic interest in this field has become possible and popular.

The variegated and very diverse reactions to SF are also signs of the changeable position of this literary genre, which continues to be the target of controversy. A large part of published criticism is mostly descriptive, and often either polemic or full of an uncritical enthusiasm characteristic of the "addicts" of this genre; a differentiated and exploratory attitude is seldom to be found. In particular the shaping of a literary theory on SF is still in progress. The long-existent lack of methodological approaches and theoretical concepts was compensated for by the introductions for SF anthologies and collections written by authors and editors who frequently went beyond short prefaces to the literary text(s) and produced instructions for the reader, information on the SF-business and especially definitions of the genre. This procedure is unusual in the modern practice of the publication of fictional texts, which are generally published without a comment. Thus SF possesses a specific form of criticism which implicitly shows that the nature and function of the literary genre need an explanation.

The following survey of SF-criticism is divided according to its typology: prefaces of editors and SF-authors, essays and studies of authors who themselves also write SF, and finally scholarly literary criticism.

This distinction of types of criticism also corresponds to a general chronological development in the history of SF-criticism.

1.1 The Self-Interpretation of Science Fiction

As a rule the self-presentation of SF by its authors, which began long before scholarship on SF, does not use specific critical methods. Most often it does not show much reflection and is rather apologetic; in many cases it has been called mere wishful thinking. Although for the literary scholar its methods of procedure and its results are often not directly useful, these self-interpretations represent very interesting resources for the SF-critic. They form the core of the genre's self-portrait, written by professional authors of SF.

In the development of the past twenty years one can see that the SF-debate led by its authors and editors is losing significance to the same extent that literary criticism has been gaining ground and has assumed the role of an SF-interpreter. For a considerable number of years the comments by SF-authors formed almost the only existing interpretation of the genre.[7]

In spite of the different aims and methods the literary criticism on SF cannot ignore this self-interpretation - as it for a long time took over the critic's role and often attained a considerable level, which was less based upon critical distance than upon a strong and positive commitment. In rare cases we find even today the "personal union" of SF-writer and critic.[8] Even in short prefaces and introductions to editions of SF texts only very few authors are able to resist making some remarks concerning the position and purpose of SF in general; often they even supply a sketchy survey of the history of the genre.[9] The growing popularity of SF and the fact that it is of immediate interest to an increasing number of literary critics are developments which are being noticed with satisfaction or, at times, with distrust. Often the author makes attempts at a new definition of SF in an era of rapid change which has been observed by many authors of prefaces to SF texts.

The definition plays a key role in the theory and interpretation of SF. Hardly a critic thinks that he can dispense with a new attempt at it. The inclination of a number of critics to consider SF a "closed-system genre", is based upon the habit of definition.[10] The tendency to write ever new definitions can be explained, however, as precisely the result of a lack of clear outlines of the genre and of its overlappings - to the point of confusion - with other genres like utopias and dystopias, detective and adventure stories, thrillers and fantasy literature. The need to write down in a definition what the constituents of this genre are is noticeably greater in dealing with SF than with other genres of literary fiction.

SF critics mostly cling to the principle that the core of their analysis of the genre is the definition of its nature, its value and its purpose. In the prefaces this habit has assumed normative functions. Often the texts presented are chosen as models. The danger of a vicious circle is obvious: the given definition is verified by selected texts often written or edited by the author of the introduction, and the scope of these texts is generally not wide enough to be really convincing. The definitions, on the other hand, have to be selective and unambiguous, if only because they have to be short. A differentiated analysis and reflection is hardly possible.[11]

More extensive than in introductions and prefaces to editions of SF texts are the fundamental definitions of the genre in the collections of critical essays in which a number of SF-authors published their theoretical reflections. They mostly appeared in the sixties and introduced the stage of writing that helped SF to a wider forum of discussion.[12]

The volumes edited by Knight and Davenport each make a greater number of SF-authors known to the general audience. It is common to all these contributions that they were published at a time when SF was hardly found worthy of academic attention. They can best be characterized as literary essays, although the requirements they make on the genre, on authors and readers seem very demanding. The contributions to the ongoing debate are generally written in the style of personal opinions. This character of a subjective and belletristic comment is especially typical of Knight's writings on SF. His book resembles more an instruction for SF-addicts or a collection of brilliant aphorisms. The author is involved in an intelligent conversation with his reader, who, because of an equal commitment to the genre is treated as his close friend. Thus an analysis of SF texts is not really intended.

Davenport's volume contains some essays (by Heinlein, Blish, Bester, Kornbluth) which, in analogy to the practice of the prefaces make visible exactly the same apparently irresistible tendency to definitions of SF, very ambitious aims and at times also a pretentious over-estimation of themselves. Especially Heinlein, in a manner that is more typical of propaganda, declares SF to be the only type of modern literature worth reading. He demands from the authors of SF great scientific knowledge and ascribes to the genre a practically unlimited didactic value.

Kornbluth, on the other hand, focuses on the psychological dimensions of SF, its symbolic value and the emotional relief it provides for the reader.[13]

The widespread idea that SF claims to supply a mythology for the space age, which later, partially from different perspectives, was also expressed by Michel Butor and Stanislaw Lem, is first expressed in Kornbluth's essay.[14]

However diverse the hypothetical reflections published in Davenport's collection of essays may be, they all have one notion in common: SF to them is still without exception a genre of popular literature or light fiction. Heinlein is trying to conceal this general devaluation by emphasizing SF's didactic purposes; Blish, Bester and Bloch are concerned with the psychological and social implications of SF as popular literature.

For a reader whose attention mainly focuses on the SF of the sixties and early seventies these interpretations are mainly of historical interest. In retrospect one recognizes in them the fore-runners of a thorough-going SF-criticism, although their own interpretations, demands and evaluations are founded in the SF texts of the forties and fifties. Their appreciation marks a period of evolution, during which SF itself was subjected to a great change in forms and functions and during which it increased in significance, variety and popularity. Therefore it is of great interest that authors like C.S. Lewis, Kingsley Amis and Brian Aldiss said early in 1965 that SF was approaching a new peak of its possibilities; as a "newcomer" its objective should be to loosen its ties to the cultural establishment and promotional purposes of the book trade.[15] The critical essays written by SF-authors between 1959 and 1968 founded a form of SF-criticism as it had been cultivated in the prefaces and partly still exists today: very subjective and not very systematic, but with strict demands on the genre, on its authors and readership. The didactic value of SF is usually rated very highly. The tradition of the fan audience with its unlimited enthusiasm and sometimes missionary zeal is obvious. The writers feel obliged to win followers for a literary art form that is still considered an outsider and still trying to establish a respectable existence with social and literary acknowledgement.

This apologetic attitude is characteristic of the position of a genre which is gaining ground but still lacking in prestige and not yet fully acknowledged. By other critics the parallel to the development of the English novel in the eighteenth century, when it was considered subliterature, has already been pointed out: the writing of prefaces with extensive theoretical and didactic reflections shows corresponding needs and pressures. Other historical parallels for this phenomenon are to be found in Sir Philip Sidney's *Defense of Poesy* or the *Preface to the Lyrical Ballads* by Wordsworth and Coleridge at the beginning of the Romantic period.[16] These examples stood at the beginning of consolidating processes of a particular literary genre, which at that respective point in time were still controversial or had only a minor reputation. The attempt to legitimate the genre, analyses of its existing imperfections and normative claims and demands - all these are signals of an unrest but also of the dynamic development of the genre in this early stage of its development.

In the years after 1968 the debate about the position and the functions of SF became more violent. Especially the relationship to other genres moved into the centre of the discussions. While James Blish (under the pseudonym Wm. Atheling) in his book *More Issues at Hand* (1970) demands that SF should no longer exclude itself from literature and seek a development outside literature and its criticism, J. Russ (1975) again decidedly insisted on SF-criticism as having completely different standards from those applied to the interpretation of other literary works.[17] The wish of some critics to underline the literary quality of SF is thus contrasted with the fear of others that SF might lose its distinctive character and blur the identity of the genre.

Simultaneous with these contrasting opinions was the criticism of the *New Wave* authors Ballard and Moorcock. Although both have remained controversial and in many instances were not fully acknowledged by the more numerous writers of "SF proper" the violence of the debate that they initiated indicated the degree to which they represented a danger and were considered a menace to the established SF-authors and their self-respect.

Of these two Ballard is the more imaginative and more progressive, both in regard to the SF he writes and to the theoretical conception of the present and future possibilities of this genre.

The decisive turning point in relation to the existing theory centers around Ballard's departure from what he contemptuously calls "retrospective literature", including in his view all the SF which so far had appeared. He demands from the genre that it fulfil the requirements of its definition as "prospective literature" and reflect in its narrative techniques its theme - the future. The outside world, especially that of the future, should be transposed into an inside world - that of the mind; instead of "outer space" the dimension of "inner space" should become decisive.[18]

When Ballard in his "Remarks from Zero point" and his essay "The Coming of the Unconscious"[19] seems to completely turn away from SF and wants to combine psychoanalytical concepts with the stylistic means of surrealism to produce a new, the "true SF", then this is the solution for a problem underlying the whole genre: Ballard defines SF radically with the concept of the future. But what is "future literature" - written by an author of the present for readers of the present? Ballard and with him Moorcock have refused numerous times to acknowledge space and technological progress as the constituent element of the future and the literature of the future; instead they identify the "New Poetry" with "time and human consciousness and with the philosophy of science."[20]

The "future literature" ought to be "evolutionary" and "prospective". "It rejects the conventional novel as well as conventional Science Fiction" (op.cit., p. 88). Moorcock consequently, though rather immodestly, calls himself a "revolutionary".[21]

The theories of the "revolutionaries" were rejected by the critics. Certainly this was partly caused by Moorcock's and Ballard's elitist arrogance, which as a result led to the partly angry, partly sarcastic reaction of the established authors. There are, however, other and more important reasons for the violent attacks on Moorcock and Ballard. The supposedly conclusive evaluation which Brian Aldiss made in his history of SF - that the New Wave is in reality a "New Ripple" - is not quite appropriate. It underestimates the initial effect which was created by troublemakers like Ballard and Moorcock.[22] They could not be successful with their elitist and eccentric ideas, but they did manage to put a finger on a sore spot. As a consequence much in SF was set into motion which in its effects and indirect results can be traced back to their provocative statements (see also chapter 3).

Finally the seventies brought a number of publications by authors of SF: several collections of essays,[23] the widely acclaimed *True History of Science Fiction* by Brian Aldiss[24] and the critical essays by Stanislaw Lem. Lem's writings got much attention in Anglo-American and British SF-criticism because they are based on a thorough knowledge of American SF in particular and often appeared as articles in American and sometimes German periodicals or collections of essays.

The volumes edited by Bretnor and Clareson, on the other hand, reflect a landscape that is very different from that of the earlier years. The thematic scope as well as the role of SF in other media, the publishing and editing business, new trends in SF, European SF as well as SF in teaching - these themes and stances reveal, in comparison to those of the fifties and sixties, more open and diversified perspectives. Authors representing the fringes and extremes of the genre are also included, e.g. Merrill, Delany, Vonnegut, and Spinrad.

At this point SF begins to relate more closely to other literary and non-literary phenomena and gives up its position in a literary ghetto, which it held for a long time, sometimes voluntarily, sometimes on account of external circumstances. This rapid liberalization is contradicted and opposed, and in the collections of essays mentioned above we find many contributions with traditional topics and intentions. Generally, however, there is an obvious tendency in SF-criticism for the emphasis to shift from apologetic and normative statements to exploratory and descriptive analysis, in the critical writing of SF-authors as well as in other critics.

Aldiss' *Billion Year Spree*, a history of SF in which its recent development is traced back to the origins in the Gothic Novel and Mary Shelley's *Frankenstein*, brilliantly exemplifies the well-read, sophisticated, at times rather casual, approach of the insider. Often original, encyclopaedic in his familiarity with authors and their works, and sometimes necessarily biased, Aldiss writes a comprehensive and in his knowledge of the material really overwhelming history of SF. Compared with the primary literature he writes, his concept of the genre in this book is well-balanced and rather conservative. He seems ironical and reserved in regard to experimental developments and decidedly claims authors whose generic category is controversial, e.g. Vonnegut, for SF.

Aldiss hypothetically anticipates a convergence of different genres of fiction for the near future. In contrast to the "separatists", who still want to consider the genre in isolation from other types of fiction, Aldiss represents those critics who announce a diversification inside SF itself and a convergence, on the other hand, of the different fictional genres, with the resulting open and flexible boundaries.[25]

The eminent intellectual among SF-authors - and in some respects a renegade from the most recent development in criticism - is now Stanisław Lem.[26] Lem's rational procedure and his variously demonstrated ability to combine the analysis of SF texts and the exploration of certain motifs with the development of theoretical reflections, make him particularly significant in the view of many scholars. Through interviews and discussions in the media he has become well-known in Western Europe.

Lem's precision in dealing with texts, succesfully combined with his speculative capacity, impresses the reader and his attempt to avoid the prejudice critics often show is helpful. As a result of a thorough examination of Lem's publications, one nevertheless recognizes that he sometimes reverts to almost obsolete positions.

One of them is the reproachful attitude towards SF-authors that had been so common in former years and had been superseded by more recent developments. Although this is typical of an early stage of SF-criticism, the reader will find it again, together with dogmatic terms and conditions for SF-writers about what SF really ought to be and the general reproach that no SF text could fulfil this expectation.

The aim of "proper" - that is ideal - SF as Lem sees it is to supply a forecast of scientific and social developments. This, however, was already termed "Gernsback delusion", because it had its roots in the early stages of modern SF.[27]

Lem's dogmatic demands in regard to the genre correspond with his global condemnation of modern SF. In his articles published between 1972 and 1974 he repeatedly expressed his reproaches of a lack of logical coherence and argumentative precision in the texts, a lack of probability and of "alternate thinking" in SF, which, he felt, only contains either the obsolete or the fantastic ("what we usually find is not what may happen tomorrow but the forever impossible, not the real but the fairy-tale like"[28]). Finally Lem criticizes the "paralysis of SF in the sociological sphere"[29] and generally its "referential nature", its "cultural ethnocentricity".

The criticism that SF only alternates between "Midland City" and "cloud cuckoo land" is not only brought forward by Lem. Michel Butor comes to the same conclusion in a delightful allegory:

> SF has given up the basis of its existence, has ruined thousands of ideas. The gates have been opened wide to let out the adventurous knights, but it turns out that they have only walked around the house.[30]

For Lem Science Fiction, if measured by its own principles, to which he also subscribes, is too provincial, paralyzed, unenlightened, and childish. The published SF texts, he sums up, "are intellectually uninspiring".[31] The genre turns out to be incapable - and therefore unworthy, according to Lem - of doing justice to its given task and true mission: to create an alternate reality by means of creative and imaginative abstraction. The weaknesses of SF criticized by Lem have been observed by many readers of SF texts. The lack of ideas presented in numerous texts as well as the frequent magnifying of one single idea to novel-length, the often annoying redundancy and need for variation and finally the trite ideas which contain scarcely any intellectually inspiring conceptions are all too familiar to the SF-reader. Lem's criticism is based on his own conception of the SF-genre, the most important principles of which are:

1. SF has to be rich in ideas and able to imagine a future which is an extrapolation of the preconditions we find in present developments.
2. These creations of the imagination have to be rational and logical; mythological principles of thinking - which for Lem are the same as wild fantasies - have no place in SF.
3. The expectations of the readers have to be very high, intellectually and speculatively.
4. SF is a very special area and must continue to exist as such.
5. Theoretical reflections on SF have to make progress; this is the first step towards the fulfilling of the above-mentioned normative principles.

The first three of these guidelines show a remarkable similarity to the less systematical and analytical theories that predominated for a long time. Their drawback is primarily the contemptuous neglect of the genre SF as a part of fiction. Lem also ignores this affiliation, when he declares cognitive, moral and didactic purposes alone valid for his concept of SF texts. Although this dogmatism and emphasized intellectualism is very inspiring for a certain group of readers, it is inimical to the aspects of playful entertainment and SF as a game which are also characteristic.

In spite of his theoretical positions Lem has obviously only little confidence in the literary use of language, in narrating and its different methods and effects - an attitude which can be reconciled with his own very successful activity as an author of SF, only because in appropriating his theories he made a number of compromises which do not fit into his abstract reflections, but are very convincing to his reading audience. In theory and in the analysis of other SF texts he is not concerned with narrative characteristics or with the interaction of object, themes and their presentation. One of Lem's critics therefore rightly remarks:

> basically he is not interested in structures of representation but in the structures of the represented: the world described. He is not interested in literature, but in the reality represented there, reconstructed in regard to its epistemological and prognostic values.[32] (my translation)

Lem applies to SF texts the measures of scientific justifiability and the sense of moral responsibility. An SF which could fulfil his demands would to a large extent have to renounce its character of telling an entertaining story; the playful element would then have to follow strict rules.

Stanislaw Lem contributes more to the development of the theory of SF than other writers. The reason for the great response he finds is less to be seen in his self-assumed role of a prophet than in the clear-sightedness and precision of his textual analysis and the inexorable questioning of the generic conventions. The danger of a progressive erosion of the genre by the mechanization of its motifs is undeniably inherent in the development of modern SF. Lem's absorption in problems of the theory of science and philosophical questions also functions as a stimulus for new questions in other authors and critics and expands the horizon of SF by one full dimension. These qualities make Lem's positions appear "modern" in comparison to other critics' opinions; that is to say in spite of his return to claims which seemed to have become obsolete they appear appropriate for the present situation of the genre.

In "On the Structural Analysis of Science Fiction" Lem takes one step towards consideration of the specifically literary nature of SF texts. More than before the relation between reality and a fictitious alternate reality and especially the process of a transformation of reality and fiction come into the foreground. Using his earlier critical approach Lem introduces the search for structural analogies which combine reality, alternate reality and interpretation. Here we find the beginning of a more differentiated development of his theoretical position. One can also assume that some of the texts which appeared in the seventies have somehow mitigated Lem's negative impression of contemporary SF.

1.2 Recent SF-Criticism

Studies written in English during the past few years primarily show a tendency towards the consolidation of the position of SF in modern cultural life. The area has become an accepted field for teaching and research, whose popularity can be recognized for example by the publication of SF-criticism in the well-known series "Twentieth Century Views".[33] The same academic usefulness is typical of the introductions to SF written by Allen and Scholes & Rabkin.[34]

The purpose of these books is clear: they were written for students of literature and popular culture. Scholes and Rabkin provide guidelines for the study of SF, but do not always fulfil their own promise of writing an introduction.

The type of publication that is best represented by articles for journals is necessarily selective; the limited length alone prevents a comprehensive study. This, however, corresponds to the present situation of the SF-debate, because it offers to the authors the possibility of officially conforming to the fact that their field has begun to develop recently and is changing fast. Of course it is also easier to avoid difficulties and contradictions in the field of research in short contributions than in book-length studies; in short publications it is not necessary to quote and debate well-known and worn definitions of the genre and its dogmas.

Very seldom have the theory of SF and its critical methods been the central theme of a publication in the form of an article.[35] Here therefore research does not progress as fast as the numerous publications on SF in recent years seem to suggest. Therefore in British and Anglo-American SF-criticism an attempt that was made in this direction has to be mentioned, which in spite of its length bears the modest title *Essay on the Fiction of the Future*.[36]

This book cannot deny its origin - it was first conceived as a series of lectures. It is composed of parts in which Scholes tries to design a structuralist theory of SF which he bases on examples from recent SF.

The innovative element in this study is the attempt to apply the instruments of a specific system of literary theory - structuralism -[37] to SF. The most obvious characteristic of SF-criticism has been for a long time a lack of methods and conceptions - a phenomenon that is typical of new literary fields. With a more systematic exploration the wish for methodological controls grows. Scholes undertakes the courageous and innovative attempt to apply a critical method to a subject that is still underdeveloped. If nevertheless he is not successful, that is to say does not achieve a thorough analysis with consequent understanding of SF texts, the reason for this lies not only in the very loose and sometimes inexplicable course of the argumentation, but equally in the deficiencies of his critical method. With his intentions of clarifying the aims of fiction in general, the nature of myth and fairy-tale, the function of the fiction of the future in contemporary reality and - last but not least - the difference between reality and fiction, the author is trying to achieve far too much, at least in my opinion. The fascination stimulated by a potentially universal method for general application like structuralism in this case leads to imaginative, but in its present form aphoristic statements (for example about the differences between conceptual and verbal alienation or about the analogy between Science and Science Fiction). In contrast to some interesting observations we also find empty phraseology (e.g. "Structural Man", "Structural Fabulation") which appears more trendy than meaningful. Generally it has to be said that Scholes does not achieve a successful combination of theory and interpretation. The application of a cultural and philosophical theory to concrete SF texts is revealed as too complicated, if one is not prepared to sacrifice a broad selection of texts and a great precision of analysis. Scholes restricts himself to exemplifying his hypotheses with a small number of texts. Because of the resulting predicament he at times withdraws to dogmas and requirements primarily of a didactic nature that are well-known to the reader of older SF-criticism.

As a result Scholes is torn between the principles of the traditional normative understanding of the genre and the descriptive methods of structuralism. What is achieved is a mixture of demands, suppositions, and exact observations. What is missing is mainly a critical examination of the SF texts and especially of a greater number of them, which alone can help to separate meaningfully recurrent elements from mere accidents or individual predilections of the authors.

The more recent criticism on SF[38] introduces the seventies by a rather devastating book: Pehlke / Lingfeld, *Roboter und Gartenlaube: Ideologie und Unterhaltung in der Science Fiction-Literatur*. The study is an attempt to reveal the "false consciousness" of authors and readers of SF from a Marxist point-of-view and to expose the mechanisms of the capitalistic cultural business. The studies by Horst Schröder, H. Linck and Martin Schäfer continue in the exploration of SF as a literature of triviality and mass consumption.[39]

Other full-length publications on the German market essentially belong to one of three categories: literary criticism, especially in the direction of a typology of SF-motifs, collections of essays with a great variety of articles by German and American, or British authors, and finally introductions that appeal partly to the general public, partly to the teacher.

This last type of publication has been expanding since the early seventies.[40] The opening up of new audiences for SF and the use they make of it as a recent and popular field of research are reflected in this increase. In the studies dating from the seventies we find new perspectives and methods of analysis as well as new results. SF is treated not only as a literary, but as a cultural phenomenon, which is evident in the articles on SF in the different media and in those about the tactics of the entertainment business.[41] A wide thematic scope is covered, and reading from the ideological contents of SF to a catalogue of its most widespread motifs. It is the explicit intention of these publications to follow the principle of supplying every reader with new ideas.

Vera Graaf's study *Homo Futurus*[42] combines an introduction to the genre - under aspects as diverse as history, definitions and marketing - with discussions of its typology and especially with analysis of SF-motifs whose objective it is to question or describe images of the world and of man. The dominant systematic principle in this study is the opposition "utopian" vs. "dystopian".[43]

Graaf's book primarily fulfils the function of a description and is inclined towards simplifications. Its most important contribution lies in the extensive description of an up to now only infrequently considered analogy between the history or rather mythological history of the United States and the SF produced in this country. Utopian SF is interpreted as history of the US and the American image of the American's historical past.[44]

The book by J. Hienger *Studie über Science Fiction*[45] puts the emphasis on the themes and motifs of SF and their common ground in the idea of change ("Veränderungsdenken"). The experiments in which SF finds such intellectual pleasure are a consequence of the presumed fundamental uncertainty of the future.

The first part of Hienger's study is dedicated to an examination of the material and cognitive components of SF[46] and is followed by a discussion of the principles of the genre. In spite of the author's extensive textual knowledge, which is obvious throughout his book, the explorations of the second part are not equal to those of the first in coherence and analytical precision. The role of narrative conventions, the interaction between the material for the game and its rules are less thoroughly explored than the various extensions of the motifs. In contrast to the first part the chapters about the literary rules of the game are of less analytical than descriptive nature. Hienger's statements about rationality as the procedure of Science Fiction, through which, according to him, the fantastic becomes explicable, about the assimilation of the conventions of the novel of adventure and the lack of clear boundaries between SF, *weird fiction* and horror literature, point to some of the most important gaps in SF-research and stimulate a further development of its theory.

In regard to its thematic scope and abundance of material Hienger's study is the most important publication of the seventies which applies methods of literary criticism to the research on SF.[47] The author's abandonment of normative and therefore controversial definitions, instead of which a temporarily open concept of the genre and a descriptive and analytical exploration are applied, turns out to be useful, considering the result.

At the same time, however, the limits of a typological study that focuses on the motifs of SF become visible: it works only in one dimension and can be extended but it cannot change its direction or achieve an additional dimension. A system of different points of reference, by means of which the correlations of the numerous elements can be worked out according to their significance, would be more suitable for finding an answer to open questions.

The effect of the collection of critical essays published by E. Barmeyer in 1972 lies less in the weight and the importance of single contributions than in the pragmatic value of such a collection of otherwise not easily available fundamental articles on SF.

The thematic scope of the book is considerable. In accordance with the sub-title of the first edition its main emphasis is on "theory and history"; "history" in connection with SF is often used synonymously for genealogy. But various SF-authors and historical trends are also discussed, as well as different SF-motifs. Contributions on Eastern European SF open up less well-known fields. - The approaches displayed here are as diverse as the themes of the contributions. The book reveals SF as the object of interdisciplinary area studies: beside literary criticism we also find essays with psychological, scientific and sociological aspects.

Of these essays those by Butor, Suvin and Blish are the most significant concerning the theory of SF from the perspective of the literary critic.[48] Butor's invitation to SF to be what it is according to its destination - and his interpretation - not only seems idealistic and far from reality, but inadequate, if measured against the reality of the texts. He demands the abolition of the playful character of SF and its function of entertainment, the latter being for him inferior in value and therefore not worth preserving. Butor, one of the founders and main representatives of the French *Nouveau Roman*, comes close to the internal criticism of SF described above, especially that of S. Lem, by the catalogue of demands and characteristics. James Blish, author of the "Epilogue to Prophecy" ("Nachruf auf die Prophetie") in the volume edited by Barmeyer, is a well-known SF-author and at the same time one of its earliest critics. In his article he denies all prognostic value to SF and also the often presumed close connection to technology. He sees two reasons for SF's abandonment of classical science: one is the turning away of contemporary SF from scientific and technological devices, and the second is the growing convergence between the sciences - especially astronomy and theoretical physics - and philosophy. The pragmatic and futurological functions of SF disappear; its role as a modern medium of free speculation is increasingly assumed by the sciences themselves.

It is Blish's opinion that SF still retains a didactic role which in Hienger's words can epigrammatically be called "Exercises in Ideas about Change" ("Einübung in das Veränderungsdenken"). It serves cognitive purposes through the method of aesthetic pleasure and thus forms a source of speculative experience in the intellectual dimension. By this capacity it is superior to so-called serious fiction, which - the author says - is essentially retrospective and conservative. This quality also enables SF to contribute significantly to the shaping of the future.

In spite of considerable differences the articles by Butor and Blish both document the continuation of SF's fundamental discussion in the traditional manner: written by enthusiasts they reflect the reception of SF in large circles of intellectual readers for whom besides a particular interest in the field and the need for entertainment the intellectual concern with the shaping of the future forms a special attraction.

Thus it is more a moralistic and didactic impulse - besides the personal involvement of the SF-author - that has always produced this type of criticism. That it has not disappeared is proved by the contributions of Blish and Butor as well as by Lem's articles discussed above.

The title of Darko Suvin's essay "On the Poetics of the Science Fiction Genre" announces a perspective and a program that are maintained in the course of his comments. For the literary scholar this is one of the most innovative and inspiring contributions of the past few years.[49]

It consists of four sections, each of which also bears a headline:
1. "Science Fiction as literature (alienation)",
2. "Science Fiction as knowledge (criticism and science)",
3. "Science Fiction as a literary genre (functions and models)",
4. "For the poetics of Science Fiction (summary and anticipation)".

Suvin is the first critic to plead with determination and with plausible reasons for an interpretation of SF as one literary genre among others, and who attempts to examine its specific procedures and its functions. He defines it as "literature of cognitive estrangement" (p. 86); for

> factual presentations of fictions have the effect of a confrontation of a given normative system [...] with a viewpoint or perspective implying a new set of norms. (p. 88)

With reference to the formalists and to Brecht Suvin modifies the traditional concept of alienation for SF; instead of the "strange view" (Brecht), Suvin says, SF alienates by its *"formal frame"* (p. 89).

The results of the attempt to define borderlines between SF and mythology, fairy-tales, *gothic* and *weird fiction* as well as pastoral poetry are not quite convincing. The method of comparison and contrast, however, proves to be an effective means of differentiation for SF-research.

In the third section of the essay Suvin outlines some of the functions and conventions of the genre that according to the author are "highly interesting and significant for the theory as well as the history of literature" (p. 93), but which so far have not been thoroughly explored. Science Fiction as the literature of the non-empirical world, as diagnosis and guideline to future actions, finally as the "drawing of maps for possible alternatives" (p. 95), uses, in Suvin's opinion, instead of the extrapolation of the empirical world more and more often analogy as a model of imaginative creations. This hypothesis abolishes the "Gernsback delusion", which had formerly been repeatedly maintained or prescribed, especially by S. Lem. Suvin, however, is not satisfied with the negation of the prognostic quality of SF; instead of a linear continuation or homology between SF-world and empirical world he claims an analogy between the two territories. The worlds of SF form "their own literary republics [...], which, it is true, lead back to the republic of man - but in their own way" (p. 96). At the highest levels of such model analogies SF texts and mainstream writing overlap, according to the author.[50]

In the last section of the article Suvin sums up his explanations and conclusively makes claims to future literary criticism of SF, the most important of which is "that it has to be based upon those features that characterize the genre" (p. 101), because this is the only way to precisely distinguish between SF and nonfiction on the one hand[51] and "the empirical mainstream of fiction" on the other hand.

Suvin's hypotheses, more than other articles, reveal the gaps in SF-criticism and theory; they also inspire the ensuing research. Possible directions in which this research could develop are the clarification of the relation between the empirical and the imaginary world, which Suvin tries to grasp with the concept of an alienation that is typical of SF and the concept of analogy, as well as the disclosure of procedures, narrative conventions and functions of SF. Besides these aims the methodological approaches introduced by Suvin as means to attain these aims are worth considering: defining SF in contrast to other literary genres in order to distinguish it; the exploration of the genre "from the top to the bottom" (p. 102), because at the top its principles reveal themselves more distinctly and more purely than in the lower ranks.

Suvin's hypotheses first show clearly that the fundamental discussions of SF can appropriately take place also on the basis of literary criticism. The question of generic distinctions and the crossing of borderlines then becomes very important.

Traditionally this problem was dealt with in connection with SF-genetics, but this inevitably leads to new problems:

> Where does the history of SF start? - There are two well-known answers to this question, which point out fundamental differences in the conception of the genre.
> One is: in Greek antiquity with Lucian of Samosate [...]
> The other answer is: on 5 April 1926, with the publication of the first volume of *Amazing Stories* [...][52]

Among the representatives of the second group, who emphasize the autonomy of SF and its uniqueness, are very well-known authors like Heinlein and Russ.

During the past few years, however, one trend in SF-criticism has gained ground which instead of a chronological approach chooses the synchronic comparison with other genres as its starting point for doing research on SF. The roots of this trend are to be found, at least partly, in the sociology of literature.[53] These critics start from the idea that the audience will receive SF in the same way as other genres of popular literature, e.g. thriller and spy novel, detective and western novel.[54] In some works of criticism the attempt has been made to compare SF with contemporary non-trivial fiction. Ketterer, in doing this, uses Leslie Fiedler's approach and also Northrop Frye's: with the mythological concept of the "apocalypse" otherwise contrasting texts are connected with each other.[55]

This concept proved to be inadequate, because it lacks discriminating qualities. Nevertheless Ketterer's approach, for finding a common basis for a comparison by themes that connect the different genres, is meaningful; in numerous modern SF texts of the *New Wave* it becomes predominant.[56] In the remarkably short time of not quite twenty years SF-criticism has gone a considerable way: from its defense by *addicts*, as Kingsley Amis called even himself, to systematic exploratory criticism in the scope of other areas of literary scholarship. None of the types of criticism has completely vanished. Even today the internal discussion continues and resembles a brilliant, though loosely connected collection of thoughts on SF. The variety of SF-criticism is preserved in spite of a recognizable progressive development.

1.3 The Aims of this Study

This study attempts to distinguish itself from two directions of the published research, whose extremes can best be illustrated in contours by an analysis of two representatives.

1. One is the trend that is especially strong in German criticism of discussing SF from commercial and thematic points of view and classifying it without exception as a branch of mass literature serving escapist and conformist purposes:

> If mass literature is conceived here as conformist literature this is not done in the same sense as Walter Nutz used this term. The idea of conformism here refers to the fact that the content of this literature has to be adequate to promote conformist purposes of governmental control; that is, it implies a far-reaching neglect of aesthetic aspects and the direct or indirect propagation of ideology for the legitimation of existing controlling relationships; it is this idea of conformity which distinguishes this literature as a part of a comprehensive "consciousness industry".[57]

This view of SF as a sociological phenomenon is certainly useful in regard to a part of SF and as a sociographic and empirical method. On the whole, however, it does not do justice to SF. Rather it can be seen as a function of a long prevailing lack of interest of the philologies in mass literature as a whole "in German research, as Nagl in 1970 concedes right at the beginning of his study (op.cit. p. 11). In contrast to this is "the uncomplicated interest of Anglo-Saxon literary scholarship" in SF (p. 81).

If one understands *dime novels* and *pulps* as the only "true" SF neither the real situation of the book market nor the interests of the audience would be correctly depicted.[58] Nagl even quotes such a well-known author as Heinlein (p. 149) in order to support his theses that, first, SF produces "incurably sound literature" and, second

> that the "unscrupulous experiment with the social fear" has remained the true profit of Science Fiction up to the present. It is SF's

contribution to the securing of command and stabilizing function of a technocratic society. (p. 61)

But nevertheless this perspective simply ignores the fact that SF has a much wider scope. In English-speaking countries it is by no means "only the fictional variety of a much broader stream [...] mainly ruling the technological and scientific popular literature and the more prestigious kinds of mass literature." (p. 219). The present study considers desirable for the research on SF that which by the representatives of sociology and by ideological critics is being condemned as a "reduction to literary and stylistic aspects" (op.cit. p. 98). The interpretation of SF with the methods of literary scholarship is certainly not the *delectatio morbosa* of a leisure class (p. 99), but a task that is suitable for literary critics and can only be adequately solved if we use the critical instruments available in the most ingenious ways.

The precondition for this use, however, is the inclusion of the so-called "superior science fiction"[59] which cannot be considered insignificant, but rather has to be seen as exemplary for the genre, as is done by this book. By doing this it continues on a way of criticism that - as the survey of SF-research has already shown - has variously been chosen - by German as well as English-speaking works of criticism - and with considerable partial success. It will more probably lead to further concrete results if the tested approaches and methods of literary criticism and analysis are applied to SF.

2. A second very interesting method of criticism from which this study will differentiate itself, is represented by a book which appeared in 1980, the aim of which is to explore SF as the expression and result of *science*.[60] Significantly this study was published by MIT. It defines SF as "the literary response of the imagination to scientific theory and technological innovation" (p. 1). In doing this it comes close to the well-known apologetic and didactic usage of defining SF from its internal viewpoint. But it takes one further step which is decisive in trying to bridge the gap between "The Two Cultures" - sciences and the humanities.[61]

Warrick's starting point for her book is the following question:

How does the literary imagination exploring cybernetics respond to this challenge of change? Does it move beyond the fascination with gadgets and adventures, typical of early SF, to consider the implications of cybernetic advances; to examine the way man's environment and his image of his nature and significance will be changed; to speculate on how man may respond to these changes? (p. 17)

Her starting point differs from the old "Gernsback delusion" in that the author does not claim prognostic qualities for SF on technological matters. It recognizes in one part of SF, which is here called "the body of cybernetic SF", (p. 17) the literary response to technological developments in the field of machine and computer technology. Significantly the author's outline of the history of SF includes Mary Shelley's novel *Frankenstein*, which it considers an incorporation of the motif of the sorcerer's apprentice and a rejection of technology, Butler's *Erewhon*, Bellamy's *Looking Backward*, Wells' *A Modern Utopia* and Forster's *The Machine Stops*. The dystopias *We* by Samjatin, *Brave New World* by Aldous Huxley, *1984* by George Orwell and Capek's novel *R.U.R.* continue her genealogy. In modern SF Warrick significantly considers Asimov with his *Three Laws of Robotics* and the *I, Robot* stories the most important author of cybernetic Science Fiction. Other representatives are Lem, Clarke and Fred Hoyle with his novels *A For Andromeda* and *The Black Cloud*, and finally P.K. Dick. Clarke and Hoyle, among these, are at the same time scientists.

Warrick links her method of analysis to Scholes' *Structural Fabulation* (1975), to Russ' "Towards an Aesthetic of Science Fiction" (1975) and to Suvin.[62] She refers to Heisenberg's essay "The Tendency to Abstraction in Modern Art and Science" as well as to A.N. Whitehead's thesis that "creativity is to the mind what energy is to matter. Energy transforms matter; imagination transforms ideas". Furthermore she quotes Arthur Koestler's definition of the creative process as *bisociation*. It involves the combining of two hitherto unrelated cognitive matrices in such a way that a new level is added to the hierarchy, which contains the previously separate structures as its members." (p. 86)

In order to define SF the author makes the following statements:

First, the work is *grounded in scientific knowledge*. [...] Second, the fiction incorporates *a sense of novelty*. It does not repeat exactly what has been written before. It may treat but not duplicate the idea that another work has used. The subsequent work on the same idea develops another permutation. SF's requirement of novelty reflects in a more informal way the importance of originality of published research in science.

Third, the fiction imagines *some dislocation in space or time* from present reality. [...]

Fourth, the fiction moves the reader toward an *awareness of unity* in the world and toward a higher level of abstraction. [...]
Fifth, the fiction *addresses itself to the mind*. [...] The literature is didactic, it aims to teach its reader about scientific knowledge [...]
The sixth criterion in the aesthetic involves a complex process [...]. When the writer achieves the right mix of the first five elements, *the reader experiences a new awareness*, a moment that surpasses his previous perceptions of time and space. (p. 82-84)

The author's method proves to be successful for the interpretation. In the course of the analysis of texts which she summarizes under the headlines borrowed from cybernetics "The Isolated-System Model", "The Closed-System Model" and "The Open-System Model" she contributes significantly to the analysis of SF and achieves her aim of recognizing the results of modern science in SF and making them evident to the reader.[63]

Nevertheless at the end of her study she arrives at a rather disappointing result, as she herself would no doubt admit:

The lover of SF is disappointed with the quality and content of much cybernetic fiction. The genre has held so much promise. It has seemed to offer the first really wordable mediation between the humanities and the sciences, a slender span that might model a means of breaching the two-culture gap. But it can mediate only if it is willing to immerse itself in both humanistic values and scientific knowledge [...]. (p. 235)

It turns out, not quite unexpectedly, that only a very small part of existing SF fulfils the requirements of her idealistic concept that takes the sciences for its model (p. 237). By far the largest part of SF is not based upon knowledge of modern technology and the theory of the sciences and is hardly interested in them.

If, following her own premises, the author is right, her conclusion that "all the rest" of SF is "nothing more than entertainment and escapist reading" (p. 237) is not truly valid. To condemn the largest part of SF because it is escapist, because it does not serve the presentation of scientific knowledge, is undifferentiated and wrong. Between Zelazny and pulp magazines there is too big a gap to render it possible simply to ignore everything inside this range!

The reason for this disappointing result lies in the approach by which she severs SF from the rest of contemporary fiction, as Scholes and Russ, to whom she refers, also did (p. 80f.). The relatively small canon of texts with which she is able to prove her theses, excluding the bulk of SF, makes obvious that the attempt to connect SF with modern scientific nonfiction creates a number of problems. Her publication is a merit to the extent that she moves in a direction with her study which in Anglo-American criticism had so far never been tried. On the other hand it reveals the gap in the research on SF.

Ideological criticism and scientific interpretation of SF represent two approaches which in spite of all the differences have one thing in common: they are founded upon the content of SF and neglect its aesthetic and literary characteristics, as they themselves admit. By doing so they continue the old dilemma of SF-criticism, which for a long time had isolated itself from the methods of literary criticism.

Summary

Against the background of the present debate we can sum up the following results:
1. Especially in Anglo-American criticism general and essayistic descriptions of SF exist in abundance. The internal discussion, the debates about definitions and apologetic treatises do not show new and useful results at present.
2. The method of literary history and genealogy has brought forth long and divergent descriptions. But decisive progress has not been made during the years 1970 to 1980.
3. Literary criticism and analysis of SF has resulted in typologies of motifs that have been applied to the texts with considerable success. Their resources are used up and at this point will not help to achieve new insights.
4. In German secondary literature the sociological approach and criticism of ideology play an important role. Especially this debate, however, only shows more clearly the gaps in SF-research in spite of all its merits.
5. The question of evaluation of SF - the problem of triviality - is being violently discussed. Whereas a part of the criticism ascribes to SF a high literary and didactic value, other critics, especially those who focus on questions of ideology, condemn it as escapist and generally redundant. For critics and editors SF has for years been a type of popular literature like the detective novel, the western and the adventure novel. In a generalising way it can be said that this attitude is uncritical and that SF as popular literature - or "trivial genre" - has not been thoroughly explored by research.

1.4 The Methodological Approach of this Study

In spite of the fact that SF can also be considered as an expression of the consciousness of its authors, as a social and cultural phenomenon or as a supplier of technological innovations and that it can become the object of different disciplinary efforts, the central interest of literary scholarship lies elsewhere. For literary scholarship the text and its interpretation are the objectives of the critical exploration, instead of diverse other phenomena like the future, capitalistic free enterprise economy, the personality of the author and the anxieties of the readers. SF-criticism has so far not taken seriously enough the requirements which were made by Russian Formalism during the twenties:

> For as the formalists rightly emphasized immediately at the beginning of their activity, not all concern with literature, not even all scholarly concern, is literary criticism. Literary works can very well be considered as expressions of an author's individual personality, as social phenomena and as historical documents, and as such they will be analyzed under psychological, sociological, historical and other aspects with scientific methods and results. But this is not yet literary scholarship. Its object is, according to Jakobson's often quoted phrase, not literature in its manifold aspects, but the literary element in literature, its "literaturnost".[64]

In spite of the flood of secondary literature literary criticism on SF is still in demand. Especially the concrete exploration verified by a great number of texts is still rare. Literary criticism on SF in Germany mainly developed from an exploration of the typology of its motifs. From there no fundamentally new insights and results are to be expected.[65] The treatment of SF and its history has traditionally been a genealogical history, SF's "pedigree". In the already published research on SF moreover, its development from and its functioning in connection with related groups of texts like utopia, travel fiction and fantastic literature occupy an important place.[66]

"I contend that it is possible to use some of the critical tools we have inherited to discuss science fiction", a SF-critic writes at the beginning of the seventies.[67] The range of "critical tools" of literary scholarship has not yet been fully explored and applied to SF-research.

This study makes the attempt against this background, to interpret a representatively large group of SF texts in comparison with and in contrast to other works of contemporary prose fiction. At the same time it gives a detailed description of a concrete process of literary history, that is the development of SF in Britain and the US during the fifties and sixties.

Before starting on this I propose to outline some significant statements from the discussion of genre theory.

1.4.1 The Concept of Literary Genre[68]

In the discussion of genres W. Kayser observed already in 1948 an "almost confusing abundance of disparate conceptions" (p. 332) and "a depletion of the concept of genre" (p. 331).[69] Literary scholarship in Germany up to the sixties simply ignores the ideas of genre theory developed by the Russian Formalists, who as early as in the twenties had already begun to connect the system of literary genres with their ideas about literary history by using the concept of evolution:[70]

> Then, however, it becomes clear that it is impossible to give a *static* definition of the genre which would include all its phenomena: the genre is *displaced*. Here we are dealing with a refracted, not a straight line in its evolution - and this evolution progresses especially to the disadvantage of the "fundamental" traits of the genre. [...] But the *genre* as such is also not a constant, unchangeable system [...]. The genre as a system may oscillate in the following manner. It develops (from infringements and advances in other systems) and again disintegrates in order to change into the rudiments of other systems. The function of a specific procedure in a literary genre is indisplaceable. To imagine the genre as a static system is also impossible because the genre only gains awareness of itself as a result of a collision with the traditional genres.[71] (my translation)

In 1927 Tynjanov made the concept of evolution the topic of a further essay, in which he claims that precisely the 'infringements' against the ruling norms and standards shape the outlines of a genre. Only the interdependence of regularity and infringements constitutes the conceiving of a literary text:

> A work is put in relation to a given literary series in regard to its 'aberration', its 'difference' to exactly this literary series in which it appears [...]. The greater the difference to the given literary series the more the system is underlined to which the difference exists.[72]

And Tynjanov affirms that it is indispensable for the interpretation of a literary text to compare it with other texts. He states:

In a work isolated from the systems we are not able to define the genre. (p. 445).

Striedter sums up the relation between the individual text and the genre with the following words:

> The producing author as well as the receiving reader relate the individual work, its components and their organization to certain familiar stylistic traditions and conventions of the genre, either because these were confirmed by the work or because they were violated or 'alienated' by it. [...] By such a confirmation or violation of existing generic norms, however, the individual work and its reception change the canonization of the genre, thus becoming the element of evolution in the respective genre and its relation to others. (op.cit., p. LXIf.; my translation)

U. Suerbaum's essay, published in 1971, is inspired by Russian formalism as well as linguistics. He departs from the concept of text types which are shaped by specific linguistic characteristics. Object and situative context influence and determine the peculiarities of the textual types. He states the hypothesis that in the field of literature we find analogous principles and defines the literary genre as follows:

> A literary genre consequently is a group of texts which share certain characteristics, a sub-system in the system of literature, which in its turn is integrated in the total system of verbal texts. For the individual work the affiliation to a genre is a limiting, a determining element for its origin as well as the reception by the audience. The author creates a work which from the beginning is integrated into a larger group and he - by assimilation or contrast - relates it to rules, conventions and expectations. For the reader or critic the knowledge of other works of the group and the ideas of the peculiarities and requirements of the genre form the basis of his understanding and evaluation of the individual work.[73]

The term 'genre', according to Suerbaum, is used on such different levels "that there are hardly any groups of texts on the same level and hardly any works that do not bear the characteristics of several groups. In literary texts we most often deal with merged forms and types." (p. 109)

The distinction between the historical and the systematic aspect is abolished here. Literary genres "are not closed systems of abstract models which exist unchangeably and independently of their realization and the course of literary history" (p. 113). For the individual text the context of the group is affirmed, but the nature of the work itself is not completely determined by this affirmation.

Genres are based upon conventions. They "only exist as groups of texts, among which the same or similar conventions are valid" (p. 123). These conventions are determined by changes.

A further important standpoint is that of a representative of Anglo-American theory of literature. Hirsch (1967) determines his concept of genre through the concepts of expectation and fulfilment:

> these expectations could have arisen only from a genre idea: 'In this type of utterance, we expect these types of traits. Since the expectations do not arise out of nowhere, they must, for the most part, arise from past experience: 'In this type of utterance, we expect these types of traits because we know from experience that such traits go with such utterances'.
> We found the types of meanings we expected to find, because what we found was in fact powerfully influenced by what we expected. All along the way we construe *this* meaning instead of *that* because *this* meaning belongs to the type of meaning we are interpreting while *that* does not.[74] (p. 76)

According to Hirsch both the literary text and other verbal communication obey the same laws in regard to their affiliation:

> All understanding of verbal meaning is necessarily genre-bound.
> This description of the genre-bound character of understanding is, of course, a version of the hermeneutic circle. (p. 76)

As a "system of expectations" the concept of genre is not arbitrary, but is provisional. The assignment of a text to a genre becomes a "narrowing process of trial and error, guess and counterguess".

> Genre ideas, then, have a necessary heuristic function in interpretation, and it is well known that heuristic instruments are to be thrown away as soon as they have served their purpose. Nevertheless, a generic conception is not simply a tool that can be discarded once understanding is attained, because, as I pointed out in the preceding section, understanding is itself genre-bound. (p. 78)

Hirsch contrasts two genre concepts: the well-known system of conventions of an established genre - which he calls "intrinsic genre"[75] -, which forms the background on which alone the novelty of a statement can be recognized, and the heuristic concept:

My account of genres would therefore be very one-sided if I were to stress intrinsic genres at the expense of provisional, heuristic type concepts. Without these broader types new intrinsic genres could not come into existence. I have defined an intrinsic genre as a shared type that constitutes and determines meanings, since the implications of an utterance could not be conveyed if the genre were not a shared type. How, then, can anyone understand a new type of utterance? How can an interpreter know which implications belong and which do not belong if he has never encountered that particular type of meaning before? (p. 103)

The affiliation of a specific text with a group of texts is therefore always a continuous assimilation: the concept of genre is indispensable in order to be able to integrate or to exclude a text; inevitably literary criticism has to cope with the hermeneutic circle.[76] The interpreter can only avoid that by accepting not only the validity of the well-known norms and conventions, but also their temporary nature; only then can aberrations and innovations be integrated.

For the interpretation of SF texts I draw the following conclusions:
1. SF cannot dispense with the concept of the literary genre. Our starting point is that SF is a literary genre, and that the individual texts exist in a historical context and also share a number of characteristics.
2. We have to examine whether in SF we are dealing with a "closed genre", whose conventions can only vary within a comparatively narrow pattern.[77]

The objective of this study is not the determination of the genre or a theory of SF as a complete system. Its aim is mainly to state on the basis of textual analysis how far significant structural characteristics of SF are being realised, varied and possibly also transcended.

1.4.2 Reasons for Choosing Comparison as the Basic Procedure

The typology of motifs in Hienger's study (see above) on SF led to further reflection on the extent to which SF shares themes with other works of prose fiction. Hienger himself has already observed that there are unusual overlappings and shared characteristics, especially concerning the themes of time and identity. Hienger describes efficiently the feeling of "déjà vu" which may overwhelm the reader of SF texts:

An experienced SF-reader at his first reading probably gets the impression that this kind of literature when it describes crises, confusion and loss of personal identity, in its fairy-tale-like manner wants to write a variation of a great theme of modern literature for which the idea of the person has long ago changed from a fact into a problem (op.cit., p. 124; my translation).[78]

When corresponding elements in regard to the themes of time and identity can be found, the question arises how they are used in the context of an SF text.

In order to answer this question it is necessary to systematically investigate the components of SF texts and to elucidate their strategies of fictionalization.

The structure of a literary text - this is one of my premises - is determined by a number of traditional individual elements that are not isolated but interdependent and which only together produce the coordination of text and genre.

Among the general characteristics of fiction are action, characters, constellations of characters, *setting*, time, narrator and reader. The narrative technique in the texts that are used for the verbal presentation of these elements is equally the object of this study.

The contours of the genre SF are outlined against the background of a group of carefully selected texts, chosen on the basis of their comparability. The characteristics they have in common with the SF texts form the starting point of this study, but only their differences are constitutive for their participation in SF.

1.5 Problems of Subject and Method: Contrastive Comparisons as Exploratory Instruments

The genres most frequently compared to SF were up to now utopia, myth and fairy-tale, novel of adventure, *weird fiction*, mystery novel, western and Gothic Novel, sometimes even pastoral prose fiction. Often the labelling for these types of fiction is ambiguous; especially the popular use of such "labels" hardly takes definitions and demarcations into consideration.

The examples of "genre fiction" mentioned above are referred to partly for historical and genealogical reasons; in some cases there are also similar or nearly identical patterns to be found in the development of the texts, as e.g. between the pattern of the adventurous novel and that of SF, between *horse opera* and *space opera*; at some points there is merely an unexplained predilection of critics. More often, however, the texts to be compared show in one particular point an intersection with SF and in many cases trigger an argument about the classification of the authors. This concerns, e.g. Ray Bradbury and the fantasy-discussion inside SF-criticism. Without doubt other forms of so-called popular literature invite a comparison between the different literary systems, such as detective story, Robinsonade, thriller and spy novel.[79]

The approach of this study - corresponding to its objectives - is different. A representative selection of texts is to be analyzed which belong to an important field of contemporary American prose fiction, namely the postmodern novel.[80] These texts do not form a "genre" in the same sense as SF does, since they rather represent one type of contemporary prose fiction. Nevertheless, they make evident the structurally necessary and typical use of narrative elements in SF and also the innovation and transcendence of traditional structural patterns of SF. The study will also in turn explore in what way SF contributes to the postmodern novel.

The selection of texts for contrastive comparisons was determined by the aim of this study: from the unlimited number of SF texts available I chose a wide selection of novels and short stories which are representative of a generation of SF-authors partly indebted to the older tradition of conventional genre patterns, but also partly experimental in using new topics and representational forms. A tendency toward "superior science fiction" in the selection is undeniable, that is to say that the "pulp" production in the manner of "Perry Rhodan" is not considered. The intellectual level of the texts has to correspond approximately in order to make a comparison feasible.

The compared texts - postmodern and SF - date also from the same period. During the fifties modern SF reached its first peak in terms of the demands of literary criticism. It had begun to leave its ghetto and to stabilize its position. In the sixties experimental trends were setting in which will be one of the main concerns of this book; these trends were international.

Since 1950, approximately, there has been a common development of British and American SF. Therefore it is possible to deal with them as one group of texts. The thirties and forties in the US brought forth "the generation of the founding fathers in the ghetto" in America, writing for "pulps" and publishing the great SF magazines *Amazing Stories* and *Astounding*, while the British authors H.G. Wells, George Orwell and Aldous Huxley were acknowledged by literary critics for their SF or anti-utopian novels; after 1950, however, there are no significant national differences. Ballard and Moorcock, the founders of the *New Wave*, are, like Aldiss, Brunner, Clarke and others, British - a fact that is often overlooked, because activities in reception, criticism and the fanzine are more widespread in the United States.

The American "mainstream" novels used for our exploration date mainly from the sixties and early seventies; some of them were written earlier and thematically focus on the search for identity.[81] Authors of fiction in America began during the forties with the analysis of the self, the quest for identity of the individual and an exploration of its different social roles which were threatened by collapse; these themes prevailed in the modern American novel, and in its postmodern development were combined with narrative strategies that left realism behind them. Interferences between postmodern fiction and SF are examined therefore, under two aspects: the thematic and the narrative. The contrastive analysis will yield new insights and results for the interpretation of SF as well as postmodern fiction.

1.6 The Different Stages of Analysis

The aim of this study - to explore SF as a *literary* genre by a systematic analysis of representative texts - led to the preliminary methodological decision to investigate SF not only from the inside as an isolated phenomenon or by means of one-dimensional categories of content, but by a contrastive comparison with contemporary prose fiction. The aim was to elucidate the multi-dimensional structure of these texts. This task implies a detailed and comprehensive description of the system of conventions used in the texts. Partly this system will reveal itself as appertaining to the repertory of contemporary prose fiction, while other characteristics that cannot be explained in the same way have to be investigated for their generic nature and function. The textual analyses will include the relevant thematic, compository and verbal strategies of SF and equally the rules of combination in the different structurally relevant elements.

The second chapter of the study serves to inquire into the opposition of SF and selected examples of American prose fiction. It forms the first and in a sense the basic part of the study; for the structural patterns of the two types of fiction from which we can perceive contrasts, parallels and analogies, are the result of this opposition of texts in the second chapter.

The interpretation of two novels whose common and contrasting traits are to be found out, forms the beginning of this chapter. The detailed analysis of individual texts fulfils mainly two functions: it tries to prove the thesis that the same critical approaches and analytical methods are applicable to a specific SF text as to other examples of modern fiction. In this sense the two juxtaposed interpretations have a paradigmatic value. At the same time they form the first stage of the systematic analysis of textual structures. Especially characteristics of the composition of *plot*, significance of *plot* and operational structures created by the *plot* become visible in this part. This means that as a result the first functional elements of a list of characteristics emerge. On this platform the construction of such a catalogue develops, not only in an additive file, but in a disclosure of existing interdependencies and mechanisms.

The next part serves to point at varieties and attempts at variation. The significance of these analyses results from the character of SF as a "genre of variation", whose pronounced tendency to be redundant and even to copy its former examples has repeatedly called forth critical response on the side of the audience.

Whereas in the second chapter - with the exception of its very last pages - the systematical juxtaposition of selected texts was chosen as the instrument of critical analysis, the explanations on the variability of the system of conventions in SF in the third chapter are limited to texts from SF. They are based on the results of the comparison between SF and postmodern fiction in the preceding chapter and include as a new aspect the historical development of the genre. The appropriation of thematic aspects and narrative techniques that are unusual for the code of the genre by representatives of recent SF reveal significant details of the relationship between continuity and innovation. Special attention is paid to the question of the flexibility and the limitations of the genre.

This exploration of the changeability or evolution of the genre forms the background for the subsequent part which interprets the work of two postmodern American writers whose novels show evidence of sharing characteristics with the "borderline phenomena" between postmodern fiction and SF: Kurt Vonnegut and William S. Burroughs.

Their novels and the published criticism support my hypothesis of intersections between the two literary fields. The "fringe areas" of contemporary SF have certainly gained ground during the sixties and seventies. Classification of individual authors is sometimes controversial. The "membership" of Vonnegut and Burroughs is discussed in these chapters, as well as the question as to what SF possibly contributes to the postmodern novels of these two writers. The results of the preceding chapters are applied there.

The concluding chapter summarizes the results of this study and offers a new perspective on remaining open questions.

Notes Chapter 1

[1] Mark Hillegas, "The Course in SF: a Hope deferred", in: *Extrapolation*, Dec. 1967.

[2] B.L. Heintz / Frank Herbert / D.A. Joos / J.A. McGee (edd.), *Tomorrow and Tomorrow, and Tomorrow* .... (1974), "Preface", p. vii.

[3] See also U. Suerbaum in his interpretation of Brunner, "The Windows of Heaven", in: Goeller / Hoffmann (edd.), *Die englische Kurzgeschichte* (1973), p. 337.

[4] Eike Barmeyer (ed.), *Science Fiction. Theorie und Geschichte* (1972).

[5] The interdisciplinary analysis of SF is represented in publications such as:
S.E. Finer, "Profile of Science Fiction", in: *Sociological Review*, n.p. 2 (December 1964), p. 239-246.
John R. Krueger, "Language and Techniques of Communication as Theme and Tool in Science Fiction", in: *Linguistics* 39 (May 1968), p. 68-86.
Klaus-Peter Klein, *Zukunft zwischen Trauma und Mythos: Science-fiction*. Zur Wirkungsaesthetik, Sozialpsychologie und Didaktik eines literarischen Massenphaenomens (1976).
Manfred Nagl, *Science Fiction in Deutschland:* Untersuchungen zur Genese, Soziographie und Ideologie der phantastischen Massenliteratur (1972).
H. Schroeder, *Science Fiction Literatur in den USA* (1978).
Robert Plank, *The Emotional Significance of Imaginary Beings*: A Study of the Interaction Between Psychotherapy, Literature, and Reality in the Modern World (1968).
Robert Plank, "Communication in Science Fiction", in: *ETC.* 11/1 (Autumn 1953), p. 16-20.

[6] See also "Science Fiction und Sachliteratur", in: Suerbaum / Broich / Borgmeier, *Science Fiction: Theorie und Geschichte*, p. 28f. (1981).

[7] The contradictory tendencies of opening the genre and of regulating it are evident in the following quotations:
1. "SF deals with change and must incorporate change.
But it is undeniable that increasing diversity brings confusion with it, and confusion has little to recommend it.
The urge to write a history of Science fiction grows from a hope that one can straighten out some of the confusion." (Brian Aldiss, *Year's Best SF 6* (1972).
2. "the term 'science fiction' gives the comment a kind of club membership which trims verity. So much which is published as science fiction is nothing of the kind. And more and more, science fiction is produced and not called

science fiction [...]" (Theodore Sturgeon, "Introduction", in: Roger Zelazny (ed.), *Four for Tomorrow*, ³1974, p. 7).

8 This is especially true of Stanislaw Lem who is famous for his published SF-theory as well as for his fiction. His most important critical publications in Germany are:
"Roboter in der Science Fiction", in: Barmeyer (ed.) (1972); "Erotik und Sexualitaet in der Science Fiction", in: Rottensteiner (ed.) (1972); "Science Fiction: Ein hoffnungsloser Fall - mit Ausnahmen", in: Rottensteiner (ed.) (1973): "The Time-Travel Story and Related Matters of Science Fiction Structuring", in: *SFS* 1 (1973/74); "On the Structural Analysis of Science Fiction", in: *SFS* 1. - Authors writing SF and SF-criticism are, besides Lem, D. Knight, Blish, Asimov, Bester, Kornbluth, Heinlein, van Vogt, Ballard and Moorcock.

9 This is done in the introduction to Wollheim's and Carr's edition of the first volume of the series *World's Best Science Fiction* (1965) and in the short story collection *Past, Present, & Future Perfect* (ed. G.F. Gerald & J.C. Wolf) (1973).

10 See also U. Suerbaum, *Studienbrief Science Fiction* (1978), p. 8f. and "Text und Gattung", in: Fabian (ed.), *Ein anglistischer Grundkurs* (1971), p. 112.

11 A few representative passages from prefaces to SF texts may serve to illustrate the wide scope and ambitious aims of these comments:
1. "A science fiction story is one which presupposes a technology, or a disturbance in the natural order, such as humanity, up to the time of writing, has not in actual fact experienced. On the hither side of this definition, the genre throws up an occasional sober tale [...]; and at the other extreme it is apt to degenerate into goblins." (E. Crispin (ed.), *Best sf: Science Fiction Stories*. (1964), p. 9).
2. "[...] science fiction being largely a literature of prophecy, the writer has to be one jump ahead of current events all the time." (Carnell, *New Writings in SF 9*) (1966).
3. "[...] it is the duty of science fiction writers to look at all our problems and warn against the obvious defects." (Carnell, *New Writings in SF 17*) (1970).
4. "[Science Fiction] has unceasingly explored the impact of the social and natural sciences on the human condition and environment." (Wolf / Gerald (edd.), op.cit. 1973, p. 9).
5. "The most powerful and compelling theme in science fiction is the fate which overcomes man when he attempts to outdo nature, when he is faced with menaces of his own making, [...]. The relevance of such a theme to our times [...] hardly needs stating." (Brian Aldiss (ed.), *The Penguin Science Fiction Omnibus* (1973), p. 11).

6. "Today is yesterday's science fiction. [...] So read on; enjoy yourself! And become acquainted with 'the only literature of relevant ideas', the literature that gives you glimpses ahead of time ..." (Heintz / Herbert / Joos / McGee (edd.) (1974), p. vii).
7. "To reach beyond the set bounds of space and time, to attempt to walk for a moment in infinity's shadow, is science fiction's essential goal" (R. Silverberg (ed.), *The Mirror of Infinity* (1973), p. ix).
8. "[...] in science fiction, which accepts no limitations of time or space and uniquely liberates the imagination, I believe we will find the governing myths of the dawning age of galactic man" (loc.cit., p. xiv).

12 The most important among these collections are:
Davenport et al., *The Science Fiction Novel* (1959); L.A. Eshbach, *Of Worlds Beyond* (1964); W. Atheling (alias J. Blish), *The Issue at Hand* (1964), and by the same author the volume *More Issues at Hand* (1970); D. Knight, *In Search of Wonder* (1967). - It is significant of the position of SF and its criticism in its "early modern stages" that all these books were published by Advent, Chicago, Ill., a publisher that has almost entirely devoted himself to the publication of SF and SF-criticism. The nature of addiction, fan audience and ghetto had not yet been overcome in America at that time, so that only later well-known publishing houses wanted to run the risk of publication. Among early SF-criticism there are two exceptions: R. Bretnor (ed.), *Modern Science Fiction* (1953) and Davenport, *Inquiry into Science Fiction* (1955). Among the articles worth mentioning the most remarkable are: C.S. Lewis / K. Amis / B.W. Aldiss, "Unnatural Estates. On Science Fiction", in: C.S. Lewis, *Of Other Worlds* (ed. W. Hooper) (1966); S.R. Delany, "About five thousand one hundred and seventy-five words", in: *Extrapolation* (May 1969).

13 Approximately ten years later the authors of the *New Wave* again focus on psychological developments; both in their theoretical texts and their SF-works.

14 C.S. Lewis is also of the opinion that "modern mythology" is the most important potential in SF, whereas he sharply rejects mere functional aims for SF - namely an SF-motif as a trigger for love or adventure stories, for Robinsonades and detective novels ("On Science Fiction").

15 See his discussion "Unreal Estates. On Science Fiction".

16 See also Suerbaum, *Studienbrief*, p. 13 and note 15.

17 J. Russ, "Towards an Aesthetic of Science Fiction", in: *SFS* 2 (1975), p. 112-119. Russ does not want to renounce the self-interpretation of SF as didactic literature - a characteristic which according to Russ distinguishes SF from all other modern prose fiction. To give up this characteristic would lead to a levelling of the genre.

[18] Ballard, "Notizen from Nullpunkt". Published in English as "Notes from Nowhere" in the journal edited by M. Moorcock, *New Worlds* 167.

[19] *The Overloaded Man* (1967), p. 140-145.

[20] M. Moorcock, "Die Neue Dichtung", in: *Munich Round Up* (1968), p. 87.

[21] The theories by *New Wave* authors are rejected by the critics as esoteric. German criticism, however, welcomed the "revolutionaries" for their condemnation of ideology and marketing of SF (e.g. Enzensberger, Alpers, Pehlke / Lingfeld, Lück).

[22] Suerbaum in Suerbaum / Broich / Borgmeier, op.cit. (1981) takes a different position, which comes close to that of Aldiss. I do not agree in considering the *New Wave* as insignificant.

[23] Bretnor (ed.), *Science Fiction. Today and Tomorrow* (1974); Bretnor (ed.), *The Craft of Science Fiction* (1976); T.D. Clareson (ed.), *Science Fiction: The Other Side of Realism* (1971); Clareson (ed.), *Many futures - many worlds: theme and form in science fiction* (1977); P. Nicholls (ed.), *Science Fiction at Large* (1976); B. Ash, *Faces of the Future. The Lessons of Science Fiction* (1975).

[24] For history of the genre see also: J. & G. Bogdanoff, *La science fiction* (1976); R. Scholes / E.S. Rabkin, *Science Fiction. History, Science, Vision* (1977), p. 3-99 and J. Griffith, *Three Tomorrows, American, British and Soviet Science Fiction* (1980), p. 33-55. Among the book-length studies completely devoted to the history of SF Brian Aldiss' *Billion Year Spree. The True History of Science Fiction* (1973) is more up-to-date and more brilliant than Armitage, Warner, Bailey and Parrinder's *Science Fiction: A Critical Guide* (1979).

[25] Cf. P.S. Warrick, *Cybernetic Imagination* (1980), p. 39: "mainstream fiction and SF are likely to reunite by the end of the century." Also T. Ebert, "The Convergence of Postmodern Innovative Fiction and Science Fiction", in: *Poetics Today* 1 (1979), pp. 91-104.

[26] For a list of his articles see note 8.

[27] In 1926 Hugo Gernsback founded the SF-magazine *Amazing Stories* and in 1927 a second journal with the title *Science Fiction Wonder Stories*. Because of his editorial activities, his own former SF-publications and his creation of the name "Science Fiction" he is often referred to as "the Father of Science Fiction". - For modern examples of the "Gernsback Delusion" see also in note 11 the quotes from Carnell (2) and Heintz (6).

[28] "On the Structural Analysis", p. 31f.

[29] "Erotik und Sexualität", p. 50.

[30] Butor, "Die Krise der Science Fiction", in: Barmeyer (ed.), op.cit. p. 84.

[31] "Erotik und Sexualität", p. 38. Lem maintains his criticism, admitting later on that the commercialization of culture filters and rejects any attempt at innovation and thus excludes the better products.

[32] Szpakowsky, "Vom Weissagen aus dem Kaffeesatz und der moralischen Verantwortung", in *Polaris* 1, p. 89). - For further criticism of Lem see also a collection of essays by Darko Suvin, D. Hasselblatt and S. Lenz edited by W. Berthel (ed.), *Insel Almanach auf das Jahr 1976: Stanislaw Lem. Der dialektische Weise aus Krakow* (1976).

[33] Mark Rose (ed.), *Science Fiction: A Collection of Critical Essays* (1976). This book includes such diverse articles as Susan Sontag's criticism of SF-movies and Lem's theories. Most of them, however, had been published before and are only made more easily available by this collection.

[34] L.D. Allen, *The Ballantine Teachers' Guide to Science Fiction* (1975); R. Scholes / E.S. Rabkin, *Science Fiction History - Science - Vision.* (1977). S. Lundwall's introduction *Science Fiction: What it's all about* (1971) is the work of an enthusiast and similar to the criticism written by authors of SF.

[35] Lem's and Suvin's essays, which are discussed at a later point, are the main exceptions published in English.

[36] R. Scholes, *Structural Fabulation. An Essay on the Fiction of the Future* (1975).

[37] See Scholes' own *Structuralism in Literature* (1974).

[38] I do not consider here studies published before Amis' *New Maps of Hell* (1960).

[39] H. Schröder, *Science Fiction Literatur in den USA. Vorstudien für eine materialistische Paraliteraturwissenschaft* (1978); M. Schäfer, *Science Fiction als Ideologiekritik? Utopische Spuren in der amerikanischen Science Fiction-Literatur 1940-1955* (1977); vgl. auch Nagl (op.cit.) und H. Lück, *Fantastik - Science Fiction - Utopie. Das Realismusproblem der utopisch-fantastischen Literatur* (1977).

[40] D. Hasselblatt, *Grüne Männchen vom Mars.* Science Fiction für Leser und Macher (1974); R. Jehmlich / H. Lück (edd.), *Die deformierte Zukunft. Untersuchungen zur Science Fiction* (1974); Leiner / Gutsch, *Science Fiction.*

Materialienband (1973); G. Seeßlen / B. Kling, *Romantik & Gewalt*. Ein Lexikon der Unterhaltungsindustrie, Bd. 1 (1973); F. Rottensteiner (ed.), *Insel-Almanach auf das Jahr 1972. Pfade ins Unendliche* (1971). *Polaris 1* and *Polaris 2* (1973 / 1974).

[41] See also Suerbaum / Broich / Borgmeier (op.cit.), p. 57f.

[42] V. Graaf, *Homo Futurus*. Eine Analyse der modernen Science Fiction (1971).

[43] H.U. Seeber, *Wandlungen der Form in der literarischen Utopie* (1970); M.W. McClintock, *Utopias and Dystopias* (1970); R. Gerber, *Utopian Fantasy* (1973); U. Broich, *Gattungen des modernen englischen Romans* (1975), p. 94-135.

[44] See also on the relation between history and SF, p. 21-29 in Suerbaum / Broich / Borgmeier, op.cit.

[45] J. Hienger, *Literarische Zukunftsphantastik*. Eine Studie über Science Fiction (1972).

[46] Especially in his chapters on time-travelling, androids, and superhuman beings Hienger shows the intersections between SF and other types of modern prose fiction, which also provided the starting-point for this book.

[47] The motifs also formed a starting point for criticism on SF in D. Wessels, *Welt im Chaos* (1974).

[48] Butor's essay also appeared in Rottensteiner (ed.), *Insel Almanach: Pfade ins Unendliche* (1971); Suvin's article in English in *College English* (1973).

[49] Suvin published his book *Metamorphoses of Science Fiction. On the Poetics and History of a Literary Genre* in 1979; it contains a debate on the history and definition of SF, but nothing new on the poetics.

[50] See note 80 for further explanation.

[51] That sporadically authors do not consider SF as fiction, but as nonfiction, is proved by J. Barthell, "Science Fiction: A Literature of Ideas", in: *Extrapolation* 13 (1971), p. 56-63.

[52] Suerbaum (1981), p. 37. The most comprehensive "pedigree" is written by W.P. Nicholls, "Science Fiction and the mainstream. Part Two: The great tradition of proto science fiction", in *Foundation* (1974). The author calls *Gulliver's Travels*, "The Rime of the Ancient Mariner" and *Frankenstein* "the more obvious forerunners of modern science fiction" (p. 9) and claims Homer's *Odyssey*, the *Gilgamesh*-Epic as well as Dante's *Divine Comedy* also

for SF and its predecessors. See also B. Appel, *The Fantastic Mirror: Science Fiction Across the Ages* (1969).

[53] E.g. Gunn, "Science Fiction and the Mainstream", in: Bretnor (ed.) (1974), p. 183-216.

[54] Rucktäschel / Zimmermann, *Trivialliteratur* (1976), especially p. 10-29.

[55] Most elaborately this is applied in Ketterer, *New Worlds for Old. The Apocalyptic Imagination, Science Fiction, and American Literature* (1974) and, at some points; in J.R. May, *Toward a New Earth. Apocalypse in the American Novel* (1972) in connection with Vonnegut.
Ketterer "Science Fiction and Allied Literature", in: *SFS* (1976) shows the same deficiencies as his book; cf. also L. Fiedler, *Waiting for the End* (1967).

[56] C. Nicol, "Ballard and the Limits of Mainstream Science Fiction", in: *SFS* (1976). Gunn (1974) also considers the authors of the *New Wave* as "crossing the border".

[57] Nagl, op.cit., p. 22; my translation.

[58] In 1980 there was as yet no empirical study on the reading audience of "superior science fiction".

[59] The term is H.G. Wells'. It is used in Anglo-American criticism and, less frequently, by German literary critics.

[60] Patricia S. Warrick, *The Cybernetic Imagination in Science Fiction* (1980).

[61] The phrase was coined by C.P. Snow, *The Two Cultures and A Second Look* (1965): "Literary intellectuals at one pole - at the other scientists, and as the most representative, the physical scientists. Between the two a gulf of mutual incomprehension" (p. 4).
He also underlined that "at M.I.T. and Cal.Tech. [...] students of the sciences are receiving a serious humane education" (p. 69), which is proved by Warrick's study.
Thus from both sides the gap is closed between the sciences and the humanities: by the scientists' interest in SF and by the intrusion of scientific concepts in postmodern fiction, as in Pynchon's short story "Entropy" and his novel *Gravity's Rainbow*.

[62] For these authors see chapter 1.1.

[63] See also Zelazny's short story "For a Breath I Tarry", which she calls "one of the great moments in cybernetic SF" and which I will interpret later in this book.

[64] J. Striedter, *Russischer Formalismus* (1971), p. XIX.

[65] In the third chapter I will extensively deal with theme and motif and their significance for the SF-discussion. See also U. Broich's chapter on the thematic scope of SF in Suerbaum / Broich / Borgmeier (1981).

[66] See Hillegas, op.cit., also Broich in *Gattungen des modernen englischen Romans* (1975).

[67] Wolfe, "The Limits of Science Fiction", in: *Extrapolation* 14 (1972), p. 30-38, here p. 31.

[68] In German literary theory especially remarkable for its comprehensiveness: K.W. Hempfer, *Gattungstheorie* (1973).

[69] W. Kayser, *Das sprachliche Kunstwerk* ([1]1948) [10]1964. In the same way Lämmert also states that little is known "according to what principles or headings their forms can be categorized or described at all" (E. Lämmert, *Bauformen des Erzählens* ([1]1955), p. 9; my translation). The historical and the systematical approach collide and form the central conflict of the debate about literary genres. According to him it seems impossible to distinguish between literary history and poetics.
Another poetics of literary genres was published by W.V. Ruttkowski, *Die literarischen Gattungen. Reflexionen über eine modifizierte Fundamentalpoetik* (1968), which is mainly based upon the classical and German traditions. The chaos in the terminology of genre poetics is well described by W. Lockemann, *Lyrik - Epik - Dramatik, oder die totgesagte Trinität*. 1973, p. 7). Cf. T. Todorov, *Genres in Discourse* (1990), in particular the chapter "Reading as Construction".

[70] Wellek and Warren ([1]1949) discuss the problem of literary genres in a rather unsystematic way and sporadically - a long time before German literary criticism - include the Russian Formalists: in their description the definition of the genre as the "sum of aesthetic procedures" emerges and also the concept of evolution. (Wellek / Warren, *Theory of Literature*, p. 235):

> The genre represents, so to speak, a sum of aesthetic devices at hand, available to the writer and already intelligible to the reader. The good writer partly conforms to the genre as it exists, partly stretches it.

Šklovskij is mentioned several times, but without being discussed (p. 235, p. 242).

[71] J. Tynjanov, "Das literarische Faktum", in: Striedter, op.cit., p. 397. This article opens significantly with the questions "What is literature? What is genre?" (p. 394)

[72] J. Tynjanov, "Über die literarische Evolution", in: Striedter, op.cit., p. 451.

[73] U. Suerbaum, "Text und Gattung", in: *Ein anglistischer Grundkurs* (ed. B. Fabian, [1]1971), p. 107; my translation).

[74] E.D. Hirsch, *Validitiy in Interpretation* ([1]1967) 1969. Hirsch's definitions are based upon the concept of textual criticism instead of literary criticism.

[75] "Understanding can occur only if the interpreter proceeds under the same system of expectations, and this shared generic conception, constitutive both of meaning and of understanding is the intrinsic genre of the utterance" (p. 80f.).

[76] Hirsch with reference to G. Müller, p. 108.

[77] U. Suerbaum in "Text und Gattung", p. 112. There it says: "On the other hand we still find 'closed genres' like detective novel and Science Fiction" (my translation).

[78] Hienger in chaps. 5 ("time") and 6 ("identity"). In his description of the connection and difference of genres Hienger achieves to describe the special problems of SF, but only at a few points, since this is not his main concern (e.g. p. 106ff. and 124f.). The question which remains open after Hienger's explorations in chaps. 5 and 6 is a definition of the treatment of "time" and "identity" in SF as components of a system of characteristics typical of the genre. The result of Hienger's analyses is a series of contrasts that have not been interpreted and put into a connection. That in contrast to our body our consciousness can escape the progress and rhythm of physical time is an idea to which particularly new narrative fiction responds both in theme as in technique (p. 106).

[79] See for this Suerbaum / Broich / Borgmeier, chaps. 4.2 to 4.5.

[80] The internal SF-discussion has for years been using the term *mainstream fiction* in a very undifferentiated way (Nicholls, op.cit.; Gunn, op.cit., p. 183; Warrick, op.cit., p. 2, 4, 7, 16, 90; Suvin in Rose (ed.), op.cit., p. 69; also Moorcock). The term "mainstream" is used for "highbrow literature" in general. One critic ironically remarks that it is used for everything, "lumping together everything from Aristotle's *Poetics* to *Love Story*" (Wolfe, op.cit., p. 31). In German criticism the term "mainstream literature" is also widespread. Since this study, however, proposes to deal with SF's connections

to one type of "mainstream fiction" only this usage of uncertain terminology is almost irrelevant.

[81] With the exception of the stories by Borges which became, however, part of contemporary American fiction the authors are Americans. The year of publication for Borges' fiction is that of the English edition.
The inclusion of examples of the French *Nouveau Roman* was caused by Aldiss' SF mainly and illustrates the tendency towards an appropriation of experimental tendencies for SF.

2. THE CONVENTIONS OF THE SF GENRE. COMPARATIVE ANALYSES

2.1 Structures of Plot and their Effects. Analysis and Opposition of two Novels: Thomas Pynchon, The Crying of Lot 49 (1966) and John Brunner, The Productions of Time (1967)

The Crying of Lot 49 and *The Productions of Time* were selected for this comparison because the analysis of their similarities as well as their contrasts reveals significant strategies of SF which point beyond the individual novel and its respective author and are thus relevant for the description of the genre.

Overlappings and analogies between the texts proved to be most intense in the following areas and subject matters:

a) structures and themes of the "riddle"-type,

b) an alternate reality as hallucination as opposed to the discovery of a "true" unknown reality,

c) isolation and performance / self-performance as *leitmotiv*,

d) disorientation as intended effect.

The main differences are to be found in a) the closures towards which the actions of the two novels move, b) in their degree of verbal and narrative complexity, and c) in the heterogeneous demands on their readers, which are partly and among other conditions predetermined by d) the conception of the protagonists.

One problem which the following part of this study will attempt to solve is the question of the evaluation of the differences. I would like to state already at this point that I believe it is possible to prove that the divergences concerning the components a) - d) are not accidental but symptomatic.

Pynchon's book continues the themes and narrative methods of his novel *V.*, published in 1963, this time in a shorter form. *The Crying* is also the history of a paranoid search in which the vision of the central characters continuously fluctuates between mutually exclusive and equally terrifying interpretations of the world, which can be regarded as "a plotted or a plotless universe",[1] as one critic concisely calls this alternative - reality as a perfect fiction or as an amorphous heap without structure or meaning.

With Pynchon's novel *Gravity's Rainbow* (1973) *The Crying* is connected primarily by its concern with modern science. The thematic importance of scientific components in his fictional works - especially significant in the short story "Entropy" (1960), apart from these novels - is one of the aspects most often dealt with by the critics.[2]

In Pynchon's novel *The Crying of Lot 49* the critic deals with a text that offers resistance of a very specific kind to interpretation: it constantly plays with the dichotomy between coherence and incoherence of the narration. The result is a narrative difficult to follow and even more difficult to analyze and describe.

This is one of the reasons for my attempting a unified and in its first stage isolated interpretation of the Pynchon text, before comparing it with the SF text. The attempt will be made first to grasp the elusive and enigmatic stream of continuity in the novel and to point out the connection of individual elements, and then to focus on references to the SF text.

2.1.1 Thomas Pynchon, The Crying of Lot 49[3]

2.1.1.1 The 'story' of the novel

The action takes place in California in 1965. Mrs. Oedipa Maas, a young woman, receives a letter from a solicitor which tells her that she has been named executor for the will of a certain Pierce Inverarity. The novel describes her attempt to fulfil this given task. It turns out that it consists mainly in the quest for the solution to a riddle: the nature of the mysterious Tristero System, in which almost everybody whom she meets in connection with the execution of the will, seems to participate. Oedipa's main clue is a secret system of communication whose acronym is W.A.S.T.E. and whose trademark is a muted posthorn, an emblem the meaning of which is known only to those initiated to the secret organisation.

Oedipa Maas is not successful in her attempt to solve the riddle; in spite of all clues and traces there is no explanation for the mysterious system.

2.1.1.2 The 'subject'

The true mystery of the system, whose different spellings (Tristero or Trystero) already indicate ambiguity, is the question of its status in relation to reality; for the protagonist it is unanswerable. In the end she can recognize a double, symmetrically structured alternative as a possible pattern of a solution:

either [a network of true communication
a plot against her   *or* [hallucination
fantasy of a plot

In a reduced form this alternative means "reality" vs. "subjective imaginings": "Either Trystero did exist in its own right, or it was being presumed, perhaps fantasied [sic] by Oedipa" (p. 80).

If we accept this dichotomy as the only possibility, then both the protagonist and the reader are deceived. Oedipa's reflections, however, point out that there might be a compromise between these opposed possibilities, where we may find an explanation:

Or a plot has been mounted against you, so expensive and elaborate [...] so labyrinthine that *it must have meaning* beyond just a practical joke. (p. 128; my emphasis)

The following section serves as the exploration of the implied meaning.

2.1.1.3 Detailed Analysis, with Special Regard to Three Elements

a) expository points of major emphasis,
b) development of imagery, primarily the metaphors of imprisonment and stage performance,
c) symbolism of names and signs.

The initial situation of the novel is extraordinarily trivial and common.

An approximately thirty year old American housewife, living in a Californian suburb, married, childless, already slightly tipsy in the early afternoon, goes shopping and prepares dinner and cocktails for her husband's return in the evening. Into this world of monotony, consisting "of days which seemed (wouldn't she be the first to admit it?) more or less identical" (p. 2) the unexpected suddenly intrudes with the letter from a lawyer in Los Angeles. The deceased, the intruder into the familiar environment, at first seems like a stranger:

One summer afternoon Mrs. Oedipa Maas came home [...] to find
that she, Oedipa, had been named executor, or she supposed
executrix, of the estate of one Pierce Inverarity. (p. 1)

Only gradually does the reader learn - in the course of a slow and
laborious process of remembering by the protagonist - that the dead person had
formerly been her friend and lover, from whom she had separated years ago
for unspecified reasons. Her first memory when reading the name of the
deceased, is that of "a hotel room [...] whose door had just been slammed, it
seemed forever" (p. 1). The image of the locked room is followed by a
recollection, the irreality of which is nevertheless nightmarish. Oedipa
remembers a phone call in the middle of the night, which - like the writing of
the enigmatic will - occurred about a year in the past. During that phone call
Pierce in a feigned voice performed a series of horror scenes over the phone
and announced to her and her husband the approaching visit of *The Shadow*.
This haunting visit has become reality by the opening of the will. The dead
("the shadow") forces them to acknowledge his existence - something he could
not achieve as a living person.

From his presence Oedipa cannot be protected by the "real" presence of
her husband Mucho. Her lawyer Roseman, too, whom Mucho, himself
helpless, refers her to, is unable to do anything on her behalf. He only
suggests that she run away with him. "'Where?' she asked. That shut him up."
(p. 9) All that remains for her, since nobody knows where to go, is the
confrontation with the testament of the deceased.

As things developed, she was to have all manner of revelations.
Hardly about Pierce Inverarity, or herself; but about what remained
yet had somehow, before this, stayed away. There had hung the
sense of buffering, insulation, she had noticed the absence of an
intensity, as if watching a movie. (p. 9f.)

The long passage at the end of the first chapter contains in many respects
the key to the meaning of the *plot*. The two basic metaphors of isolation
("buffering, insulation, couldn't feel much of anything, escape") and of
fictitiousness, that of the illusionary nature of reality ("as if watching a
movie") are at this point condensed and enlarged to an allegory in which all
the details are linked together, after having been used sporadically before. This
gives them an emphasis which indicates their future significance.

The picture which is called "revelation"[4] seems unreal: Oedipa sees a
reflection of herself in it as the character from a fairy tale: Rapunzel, eternally

locked up in her tower, "looking for somebody to say hey, let down your hair" (p. 10). The fairy tale prince who seemingly succeeded in penetrating to her, was Pierce. But the narrator changes this source in significant points: on the one hand he enhances the sexual connotations of his images so that the reader can get the impression that he wants to point to the psychoanalytical interpretation of fairy tale and dream, as might be expected from a novel whose protagonists are called Oedipa and Pierce:

> dauntless [...] he'd slipped the lock on her tower door and come up the conchlike stairs, which, had true guile come more naturally to him, he'd have done to begin with. (p. 10)

On the other hand, however, the text leaves no doubt that the imagery is intended also to signify something else. The closing sentence of the fairy tale, we are told here, is not "and they lived happily ever after", but "all that had there gone on between them had really never escaped the confinement of that tower" (p. 10). The isolation has proved irrevocable, the tower prison "is everywhere and the knight of deliverance no proof against its magic" (p. 71). The reason lies outside: "that what really keeps her where she is is magic, anonymous and malignant, visited on her from outside and for no reason at all" (p. 11). There is no way out, because the enemy is invisible. The surrogates for meaning and relationship which should help to secure the survival of the self - really desperate efforts - are therefore magic or exorcisms: "fall back on superstition, or take up a useful hobby like embroidery, or go mad, or marry a disk jockey [her husband]" (p. 11).

Her meeting with Pierce was the point for the protagonist where she came closest to escape. The paradoxical character of the situation consisted in the fact that the perception of an insurmountable isolation and of being locked up was the only existentially "real" experience of the protagonist. Here a fundamental contradiction - at the same time the central message - of the theme of the novel reveals itself: the experience which possesses the highest degree of authenticity - and therefore the strongest claim to the status of reality - is a denial.

This moment of truth for Oedipa happens - in the novel remembered by her in a flashback - significantly in front of a painting which continues the representation of the Rapunzel-motif:

> a number of frail girls with heart-shaped faces, huge eyes, spun-gold hair, prisoners in the top room of a circular tower, embroidering a

kind of tapestry which spilled out the slit windows and into a void, seeking hopelessly to fill the void: for all the other buildings and creatures [...] were contained in this tapestry, *and the tapestry was the world*. Oedipa, perverse, had stood in front of the painting and cried. No one had noticed. (p. 10; my emphasis)

Reality is experienced with such distance and with such a lack of emotional commitment that it appears fictitious and *is* fictitious for those involved.[5] As a complementary experience the artefact becomes real; the artificial alone is capable of exciting emotions and concern and redeeming the self from its alienation. This paradox is not only exemplified in the central character alone. Thus Roseman's closest "tie" is the TV lawyer Perry Mason; and Mucho Maas, who as a rule refers his wife to her professional problem-solver, suffers from his lack of emotional commitment to his job as a disk jockey. The fact that in the "primary world" of the novel these paradoxes are covered up or silenced is the precondition for the existence of a *plot* and its structure as a riddle.

The second chapter shows Oedipa's departure from her world of routine. It mainly serves to enlarge the statements made in the opening chapter and to intensify their effect. On her trip Oedipa meets the second executor, whose name is Metzger, and sleeps with him. Instead of a new definable reality she begins already to recognize increasingly the indefiniteness of reality. Her environment gradually becomes shadowy and the presence of the "shadow" even more overwhelming: "She wondered then if this were really happening in the same way as, say, her first time in bed with Pierce, the dead man." (p. 21) Inverarity turns out to be the controller, maybe even the manipulator, for he was able to shape reality in such a way that after his death it became a plot staged by him and a sophisticated artefact. The reality Oedipa finds is synthetic, the boundary to fiction fluid. This is also true of the characters of the novel: Metzger is an actor by profession. When Oedipa is sitting in front of him, the TV program shows an old movie with him as a child star; but in spite of all the expectations from the audience he does not survive his adventures; he dies "trapped inside the darkening 'Justine', as the water level inexorably rose" (p. 27).

In the second chapter the two central metaphors of the text, imprisonment and performance, are combined. They are also the fundamental experiences of the protagonist.

It seemed unnatural. To her left appeared a prolonged scatter of wide, pink buildings, surrounded by miles of fence topped with barbed wire and interrupted now and then by guarded towers (p. 14).

A stage begins here that is called by the narrator "sensitizing". The revelation of the Tristero System has for Oedipa the character of a "unique performance" (p. 36), in which she is on the audience's side, but nevertheless shares with others the feeling of being observed. Allusions to the Mafia which the customers in the bar in Los Angeles make ("Cosa Nostra is watching", "I have relations in Sicily", "his contacts in the 'family'", p. 40, 43) and to Inverarity's secret connections to their sinister activities accompany the first secret distribution of the mail and Oedipa's discovery of the Tristero symbol in a bar toilet. The second hint at the existence of a conspiracy significantly occurs during the performance of a Jacobean revenge tragedy entitled *The Courier's Tragedy*. Other indirect suggestions of the secret communications system and Inverarity's involvement accumulate; yet it remains elusive. Thus Oedipa writes below the symbol she has copied from the graffitti on the toilet wall the key sentence "*Shall I project a world?*" (p. 59). The fear of being or becoming the prisoner of her own mere fantasies is constantly growing:

> All she could think of was to put on her shades [...] and wait for somebody to rescue her. But nobody noticed [...] nobody spoke to her [...] panic growing inside her head: there seemed no way out of the area. (p. 60)

In the same measure as the ghostliness of reality increases the Tristero system gains structure and actuality: "a pattern was beginning to emerge, having to do with the mail and how it was delivered" (p. 64). Oedipa now more frequently discovers the symbol of the secret organization and learns more about its history and function. The "misfits" of American society have gathered under this sign. Tristero is a communications system of those lacking communication, "a whole underworld of suicides who failed. All keeping in touch through that secret delivery system" (p. 85). Like the couriers of the historical Trystero system its members are "outlaws" and "disguised" (p. 80). "Decorating each alienation, each species of withdrawal, [...] there was somehow always the post horn" (p. 91).

The central secret of the community is again a paradox which is also symbolized by the emblem of "the muted post horn" from which no sound or message will come. "My big mistake was love", says the religious founder of the Tristero system. "From this day I swear to stay off of love: hetero, homo, bi, dog or cat, every kind there is. I will found *a society of isolates*, dedicated to this purpose, and this sign [...] will be its emblem" (p. 85, my emphasis). Oedipa is already a member of this society when she learns about its existence:

> Oedipa sat, feeling as alone as she ever had, now the only woman, she saw, in a room full of drunken male homosexuals. Story of my life, she thought, Mucho [her husband] won't talk to me, Hilarius [her shrink] won't listen, Clerk Maxwell didn't even look at me, and this group, God knows. Despair came over her, as it will when nobody around has any sexual relevance to you. (p. 86)[6]

Silence and the night's darkness create the room where the irrelevance of the surrounding reality overcomes her; existentially relevant would only be what can be communicated:

> Nothing of the night's could touch her; nothing did. The repetition of symbols was to be enough [...] 'clues' were only some kind of compensation. To make up for her having lost the direct, epileptic word, the cry that might abolish the night. (p. 87)

To the illusionary and synthetic character of "true life", where one is present less as an actor than as an onlooker, is opposed the secret parallel reality of the Tristero System, which manifests itself more and more unavoidably. The final evidence of its reality, however, is denied her; for the Tristero and Pierce Inverarity are dependent on each other, which renders it impossible to find a reference point outside the system - it is auto-referential; as a consequence its existence cannot be verified beyond doubt. Pierce is dead - perhaps the only one who would be able to solve the riddle. All the other relationships Oedipa has gradually dissolve into nothing; for each of these characters disappears into his own peculiar form of isolation:

> They are stripping from me, she said subvocally - [...] they are stripping away, one by one, my men. My shrink, pursued by Israelis, has gone mad; my husband, on LSD, gropes like a child further and further into the rooms of the elaborate candy house of himself and away, hopelessly away, from what has passed, I was hoping forever, for love; my one extra-marital fella has eloped with a depraved 15-year-old; my best guide back to the Tristero has taken a Brody. Where am I? (p. 114)

The novel has no real *closure*, but instead an open-ended structure. Oedipa attends a stamp auction to have one part of Inverarity's collections auctioned as "Lot 49", among them stamps from the secret postal system. The title of the novelette is derived from the usage of auctioneers, "We say an auctioneer 'cries' a sale" (p. 137).

To Oedipa the anonymous representative of the Tristero System has been announced as a potential bidder. But there is no "revelation", not even at the end, which would abolish all doubt. Indeed the elements and images of the text are reaffirmed: Oedipa as the victim of isolation and imprisonment. On the other hand there are signs of that other reality, without any interpretation.

The auctioneer, Passerine, "like a puppet master [...] relentless" opens the auction:

> Oedipa sat alone, toward the back of the room, looking at the napes of necks, trying to guess which one was her target, her enemy, perhaps her proof. An assistant closed the heavy door on the lobby windows and the sun. She heard a lock snap shut; the sound echoed a moment. Passerine spread his arms in a gesture that seemed to belong to the priesthood of some remote culture; perhaps to a descending angel. (p. 138)

Instead of answering the open questions and offering conclusive evidence the text continues with its "repetition of symbols [...] to make up for [...] having lost the direct, epileptic word" (see quote above).

It is characteristic of Pynchon's elaborate use of metaphors and symbols - including their ironic use - that he carefully creates telling names. From the meaningful acronyms W.A.S.T.E. ("We Await Silent Tristero's Empire"), N.A.D.A., Spanish "Nothing" ("National Automobile Dealers Association"), and D.E.A.T.H. ("Don't Ever Antagonize The Horn") to allusive associations with names which really exist ("Jesus", "Arrabal", "Oedipa") to purely parodistic surnames ("Dr. Hilarius", "Mike Fallopian", "The Paranoids").

Several critics recognize a similarity between Pynchon's characters and cartoon figures on account of the telling names, and indeed detect particular reference to some of the flat minor characters of *comics*.[7] The underlined fictitiousness of these figures, their remoteness from reality as the reader knows it, their grotesqueness, which is mainly a result of the typifying reduction - all these characteristics lead to shadowy borders between illusion and reality.

The meaning of the names is rather too obvious to be taken seriously or as their true purpose. The secret wish also of the reader to find "another mode of meaning behind the (all too) obvious" (p. 137) provokes the author to playfully grant this wish. As a result we find the characteristic ambivalent tension of *black humor* which we will also encounter in other contemporary authors whom we are going to discuss.[8]

The Crying denies unequivocal statements - and in this sense also meaning - to the central character as well as to the reader. The ambiguity of reality becomes evident by the opposition of two worlds which we may call primary and secondary world and of which we do not know with certainty whether they are not perhaps one and the same: America and Tristero.

What the protagonist experiences is called in the novel "another world's intrusion into this one. Most of the time we coexist peacefully, but when we do touch there's cataclysm" (p. 88). This phrase could very well describe a SF text. It remains an objective of our comparison to find out what the implications of a "collision between two worlds" are in SF as well as in postmodern fiction.

The ontological status of the parallel world in *The Crying*, cannot be explained, but this has also become irrelevant, in a sense. The antinomy of the beginning has partly lost its impact. The world of the Tristero System has become real in the course of the story, even if its protagonist sometimes wishes that it were the hallucination of a sick mind. It is the concept of reality, we learn as a result of the novel, that has to be defined anew.

The possibility of assuring oneself of one's own existence as well as of that of others lies in the communication with others; if this is missing no evidence of reality can be supplied. Oedipa recognizes this: "Either she could not communicate, or he did not exist" (p. 122).

Tristero becomes a "miracle", its emblem a sign of hope for a coming together and being close. This sign, which seems to signify only negation and inward emigration, points to the utmost goal in terms of community:

> either an accommodation reached, in some kind of dignity, with the Angel of Death, or only death and the daily, tedious preparations for it. Another mode of meaning behind the obvious, or none. (p. 136f.)

In the parallel reality of the Tristero System the search for a dimension "behind the obvious" manifests itself. The search alone can be experienced, while it remains uncertain whether "another mode of meaning" exists at all.

There is an analogous relationship between the world represented in the novel and the structure of the relation author-text-reader. The *plot*, in the double meaning of the word as "conspiracy" and "action of the novel", is relevant in both worlds, that of the text and the "real" one: the narrator is -

like Pierce for Oedipa - the creator of a "plotted universe", the reader being the one for whom this plot is meant.

The narrative itself becomes what it signifies: a system of signs by means of which a message can be sent and a relationship established. The receiver of the signs, the reader, gradually discovers - as does the protagonist - an implied system of communication - or perhaps only thinks he has discovered one - whose signs are ambiguous. This lack of determination equally characterizes text and *plot*. The novel becomes an incorporation of what it narrates, its style directly reflecting its subject.

2.1.2 John Brunner, The Productions of Time[9]

2.1.2.1 Plot

The action takes place in and around London; time: the present, without further definition.

The protagonist Murray Douglas, a 32-year-old actor, is looking for a new engagement after having recently returned from a course of treatment for alcoholism. Unexpectedly he receives an offer to play a role in a play directed by the Argentine playwright and director Manuel Delgado. Douglas joins Delgado's company, who rehearse in a completely isolated manor, cut off from the rest of the world. The cast, Douglas finds out, consists of runaways only: a former drug addict, a male homosexual, a sadist, a lesbian etc.

The novel chiefly deals with the protagonist's attempt to clarify mysterious events that are connected with Delgado and the actors. For Douglas the impression arises that each of them is approaching a breakdown systematically planned for him and that he is being observed on his way into the catastrophe. He discovers evidence of the manipulation which is to lead into chaos: monitoring, hypnosis, isolation; but for a long time be tries in vain to get hold of the evidence for these observations; for it is part of the plot that it should not be discovered by the victims or should only be perceived as a subjective hallucination. Finally Douglas succeeds in eavesdropping on Delgado and his servant Valentine and thus partly lifting the veil of the secret: Delgado himself is controlled by an alien power on whose behalf he experiments with chosen human individuals whom he in turn keeps under surveillance.

The solution to the riddle is brought about in an apparently apocalyptic final scene. The burning of the building literally brings the truth to light. Delgado explains before his death that he has come from the 25th century as a time-traveller in order to study extreme situations of human beings and unstable characters and to write down his observations. By means of this record individuals living in the 25th century are to be cured from stress and psychological tensions by finding an outlet in reading these case histories. Delgado's employers are the clever businessmen of the future who know how to make money from the problems of their contemporaries. Delgado himself is a kind of agent, a time-traveller in decadence and neurosis.

2.1.2.2 Interpretation of the Novel and its Points of Comparison to The Crying of Lot 49

The Productions of Time confirms the definition of SF as "thriller". Its *plot* is a riddle that has to be solved by the protagonist in the course of the events. Murray resembles a self-taught detective involved in the action of the novel. The fact that in spite of being an amateur he as a loner is able to cope with the given task, which among other things consists in liberating a girl and fleeing with her, furthermore enhances the impression that this novel functions as a kind of spy thriller.

The riddle structure reveals itself very early in the novel. Delgado arouses attention as a director, even before meeting Douglas because his crew usually consists of "a gang of no-goods, has-beens, and dead beats scraped off the bottom of the barrel" (p. 11). Strange circumstances accompanying his productions have been disclosed: one of the actors committed suicide, an actress was referred to a lunatic asylum, another one attempted murder.

A series of mysterious events shocks Douglas immediately at the beginning of his strange cooperation with Delgado and other members of his cast in the isolation of Fieldfare House: he himself discovers alcoholic beverages in his cupboard after having removed them before; the successfully treated former drug addict finds enough heroin for more than one fatal shot in his room. Later Douglas even wakes up in a state of total intoxication, that is to say with all the symptoms of alcohol abuse although he is quite sure that he has consumed no alcohol. The others have similar experiences: it seems as if each of them is being tempted by an anonymous manipulator in the area of his greatest instability and is thus being driven into ruin and despair. Douglas is the only one who begins to suspect behind all this Delgado's manipulations, especially since he discovers more and more technical devices serving the control and manipulation of the individual: a tape recorder in the mattress of his bed, hidden TV-cameras, hypnopaedic devices and the hermetic isolation from the world surrounding them.

The protagonist, who also supplies the point-of-view of the novel, is the only person involved who behind these strange events is certain that he has discovered a planned procedure and who restlessly and desperately tries to disclose a conspiracy. The other characters repress what is happening or interpret it merely as the eccentricities of a star director. Thus Douglas is pushed into an isolated situation in the midst of those who share his fate. This position and the total screening from the external world almost make it impossible for him to verify the actual significance of these events; reality reveals itself as something you share with others. As a result for a considerable time all the events lead to doubts about his own mental health. The "sense of unreality" (p. 19) which had seized him already on his arrival in the former country club intensifies to a nightmare, "this nagging feeling of something being wrong, like nightmare" (p. 68f.). All the other characters respond in different ways, so that he finally doubts his own sanity: "Am I going crazy? Am I crazy already?" (p. 101). Paranoia seems to have become the only possible explanation of the riddles.

Isolation is the fundamental condition for the experience of the protagonist. The actors are in several respects prisoners: on the one hand they are isolated by Delgado's idiosyncratic method of rehearsing the play under conditions similar to imprisonment; but on the other hand each of them is also the prisoner of his or her addiction. By this dependence and the resulting social and professional stigmatization they are isolated and easily manipulated.

The artificial nature of the situation and of the events is often underlined by the characters. They explicitly compare Delgado's play with works by Poe, Dali, Genet, Ionesco, and Beckett. Several times the question is discussed and answered in the affirmative by the other characters as to whether Delgado's nightmarish productions are only artistic forms of representation, in other words metaphoric expressions of the world we know. Douglas rejects this interpretation. He cannot overcome the impression that he is dealing with something "more real". Delgado - he believes - is forming his actors to provide themselves the material for a play. For Douglas he is less a stage director than a sadistic onlooker, who only makes the actors put their own catastrophe on the stage:

> 'You keep talking about Delgado's personal way of working - well, is part of the idea to coop us up together like a real-life *Huis Clos* until we're all ready to scream, and then put the screaming on the stage?'

Here, in the protagonist's opinion, the fiction is becoming reality.

At the climax of his growing insecurity about what he experiences the relationship between fictional and real world is reversed for Douglas:

> This place was sick, with a kind of all-pervading nastiness copied directly from a Delgado play. It was one thing to see it, quintessential on the boards; it was altogether different to be living it, knowing that there was no automatic escape at curtain time, back to the familiar world of long-standing friendships and outside interests. (p. 105)

Life as a play, the world as a stage - as we can see from the *closure* of the novel this is not a metaphor here, but literal and material reality.

In *The Crying* as in *Productions* an effect on the reader is aimed at and achieved which I would like to call disorientation. Both novels have in common that this effect is brought about by the reader's perspective being determined through the protagonist's point-of-view. Both novels use the past tense and a third-person narrator; since, however, to the reader no other means of orientation, no textual landmark, is offered he is only at times and partially able to separate his own perception from the protagonist's point-of-view and to gain a new perspective. This fact that the reader heavily depends on the protagonist of the story results in a double disorientation: the uncertainty as to whether what is perceived is a hallucination or the discovery of a parallel reality dominates the protagonist as well as the audience.

It is true that the linking of the reader's perspective to the central character is closer in Brunner's novel than in Pynchon's. This, however, is balanced by the advantage the reader has over the protagonist in *The Productions of Time*, which he owes to his awareness of the fact that he is reading a text labelled as SF; for the protagonist only learns at the end about phenomena that the reader is familiar with: time-travelling, aliens, and parallel worlds. The SF-reader can expect an ending of this kind; the reader of Pynchon's novel cannot be sure of his fate as a reader from beginning to end.

2.1.3 Contrasts

2.1.3.1 Differences in Plot Structure

While the question "reality" vs. "subjective hallucination" supplies the *plot* for both novels and initiates a riddle structure, the solution for each is quite different. This is the most conspicuous contrast. Its significance will be explored in the following analysis.

In contrast to *The Crying of Lot 49 The Productions of Time* has a "closed" structure and an execution finally directed to unequivocal message and effects. Ambiguity and lack of determination are only used by Brunner for a limited time to motivate the protagonist's curiosity, which resembles that of the detective, and the reader's tension. He uses them as means of narrative technique, whereas for Pynchon they are theme and intention.

This difference has consequences for the reader and interpreter that will be discussed at a later point.

The disorientation of protagonist and reader is in both novels founded on the premise that for the perception of the central character the frame of the familiar and expectable is transcended. A considerable part of the narrative shows the protagonist's effort to find out the nature of this change and the ontological status of the newly perceived dimensions. In Brunner's case this attempt leads to the discovery of another parallel and not fundamentally different reality, which is merely displaced in time. - The result of Pynchon's riddle is more intricate: *The Tristero* has the status of reality, but of a heteronomous system, whereas the world Delgado comes from is meant to be understood as autonomous, - at least on the terms and conditions of the novel.[10]

The change described takes place in Pynchon's novel primarily in the characters' consciousness; Oedipa gains deeper insights into her environment. The Tristero System opens up a new dimension of perception. - Brunner, on the other hand, describes the discovery of a new world which in fact is not identical with the empirical world, which can be located by coordinates of space and time. Pynchon realizes a mode of representation in his book, Brunner an alternate reality, which, however, remains as such a *terra incognita*.

Whereas the technological course of the action of the SF novel ends up in a gradually emerging rational solution, each attempt of Pynchon's protagonist to verify the Tristero System only leads to new riddles; the end resembles an anti-climax.[11]

2.1.3.2 Effects of the Different Plot Structures

Some consequences of the respective narrative technique in the two texts are evident in an initial comparative juxtaposition of the two novels. Since Brunner provides a solution to the problem and riddles that is direct, logical and without "loose ends" - of course on the premise of a general "willing suspension of disbelief" - no network of implied signals is necessary, whereas these are essential elements of Pynchon's text. Elements with a prevailing connotative and allusive function, elaborate imagery and symbolism, passages mirroring other passages, long interior monologues and flashbacks are missing in *The Productions of Time*. The range of narrative techniques of course is considerable in recent SF, so that only a series of detailed interpretations will make it possible to evaluate the result of this comparison. In this case, however, Brunner's descriptive narrative technique makes the SF novel easier reading. On the other hand it has a certain degree of literary intricacy enriched by reminiscences from the drama of the absurd and surrealism, so that the described "clean" solution at the end, which is mechanically achieved by technical devices for bugging, inconsiderate behaviour of the aliens, and spontaneous combustion, appears slightly inadequate, especially since Delgado has to give a long epic report to inform the protagonist very quickly about the essential facts. Thus the novel forms a curious but for the recent development in some respects a significant combination of standard SF-motifs and several themes and techniques which one encounters more frequently in postmodern novels. Timetravelling, one of the stock motifs of SF, is not a central issue, but is used for a retrospective justification of a *plot* in which the themes of a shadowy concept of reality, the possibilities of a verification, and the unveiling function of play are much more emphasized.

The open-ended structure of *The Crying of Lot 49* makes considerable demands on the reader. Only in interpreting the novel can he read it till the end. This novel forces its reader to interpret, because it preferably applies strategies creating ambiguity. This results in a constant provocation of the reader by the text.

Like every literary text *The Productions of Time* appeals to its readers, but these appeals significantly differ from those of Pynchon's novel: the reader is a detective; he tries to anticipate the solution and will presumably be more or less successful in his guesswork, depending on his expertise as an SF-reader. Finally at the end he will learn whether his combinations were right or wrong. In this novel, nothing remains to be explained regarding the solution of the *plot*.

2.2 The Fictional World in SF and in Postmodern Fiction

2.2.1 Fictional World, Narrative Situation, and Role of the Reader

Two thematic fields where SF and the postmodern novel overlap have already been mentioned in contrasting *The Crying of Lot 49* and *The Productions of Time*:
1. the world that is controlled and directed by an outside manipulator and
2. the synthetic artificial universe.

Pynchon's novel tells of an anonymous power proceeding according to mechanical rules ("They, somebody up there", "the Republic's machinery", "Cosa Nostra"), whose representative or victim is "The Shadow" Pierce Inverarity. While the universe of the Tristero System may be merely fantastic, the intrusion of a "secondary world" into the familiar in *The Productions of Time* is empirical reality guaranteed by the narrator. The unknown, strange elements which in this book make the protagonist doubt his own perception and mental health come from the future. In this novel the aliens are manipulators of reality.

In the following contrastive and comparative analyses these themes - the controlled and the artificial universe - will form the centre of our attention. The focus of interpretation will shift from *plot* structures and their possible effects to the differences in narrative discourse.

2.2.1.1 Illusion vs. Reality

In Borges' *Ficciones*, the work selected for this contrastive analysis, the title already indicates the illusionary character of the fictional worlds.[12] In the same way the author provides a label for his narrative by using the term "fantasies" in his preface (p. 15) - in other words an exceptional case of narrative prose. Our comparison of several texts will reveal what this definition implies and what the relevant differences to SF are.

Three tales were chosen from the first part of Borges' *Ficciones* that to me form variations on the same theme, but also a series resulting in a climax: the first tells of an invented universe and its relation to reality, the second of a process of the imaginary creation of a man and his discovery of his maker, the third finally about a world that is meant to be a metonymic *pars pro toto* and a symbol of reality.

Tales by Borges are at times to be found in SF collections[13]; a similar categorizing sometimes occurs with Kafka's works, which Borges translated from the German. The tales by Franz Kafka most often claimed for SF are *Die Strafkolonie* ("Penal Colony") and *Die Verwandlung* ("Metamorphosis"). If admittedly the wish of SF-authors and -editors to bestow more literary prestige on their genre plays a considerable part in the attempts to annex famous literary works, this usage also shows that critics suppose Kafka and Borges would have an effect on the reader similar to that of SF - for some critics obviously the same effect. From this we can recognize a growing uncertainty in relation to the ordinary SF-definitions. The contrastive analysis as an instrument of verification or rejection of this tendency to see a seamless merging of the two fields is therefore of paradigmatic significance.

The general topic of the chosen tales by Borges is the discovery, creation and interpretation of a universe. The SF texts selected for comparison describe the discovery of a fictitious or simulated reality.

J.L. Borges, "Tlön, Uqbar, Orbis Tertius" and SF

The first-person narrative Borges uses deals with the discovery of an invented world in three sections[14]

1. "a brief description of a false country" (p. 21), called Uqbar,
2. "a substantial fragment of the complete history of an unknown planet" (p. 21), called Tlön, and
3. a postcript that interprets Tlön's connection to reality.

Section I of the story by Borges describes the discovery of Uqbar by the first-person narrator: "I owe the discovery of Uqbar to the conjunction of a mirror and an encyclopaedia" (p. 17). The counterpart of the narrator, Casares, tells about the layout of a novel that is only to be decoded by a handful of readers. At an advanced hour Casares remembers a reference from the *Anglo-American Cyclopaedia*, which quotes an anonymous heresiarch (a leader or a founder of a heresy) from Uqbar as saying "that mirrors and copulation are abominable, since they both multiply the numbers of man" (p. 17). It turns out that the above-mentioned reference book actually confirms the existence of the country Uqbar, but only in a single copy - that of Casares. Nowhere else is a hint to be found. Altogether the memory of Casares proves reliable, although the quotation has not been correctly cited:

> He had remembered: "Copulation and mirrors are abominable." The text of the encyclopaedia read: "For one of those gnostics, *the visible universe was an illusion or, more precisely, a sophism.* Mirrors and fatherhood are abominable, because they multiply it and extend it." (p. 18, my emphasis)

The existence of Uqbar can neither be proved not disproved. The narrator meticulously traces the question of verifiability of the unknown country; for its existence has doubtless been documented by a serious work of nonfiction:

The result of the investigation only enhances the ambiguity:

> Reading it [the article] over, we discovered, *beneath* the *superficial authority* of the prose, a *fundamental vagueness.* Of the fourteen names mentioned in the geographical section, we *recognized only* three - Khurasan, Armenia, and Erzurum - and they were *dragged* into the text in a *strangely ambiguous* way. Among the historical names, we *recognized only* one, that of the *imposter,* Smerdis the Magian, and it was *invoked* in a *rather metaphorical sense.* The notes *appeared* to fix *precisely* the frontiers of Uqbar, but the points of reference were all, *vaguely enough,* rivers and craters and mountain chains in that same region. (p. 18f., my emphasis)

The predominant impression on the narrator of this passage, which he communicates to the reader is ambiguity. This effect is brought about by lexical means (cf. my emphasis) as well as by the syntax, which in a series of three binary oppositions with clauses and sub-clauses respectively affirms the equivocation of the object described. The three clauses present objections or restrictions in the second part of the sentence, respectively; this becomes evident, however, only in the grammatical structure of the third sentence ("The notes... but..."). What was phrased as an opposition (on the one hand - on the other hand) first appeared in the two preceding sentences as parallelism (as well - as), although the content of the clauses connected by "and" ("and they were dragged into the text in a strangely ambiguous way" and " and it was evoked in a rather metaphorical sense") each modifies the content of the first part to a degree which almost supersedes it.

The impossibility of defining Uqbar's ontological status as illusion or reality remains. In all fields, geography, history, literature, it turns out that Uqbar has no reference point outside itself, it is totally self-referential, and therefore it may be a purely imaginary thing.

Two years later - as the second part of the story reveals - the first-person narrator receives a book, *A First Encyclopaedia of Tlön* which contains "the complete history of an unknown planet" (p. 21), including all fields of the sciences and all areas of life, "all clearly stated, coherent, without any apparent dogmatic intention or parodic undertone" (p. 22). Obviously this is not a piece of fiction. In this section, however, the narrator considers it confirmed from the beginning that Uqbar as well as Tlön are fictitious phenomena and that their existence depends on the consciousness of certain unknown individuals:

> who were the people who had invented Tlön? [...] We conjecture that this "brave new world" was the work of a secret society of astronomers, biologists, engineers, metaphysicians, poets, chemists, mathematicians, moralists, painters and geometricians, all under the supervision of an unknown genius. (p. 22)

The whole universe of Tlön is a secondary world derived from empirical perceptions, and as it turns out it was invented by learned men in the seventeenth century. *Orbis Tertius* is a name used for the report of Tlön on the imaginary world (p. 32), and it is also the wording of an inscription in the encyclopaedia of Tlön (p. 21).

The third part, "the postscript" (p. 30-35) again transcends the newly gained coherence and determination, because it turns out for the protagonist that the derived world Tlön in its turn influences the primary world. The fact that in an artificially created system the premises of human thinking and of human perception naturally dominate and are openly visible gives these creations an enormous power of attraction - at least this is the only explanation the first-person narrator thinks plausible (p. 34). The ruling principles are more evident, fictitious worlds are more anthropomorphic and therefore more fascinating than the "real" ones, which to the human perspective are without structure or difficult to structure. The universe created by men is open to human understanding and is easily accepted. The fiction of Tlön therefore gradually supersedes reality, until in the end reality has been totally suppressed.

The special effectiveness of this text is chiefly to be found in the relation between the story and the "story within a story".

The function of the first-person narrator as a discoverer of papers, as editor and witness of events reminds one of the early English novel, especially of Defoe's fictitious editors. In Borges' tales the cross-references the protagonist makes to well-known and proven facts are also frequent, as well as to personally known individuals and historical data; they recur at several points in the story. Whereas in Defoe, the framework primarily serves as the verifying documentation of the work, it is used here in order to constantly point to the illusionary character of the "story within a story". Thereby the narrator can clearly distinguish himself and the reality he represents from the world of Tlön and Uqbar. From what distance he reports on them to a gracious reader results from the fact that sections I and II of the tale according to his own information appeared as articles in the *Anthology of Fantastic Literature* in 1940. In the end, however, he has to discover that there is no clear borderline - in contrast to his suppositions - between reality and fiction. The narrative perspective develops in the three parts of the story dialectically from uncertainty (fiction or reality?) to certainty (clearly fiction) to the recognition of final ambivalence (fiction and reality are mixed together).

The "postscript" occupies a special position. What the narrator relates there includes his former knowledge and presentation. Whereas before he had classified Uqbar and Tlön as "another world" from which the empirical world had to be clearly distinguished, he is now the witness of their mutual integration. There is material evidence which shows that Tlön - which he refers to as fictitious - mixes with the real and increasingly suppresses it. From "Such was the first intrusion of the fantastic world into the real one" (p. 32) to the narrator's prophecy "the world will be Tlön" (p. 35) a gradual development extends which not only by its content shows analogies to SF texts. From the author's and his contemporary reader's viewpoint indeed the whole postscript lies in the future.[15]

The author uses for the fiction of time in his tale the same procedure as the SF-author usually is obliged to use: he tells future events - that is events that have not yet happened at the time of publication - retrospectively in the past tense.

The use of tenses changes at the end of the postscript. The empirical report of the first-person narrator about the discovery of Tlön and Uqbar and their creators, which ends with the words "Here I conclude the personal part of my narrative" (p. 33), is followed by attempts to explain events which supposedly can be remembered by all readers. These memories of the future are, however, largely left to subjective interpretation due to restrictive additions, by which their previously postulated character of generally known and historically certified facts is essentially undermined ("Even now it is uncertain... the second alternative is more likely... the more probable features... it is reasonable to suppose"; p. 33).[16]

The last but one paragraph of the story at first uses the present perfect tense to describe most recent developments and then continues in the present tense; this is, with the exception of the futuristic statement "The world will be Tlön", continued till the end.

The postscript provides a turning point to the whole tale and radically changes the position formerly taken by the narrator and understandable to the reader, according to which worlds can very well be imagined and equipped with details, but for the observer they have to be clearly distinguished from the primary world of reality: while the first-person narrator emphasizes and "proves" the illusionary character of the object of his narrative, he implicitly confirms the stability of empirical reality and its autonomous nature. The radical reversal on the final pages is provoked by the narrator's feeling that he is compelled to completely revise his *concept* of reality.

The relationship of "authentic" and "derived" reality is turned around: at school the language of Tlön is taught, the sciences of the imaginary planet replace the former disciplines, fictive history has replaced history. That exactly this is not an unknown event, that already several times a projected model was able almost without resistance to put aside reality is recalled to the reader's mind by the narrator:

> Almost immediately, reality gave ground on more than one point. The truth is that it hankered to give ground. Ten years ago, any symmetrical system whatsoever which gave the appearance of order - dialectial materialism, anti-Semitism, Nazism - was enough to fascinate men. Why not fall under the spell of Tlön and submit to the minute and vast evidence of an ordered planet? (p. 34)

The end presents the narrator in a situation which only seemed to be new because its relations had been reversed: he lives in a private universe, which only exists in books and surrounds him like a shell of fictions. In reality he is the only one who has not changed his position: "I take no notice. I go on..." (p. 35).

Whereas humanity continues to think of Tlön as the "true" reality, the protagonist conserves the truth which here is identical with the knowledge about the mechanisms of effect and the suggestive power of fiction.

The focus of this story and its interpretation is the first-person narrator and demiurge. He not only enters the story at the beginning and at the end but is constantly present.[17] Borges' story resembles a mirror cabinet - as a verbal construction as well as by its content, the world represented in it. The mirrored image of the narrator, in a double sense, opens the text:

> Casares had dined with me that night and talked to us at length about a great scheme for writing a novel in the first person, using a narrator who omitted or corrupted what happened and who ran into various contradictions, so that only a handful of readers, a very small handful, would be able to decipher the horrible or banal reality behind the novel. From the far end of the corridor, the mirror was watching us; (p. 17)

In the relativistic theorem dominating the textual structures the figure of the narrator is included: a Cretan who says that all Cretans are liars.[18] Thus he reports about his thorough investigations about a not very well-known world - but the results of his research are published in *The Anthology of Fantastic Literature* (p. 30)! - The discovery of Uqbar is based on the article in a reference work and therefore at first seems unquestionable and objective - but the chief witness of the world of Uqbar is called "anonymous heresiarch" (loc.cit.). Here we find the same contradictory ambiguity as in those passages from the text that at first sight seem to reflect unequivocal plausibility. The reader responds to this irritation with indecision - an indecision that has been evoked by the narrator, from which he himself, however, wants to keep his distance. Here the reader's uncertainty about the ontological classifications "fiction" and "reality" contrasts with the determination of the first-person narrator.[19]

The theme and its presentation in the narrative reveal analogies with various texts from the field of SF.[20] These are not simply vague, perhaps accidental similarities between individual texts, but significant intersections with various types of modern SF. The differences, nevertheless, are equally revealing.

The following explorations will first point to some sporadic intersections with several - otherwise very divergent - SF novels, and will then turn to a detailed comparative analysis of an SF short story.

The predominant line of thought in "Tlön, Uqbar, Orbis Tertius" is the question of the fictitious nature of reality, of the power of ideas and the foundations of human knowledge. It may be a surprise to find the elements again as components of SF texts. But the statement of "Tlön's" narrator that metaphysics is "a form of fantastic literature" can also be applied in reverse: modern SF often contains a strong philosophical and speculative component.

J.L. Borges and SF

a) Borges vs. Lem

With special intensity the Polish author Stanislaw Lem deals with fictional and theoretical works on epistemological problems. In his novel *Solaris* (1968) he has his protagonist explore a world which like Tlön is anthropomorphous; everyone who arrives there meets exclusively the materializations of his own thoughts, fantasies, and fears. The human consciousness, unable to perceive anything totally alien, creates in its solipsistic insulation continuously the same "world" - an imitation of its own self.

This position, which comes close to phenomenological theorems, is fictionalized by Lem in *Solaris* in a way that is significant of generic distinctions. The most important differences are outlined in the following analysis.

First, *Solaris* lacks the radical subjectivity which characterizes "Tlön". Solaris, the strange planet, confronts the individual in wellknown shapes but the question never arises as to whether it leads an autonomous existence of its own outside the mind - this is simply taken for granted. Its reality is ontologically not different from that of the planet Earth. The problem is not the question of reality or fictitiousness of reality, but the question of a possibility of communication between two fundamentally different systems. Lem leaves no doubt that it is impossible for the two systems to communicate and acquire knowledge about one another.

This is a difference that explains the generic coordinates of SF; one of its preconditions is the assumption of a *supposedly real* world.[21]

This world can be moved to another place or time, compared to the reader's empirical reality; apart from experimental developments of modern SF - chiefly the *New Wave* - the author presumes that the level of reality where his story is placed is only subjective and inside the mind.

Second, one major difference concerning the treatment of the philosophical subject connecting "Tlön" and *Solaris* is the representational mode. *Solaris* as a novel has a great similarity with a scientific experiment: courses of argument are rigorously followed, research is done, evidence brought forward, conclusions drawn. All this is missing in Borges' work, or where he does make use of it (e.g. in the literature quoted on Tlön) he soon arrives at a point where logical conclusions turn into paradoxes. The character of ambiguity as principle is missing from Lem's novel. It is true that Lem also questions the concept of reality, but it is not reversed and then left unsolved by creating a discrepancy between the perspective of the narrator and that of the reader, as Borges does.

b) Borges vs. Moorcock

The interest in the question of the fictitiousness or reality of our world, in the relation of psychological effectiveness or factual reality is shared by Borges with the SF-authors of the *New Wave*, especially with Moorcock and Ballard.

"Centuries and centuries of idealism have not failed to influence reality". This sentence from "Tlön, Uqbar, Orbis Tertius" depicts the degree of power which Borges gives to the imaginary, the fiction, in his tales. In order to prove his thesis he refers in his story to the historical figure of J.V. Andreä, whose *Rosenkreutzer*-fraternity only became a fact *after* he had given it an existence in his books (see "Tlön", p. 19f.). The fictive is real because it exists in the intellect and mind of the audience and gains there an existence of its own. The frontiers between reality and fiction, between identity and non-identity are blurred, as the tale by Borges claims with increasing intensity:

> Nowadays, one of the churches of Tlön maintains platonically that such and such a pain, such and such a greenish-yellow color, such and such a temperature, such and such a sound etc., make up the only reality there is. All men, in the climatic instant of coitus, are

the same man. All men who repeat one line of Shakespeare are William Shakespeare. (p. 27 n.)

A noticeable reflection on the creative power of fiction is Moorcock's SF novelette *Behold the Man*[22]. Its protagonist Glogauer, who is by time-travelling brought back to the year 28 A.D., finds out that Jesus as He is described in the New Testament did not exist. He is a fiction of the gospel. The myth created and passed on by its authors exists nevertheless, and it possesses such an irresistable attraction that Glogauer by accepting the transmitted role gradually becomes the prophetic figure of the historical Jesus of Nazareth himself; in the end he dies on the cross. Now the myth has acquired a basis in reality; as in "Tlön" fiction has become reality.

In contrast to Borges, Moorcock makes the evolution of the theme depend on a stereotype motif of the action - a functioning time-machine. Travelling backwards in time is presumed as feasible and factual and makes the theme of fictitiousness on the one hand more contradictory, because a linear and irreversible concept of time is denied. On the other hand, however, the introduction of the motif "time travel" which explains all inconsistency, mitigates the contradiction, literally in the guise of a *Deus ex machina*. The abolishment of logical principles is for the reader sufficiently legitimated by the introduction of recent technological developments. Borges opens up a surrealistic dimension, a state of indetermination which increasingly releases itself from the pressures of claims for plausibility. The SF novel regains this premise; for it acquires the free space for speculative subjects by the combination with a technological gadget, the time-machine, an "Open, Sesame" for innovative thoughts and jumping to conclusions. This and the flashbacks in Glogauer's life before his journey into the past are instruments with which Moorcock works against the development of the suggestive force of the fantastic, which is so characteristic of Borges.

Philosophical questions - identity, idea and materialization, fiction and reality - form in *Behold the Man* with conventional SF-motifs and rational ways of explanation a peculiar, but for a part of the genre SF very typical *Mixtum compositum*.

c) Borges vs. Pohl

In "The Tunnel under the World"[23], a SF short story from the fifties frequently to be found in anthologies, a third-person narrator whose perspective closely follows that of the protagonist Guy Burckhardt tells of strange events in the past tense: nightmares, changes in the accustomed environment, disappearance of individuals, especially aggressive advertising methods for commercial products. For others these changes do not need an explanation; only the protagonist can perceive them.

Burckhardt finally discovers that his universe is at least partially only a simulation of the former "real thing". As was to be expected he at first doubts his own mind, but another character helps him to discover the true facts: through a tunnel the two men can reach a large chemical plant which is well-known to Burckhardt. A show-down with its boss, Dorchin, who obviously keeps a host of robots to manipulate the unknowing inhabitants of Tylerton, at first remains indecisive. But soon the revelation follows: the recurring nightmare of the world catastrophe was the last straw of reality that he could grasp; on this day Burckhardt and most of the inhabitants of the small town Tylerton died in an explosion of the chemical plant. Dorchin rebuilt Tylerton in order to have a perfect proving ground for testing new articles and new methods of advertising. This whole "world" is a model on a table in a laboratory, its time is standing still. Its inhabitants are electronic simulations of the deceased. Of course they do not know anything about the illusionary character of their world and their own individuality. Burckhardt's capability as a discoverer reveals itself as the result of a faulty technical service of his "mind".[24]

My analysis is based on the premise that the selected short stories contain structures revealing the procedures and strategies of SF which are peculiar to the genre when dealing with themes transcending its borders.

The exploration of the text by Borges made it clear that the narrative situation is an especially important means of influencing the readers. It has the effect that in the reader uncertainty about the ontological classification of what is related is evoked - an uncertainty which finally leads to a question of our understanding of reality in general.

The discovery of a fictitious universe takes quite a different course in Pohl's story and leads to quite different results.

The most radical difference lies in the fact that the concept of reality is not questioned here. The original, "true" reality which from the narrator's point-of-view lies in the past, has disappeared. The world which has replaced it is emphatically called "ersatz city" (p. 367). The likeness between the image and the original is confusing - a perfect illusion that includes the subjective feeling of the artificially reproduced characters. Nevertheless the fundamental difference between "true" and "false" reality remains untouched inside the narrative situation: reader and narrator can recognize the artificial character of this "brave new world".

That it is in principle still possible to distinguish between them is made evident in the character of Dorchin, the creator of this synthetic empire" (p. 367). He possesses not only the knowledge about the true facts but also the ability to exchange his real shape as a "true" human being with that of a "true" robot that is identifiable as such (p. 366 and 368, respectively).

But when the principles of an understanding of world and reality cannot be shaken, the great change which reality has displayed can only have two possible explanations: either the subjective consciousness of the narrator is dimmed - and many protagonists of SF texts at some point or other are close to psychosis or nervous break-down only to have this disproved by the subsequent development - or a change has made itself felt which nevertheless does not contradict the principles of rational thinking. The latter takes place in this SF story. It is exactly by following logical principles and the unfailing instinct of his common sense that the protagonist finally reaches the knowledge of truth. This truth, however, contains finally a kind of logical *salto mortale*: the protagonist inevitably has to recognize that his own self is also synthetic. At this point he is forced to give up. Many of the elements in the text that point to a solution of the riddle and the fact that it can be achieved by exploring, logical thinking and experimental proof - but outside the empirical categories of the characters and those of the reader - remain concealed at a first reading. In this point "The Tunnel under the World" like numerous SF stories resembles a detective story. The reader follows - in conjunction with the protagonist - at first a shadowy track. The indications increasingly restrict the play with different possibilities until only a single solution seems feasible.

This short story finally leads to a confrontation between the representatives of two worlds, Dorchin and Burckhardt, in the course of which the latter kills a girl and discovers that she is a robot. He thereby causes a chain reaction of further steps to a clarification. The expository information that has now become indispensable is provided by a game of question and answer between the two opponents. The pattern of progress is common to many SF texts. The secret, the solution of the riddle which contributes to the tension of the *plot*, often lies in the past - which in SF is the past of a fictitious future.

In the case of this story a part of the postponed exposition is reserved for the climax at the end, namely the shocking revelation that "Tylerton" is a model in reduced scale but true to life, and that the protagonist himself is part of a miniature world. The reader's perspective generally develops parallel to the development of the protagonist's consciousness. Yet the reader from the beginning has an advantage in information which results from his knowledge of the genre SF and its rules. Where the protagonist is still at a loss, the reader already expects a solution in a certain direction. In this respect the narrative situation is reversed compared to that in Borges' story: in "Tlön" the security of the protagonist and first-person narrator forms a contrast with the confusion of the reader, whereas the opposite is true of Pohl's story.

In spite of his privileged situation, however, the reader of "The Tunnel" totally depends on the role of the protagonist; for on its conception his experience as a reader and his conclusions depend. Burckhardt's defective cybernetics allows a glimpse into "true reality". The perfect simulation, on the other hand, is based upon the premise that it cannot be recognized as such. In his conclusive climax Pohl makes his protagonist part of the fictitious universe. The consequences of this final effect, however, are no longer a theme of the story. Pohl does not go as far as Borges does in "Tlön" where the ambiguity of relativistic theorems extends to narrator and reader in particular.

The following analysis deals with details from the story by Pohl, which make a specific solution plausible to the reader. Part I of "The Tunnel under the World" creates a foundation for the subsequent development of the *plot*. Here we can see how and why mistrust and a detective curiosity are awakened in Burckhardt. In a climax the following sections II to VI are built on this foundation and step by step disclose the truth. In these sections Burckhardt reaps the fruits of his obstinacy and his spirit of discovery; he finds out the cardboard character of his environment (p. 349), finds the tunnel by the help of somebody else (p. 354), recognizes the connection of the riddle with the central computer of the chemical plant and advertising (p. 357 and 359), discovers the artificiality of the girl April Horn (p. 363), of his whole environment (p. 367) and finally - this now involuntarily - of his own self (p. 368). His initiative has led him to the point of no return where he can no longer deny a shocking revelation.

The first part of the tale does not yet contain discoveries and evidence. The reader has to rely on the initial effect of connotations which only gradually reveal their significance: Burckhardt's nightmare, for example, is described as "more real than any dream he had ever had in his life" (p. 337). This may appear to the reader a mere affirmation, but it possesses a literal meaning which gradually reveals itself.

The intuitive distrust of the protagonist in regard to the events of this day is the decisive element for his and the reader's investigation: the nightmare, the fact that his wife had the same nightmare, the absence of familiar characters in the daily routine - all this condenses into the terrible suspicion that there is some kind of fundamental disorder. Here Burckhardt resembles the detective who is not convinced that the dead person was the victim of suicide or accident. There are some points where he is ready to dismiss everything as fantasy, but he is again alerted. "Things weren't going right", he finally concludes at the end of the first section, and he tries to found his conclusion on systematic reflections. The result of these is the discovery of a basic incongruence in his empirical reality the cause of which remains concealed for a while.

The process of development in this first section intensifies and directs the reader's attention. Against the background of an accumulation of alarming signals the formerly trivial now appears significant. The opening of the second section - a literal repetition of the beginning - now appears no longer trite. In conjunction with the protagonist the reader notices the identical course of the two allegedly succeeding days and also recognizes by means of recurring details that his suspicion about the reality of what is being described is justified. That something is wrong with the ordinary appearance of reality is now certain, but it is unclear what it is. The decisive step has been made: he is alerted, his awareness sharpened.

The structure of the *plot* in this SF story now subdivides itself into a shorter phase of construction and a much longer gradual solution, the climax at the end leading to and at the same time transcending the series of discoveries. Under the aspect of dramatic development the story is very carefully constructed. This characteristic in particular exemplifies important components of the SF genre which it shares of course with other forms of popular literature written for the purpose of entertainment: the text is dominated by elements which serve the advancement of dramatic tension and cause the audience to expect a development heading towards a *closure* of the story. These expectations are fulfilled. The two parts of the dramatic structure, construction (section I) and solution (sections II to IV), are in spite of their difference in length identical in effect. Discrepancies like that between expectation and fulfilment are avoided. This observation even extends to the concluding climax of "The Tunnel under the World" which is foreseeable for the reader after a certain point (p. 363).[25] That it is not foreseeable to the protagonist and shocks him does not move the reader; for in contrast to Borges' story his role is not included in the narration as a theme. The reader in Pohl's story exists as a function of textual structures, but he is not a character in the fictional text; he has to be imagined as the invisible audience.

The emphasis on the *plot* and the teleological dramatic action are landmarks of this and many other SF stories which also become evident in their micro-structure.[26] In connection with the already discussed texts by Pynchon and Borges it has been stated that a correlation exists between the thematic focus and the narrative situation: where the semantic function of a fictional text consists in an abolishment of borders between reality and fiction the narrative process itself becomes the objective of fictionalization. As a result the signifier and the signified then mirror each other - a well-known characteristic of postmodern fiction. Thus we can find numerous hints in this text pointing to a conception of the role of the reader. The narrative process becomes the focus of narrating in the following discussion on metafiction.[27]

Where, however, the narration makes us believe in the reality of the fictitious universe[28] the reader is "absent". He is left outside. As a consumer he is not part of the fiction.

In analogy to this there is also an interdependence of compository accents and verbal strategies. In the text by Borges the narrative world is chiefly evoked by syntactical and semantic means which move in opposite directions and thereby achieve an effect of pure relativity. The surrealistic traits in Pynchon and Borges are largely a result of such verbal strategies of organisation.

Another result of the previous comparative analyses is the theory which follows from these statements that a priority of the *plot* and its structural patterns[29] as in the case of "The Tunnel under the World" and *The Productions of Time* correlates with a predominantly realistic discourse. The suggestive force of these works depends on components different from those described above. Their verbal utterances are primarily direct and explicit. The impressions of the protagonist or the narrator are stated openly, not mirrored indirectly.[30] The narrator tries to be unequivocal in his description, even where ambiguity rules the world of the fiction. A frequently occurring example of this strategy is the description of the doubts which the protagonist of SF nourishes concerning his mental health. His insecurity is explicitly stated; this can be done by a personal narrator in interior monologue or reported speech or by dialogue. In this case the insecurity is not transferred to the reader, since between him and the protagonist and narrator a narrative distance is established, separating the real from the fictitious world. It can only be transcended by drawing the reader into the narration and making him part of the fiction, as is done in the narrative structures described above.

Evaluation of the Thematic Focus

The treatment of the topic "artificial universe" can be explored with significant results in a large number of SF texts. It deserves in my opinion major attention and has a special fascination because in it the structures of a larger system are reflected in small scale. General poetological problems and characteristics become the subject of fictional texts. The fictitious universe as a result of intellectual and / or technological creative acts realised by verbal means is a privilege of literature. In SF "to invent" in the sense of "to fake, to imagine" is linked to the other, non-figurative meaning "to discover, to find out". With the instruments of fiction scientific invention is treated and at the same time imitated.[31]

The thesis that SF applies and counterfeits scientific principles with the means of language can be contrasted with a second, analogous one. SF is a model variation of the art of fiction. It imitates scientific activity - functions as an example and symbol of the effort of literary fiction.[32] In this framework it forms an extreme variation: in SF a construction - the future, a strange planet, aliens - something which does not exist is fictionalised. The reality guaranteed in the texts is removed from the author's and the reader's empirical reality by a double refraction: first as fiction and second as fictionalisation of the unreal.[33]

These theses are the result of my earlier explorations and serve as a starting point for later textual analyses.

At this point the building up of contrastive structural patterns is to be continued. SF is conceived in doing this as a system of literary functions against the background of other fictional texts, whose elements correlate inside the whole system. The question as to whether these components and their coherence are flexible or static will then be mainly the subject of further partial analyses concerning their variation.

2.2.1.2 Illusion vs. Simulation

The *plot* of the short story by Borges with the significant title "Circular Ruins" strongly resembles that of an SF story: a man creates another human being and then sends him out into the world.[34] In the end the protagonist recognizes that be himself is also the work of his Creator, in analogy to his own creature.

A fundamental difference in comparison to SF lies in the fact that "create" here means "invent, imagine". The creation is a dream of its creator:

> The purpose which guided him was not impossible, though supernatural. He wanted to dream a man; he wanted to dream him in minute entirety and impose on him reality. This magic project [...] (*Ficciones*, p. 58)

"Magic project" and "supernatural purpose" as paraphrases of a planned act of creation point to a surrealistic dimension. The nameless creator also takes on the semblance of a ghost for the reader. This effect is chiefly based upon the complete elimination of the environment. The "Dreamer" lives more and more exclusively in the cosmos of his own consciousness; no world beyond that exists in the story. Since the protagonist does not perceive anything beyond his own mind the question as to whether anything else exists becomes unanswerable and irrelevant. There is no external world; the interior expands so far and is so clearly outlined that it fills the whole space of the perceived reality.

In the climax of the creative process shortly before the end of the story a decisive step is taken:

> (...so that his son should never know that he was a phantom, so that he should think himself a man like any other) he destroyed in him all memory of his years of apprenticeship. (p. 61f.)[35]

Only one indication of the immaterial nature of the creature is preserved: it cannot be harmed by fire.

> He feared lest his son should meditate on his abnormal privilege and by some means find out he was a mere simulacrum. (p. 62)

At this point a new cycle starts in the circle of knowledge and the evolution of worlds indicated by the title of the story:

> With relief, with humiliation, with terror, he understood that he also was an illusion, that someone else was dreaming him. (p. 63)

Here the text of the story ends, after illusion and reality have been unmasked as relative and subjective concepts. The third-person narrator is totally absent and instructions to which conclusions the reader has to draw from the descriptions are also missing.

In spite of the striking parallels with certain themes and motifs of SF the development in the story "Circular Ruins" summarized above clearly transcends the limits of SF. Evidence for this hypothesis is best to be found where the similarities of the objects of demonstration are conspicuous at first sight.

The parallel text from SF is a novel published in 1964 by Daniel F. Galouye with the meaningful title *Simulacron-3*.[36]

In order to be able to compare the two texts, which are very different both in volume and in narrative technique, the analysis of the novel focuses on two aspects that have a special meaning for the possibility of drawing a borderline between SF and other fictional texts, in particular fantastic literature. It is the construction of the world concept on the one hand and of the protagonist on the other.

The *plot* of the novel is rich in action and intrigue. In its centre there is the first-person narrator Douglas Hall, the co-inventor of a "total environment simulator". By electronic means and in conjunction with his boss Fuller he creates a world, including its inhabitants, from nothing - similar to the artificial place "Tylerton" in Pohl's short story "The Tunnel under the World". The world of the Simulacron, which from the narrator's point-of-view only consists of very precise electronic connections, is in no way different from the real world, seen from the perspective of those who live in it. The *plot* with its numerous adventures and involvements is mainly concerned with two aspects, the combination of which makes the novel very interesting, although it is not conducive to its homogeneity: first, a political and economic component which supplies the material for a *sub-plot* because of the ability of the simulator to make precise predictions about how people will behave as consumers and voters.[37]

This part of the action proves to be a *red herring* in the middle of the novel, after Hall has contributed to preventing a revolt. The danger, represented by the technocrat Siskin, of a compulsory collective favouring a small group of politicians and economic leaders, is thereby backgrounded.[38]

The second topic which runs throughout the novel is the question of the ontological status of reality. It forms the core of the carefully built and suspenseful *main plot*.

The fictional preparation of this theme is achieved by the help of the motif from a detective novel: the scientist Fuller mysteriously dies. The explanation that this is an accident becomes increasingly suspicious to Hall. Obviously there are institutions working against clarification which do everything to destroy any trace that might lead to an explanation: important persons disappear; it seems that they never existed. Obviously there is a conspiracy against Hall by which his life is placed in danger several times. In particular attempts are made to prevent him from knowing more about a well-kept secret Fuller had discovered shortly before his death. The only indication for this obviously very dangerous discovery which Hall sees once more before it also disappears without a trace is a drawing made by Fuller. It represents the famous paradox by Zenon of Achilles and the tortoise.

After Hall has become involved in a psychological crisis or has been manipulated into it, the first step is taken towards a clarification. It is significant of the enigmatic situation produced in the novel that it can no longer be solved by the central character. He needs help from outside to solve the ambiguity of the events described in the first third of the novel:

> There were only two possible explanations that would cover all the incongruous circumstances. One: Some vast, malevolent agency of a capacity both fierce and unguessable was pursuing an unfathomable course. Two: Nothing at all of an extraordinary nature had occurred - except in my mind. (p. 43)[39]

Help for Hall comes from a *deus ex machina*, an individual from the simulator who successfully leaps into the world of his creator Hall. Phil Ashton is a so-called "Contact Unit", the only identity unit who has knowledge of the character of simulation of his world and of his own irreality. This knowledge is in the long run unbearable for Ashton. From Ashton Hall learns the reasons for Fuller's death and for the *plot* against himself:

> "Up here", he shouted, "I'm a step closer to the *real* reality! You've got to let me go on and find the material world!"
>
> "What do you mean?" I asked, trying to humor him. If I didn't steer him carefully through this experience, he might go completely irrational and have to be wiped out of the simulator.
>
> He laughed hysterically. "You utter, damned fool! You're worse off than I am. I *know* what the score is. You don't!"
>
> [...]
>
> "[...] *your world too* doesn't exist! *It's just a complex of variable charges in a simulator - nothing more than a reflection of a greater simulectronic process!*"
>
> [...]
>
> A simulated environment designed by some vaster world of absolute existence.
>
> [...]
>
> *That* was the basic discovery Fuller had stumbled upon. As a result, he had been eliminated. But he had left behind the Achilles-tortoise sketch. [...]
>
> And everything that had happened since then had been the result of the Operator's reprogramming to cover up Fuller's discovery! (p. 74f.)

This discovery stands exactly in the middle of the novel and forms the crucial point of the *plot* construction. It solves indeed Hall's question as to whether all this is fantasy or whether the mysterious events really happened, but after the dramatic climax with Ashton he is confronted with new anxieties and doubts. Epistemological and ontological problems plague him and drive him to the brink of despair. But he does not give up: like his *doppelgaenger* Phil Ashton he does not abandon his quest for a "true reality".

A second climax leads him to a new discovery; this time the decisive information also comes from outside. Now it is the Contact Unit of a world above the first, namely Hall's friend Jinx Fuller, who reveals a secret to him: the operator's name in the "true reality" is also Hall and he is a negative double of the protagonist. Since the simulated reality of the "first degree" serves the same purposes of research and manipulation as Fuller's simulator does for his master, the true Hall has the idea to program himself into his electronic universe. What he creates is an ideal self: the hero and narrator of the novel. He finally succeeds with the help of his friend in switching places with the original model, and the sadistic and megalomaniac Douglas Hall from the world Up There is banished to the simulated analogous world; the "good" Hall, our first-person narrator, is rewarded by being transferred to the "true", the "world of absolute reality" (p. 152).

The construction of these worlds is not cyclical in shape, as in Borges, but hierarchical; there is a true, real world, but it is not the one which narrator and reader believed in for a long time. It only lies a step above the other one, but by this further step the *non plus ultra* has been reached, the original as it were. The fact that the central character reaches this step at the end, or rather that he is transferred to it, is in the layout of the narrative the strongest emphasis on his awareness of reality - a kind of poetic justice.

It is the special characteristic of this SF novel that *plot* and narrator are placed on the middle level, not on the highest of the levels of existence, equally far away from genuine reality and from the simulated one of Phil Ashton. The narrator's position is comparatively - not absolutely - "real". Nevertheless reality and illusion remain distinct; significantly the protagonist does not have to suffer the fate of the nameless protagonist of the Borges tale, "not to be a man, to be a projection of another man's dreams - what an incomparable humiliation, what madness!" ("Circular Ruins", p. 62).

Here we can recognize again an important generic characteristic of SF: it leads - in any case inside the story - to a confirmation, not to a questioning of the concept of reality and identity. The paradox of Zenon of Elea finally leads to a rational solution in the last part of the novel.

The solution chosen by the author Daniel Galouye, it is true, results in considerable difficulties of narrative technique and, in my opinion, it also deeply affects the achievement of the text. The fact that the third world is made to be the "true reality" is not prepared for in the text; it is confirmed but not made believable. Instead the embarrassment of the author clearly shows in the text:

> [I] saw my reflection. Feature for feature, it was I - as I had always been.
> Jinx had not exaggerated when she had said the physical traits of Hall the Operator and Hall the analog were identical.
> At the window, I stared down on an altogether familiar street scene - pedistrips, air cars cushioning along traffic lanes, landing islands, people dressed just as the reactors in my own world were. But why *should* anything be different? My analog city had to be a valid reflection of this one if it was to satisfy its purpose, didn't it?

Looking more closely, I saw there *was* a perceptible difference. More than a few persons were nonchalantly smoking cigarettes. [...] And it was clear that one of the simulectronic functions of my counterfeit world was to test out the feasibility of a prohibition against tobacco. (p. 151)
[...] "What about - the world down there?"
She [Jinx] smiled. "We can patch it up like new."
[...]
I settled down in Hall's chair, only then beginning to realize that I had actually risen up out of illusion into reality [...] soon I would become accustomed to the idea. And eventually it would be almost as though I had always belonged to this material existence. (p. 151f.)

The impossibility of finding differences which believably prove the reality of the final place of action has the consequence that a new paradox not intended by the author is conceived: true reality is experienced by the first-person narrator as a merely abstract concept ("beginning to realize", "become accustomed to the idea").

The process of relativity introduced by the author suddenly stops at a reality depicted as absolute and obligatory. This leads to a rupture in the intellectual and aesthetic structure of the text which leaves the audience unsatisfied.

In my opinion the reason for these difficulties does not lie in the incapability of the individual author alone. It is primarily a necessary element of the general structure of the text. For another author a topic of this kind would perhaps have led to a modified development and conclusion; but the reception and confirmation of a material, objective, collectively perceived reality is a *conditio sine qua non* of SF, the verbal realization of which puts considerable difficulties on the author.[40]

The affirmation of an objective concept of reality typical of the genre and verifiable in novels and short stories can either be the premise on which an SF text is based or - as in our example - can finally emerge as a result after complications and doubts. Whether it is reflected or assumed implicitly - the precondition of a "material, objective reality" existing outside the self is the cornerstone of SF.

If we depart from this thesis an allegorical text transcends the borderlines of SF. Borges' tale *The Library of Babel*, several times printed in SF anthologies, cannot be considered an SF story for this reason; for the library in this story is from the beginning introduced as a metaphor, the signifier, of the universe, the signified. From its description the reader is to see more clearly the profile of our reality. The primary object is not the library, but the world. Several times the reader's attention is explicitly drawn to the really intended signified (*Ficciones*, p. 79, 82f.), so that the possibility of considering an allegorical meaning as the result of a subjective interpretation is excluded.

The allegorical interpretation of an arbitrarily chosen SF text, where each element has a definite figurative meaning, is impossible. At this point I want to hypothetically state the opposing theory which is to be verified later in this study: that there is a tendency typical of the genre to reverse the process of metaphorizing and to activate the literal meaning as that really intended, which is often surprising to the reader used to metaphors and the use of imagery in literary texts.[41]

The rejection of the allegorical understanding of SF cannot - this has to be admitted -, be equated with a total exclusion of any figurative meaning. Yet it is not a legitimate attitude for a reader to regard every SF text merely as an "extended metaphor", in which the literal meaning of each element has a correspondence on the evoked level of meaning, the signified being the meaning behind which the primary meaning disappears.[42]

As a result of the exploration of concepts and images of reality in SF and postmodern fiction we can draw the following conclusions and discover a fundamental pattern:

The signified in the texts by Pynchon and Borges is empirical reality, metaphor, parody and analogy being essential narrative instruments. In contrast to this the signified in SF texts is a non-existing reality, whose plausibility is assured by the *setting* and the teleological action, which aims at a *closure*. The explicit reference to the "really intended meaning", the signified, of the signifying is missing from SF texts. The reader may ask himself what is behind this SF-code of an irreality presented as real; but he can also - and that is doubtless what the majority of SF-readers do - devote himself to the shaping of illusions and accept the code without trying to decode it. This attitude for the reception of SF is impossible in regard to the texts by Pynchon and Borges where the decoding is indispensable in order to recognize something like coherence and meaning. Very often they may deny meaning, thereby provoking the reader.

The reduction of empirical reality to the kind of fiction the following section deals with, is the paradox which numerous postmodern American texts are based upon and which one of their greatest representatives, John Barth, calls "The Literature of Exhaustion".[43]

2.2.1.3 Borderline Cases of Postmodern Fiction:[44] Metafictions

To the largely "realistic" narrative techniques of SF are opposed the innovative trends of modern and postmodern fiction. Consequently, the process of reflection leads to a dissolution of realistic narrative conventions and to a cyclical autoanalysis best summarized in John Barth's phrase "I must get to where I am"[45].

Actually, in literary texts of the avant-garde we occasionally find an almost morbid indulgence in unmasking the medium from its own discourse, including the self-destruction of fictional prose language.

Apart from the action it is primarily narrator and protagonist - the characters as a whole - who become victims of the autoreflection of the narrative. Vladimir Nabokov's novel *Pale Fire* (1962) is one example of fiction being the main subject of fiction.[46]

As in Borges' story "Tlön..." its *plot* is the writing of a critical comment of a fictional work. The title is a hint at the unusual configuration of the narrator, which, first, is a variation of the *doppelgaenger* motif and, second, associates and mirrors in multiple refractions the medium "narrative fiction".

The splitting into the author's double identity Shade and Kinbote corresponds to the division of the text into Shade's epic poem "Pale Fire - A Poem in Four Cantos", and its commentaries, written by the fictitious editor Kinbote. In it Kinbote sees himself as the one who receives his glamour from "Shade", ironically. - The longer part of the text is formed by the "commentary" relating the editor's associations awakened by the primary text.

The narrator's identity, his world and the medium of narration are repeatedly reflected in *Pale Fire*. They cannot be pinpointed but are refracted in different shades, characterized by paradoxes, subjective associations and imagery. A binding and objective idea of reality founded on a common agreement and the idea of the rational explicability of the universe are depicted as totally inadequate:

Space is a swarming in the eyes; and time,
A singing in the ears. (p. 28)

Reality withdraws and vanishes before realistic principles of thinking and telling as

Impossible, mad, unutterably weird,
Wonderful nonsense (p. 28f.).

The refraction and multiplication of the roles of protagonist and narrator is also characteristic of Nabokov's novel *Ada* (1969).[47] The linear concept of time is dissolved there and the narrative is reflected. Apart from being *A Family Chronicle* (subtitle) the novel is also a history of its own development. Ada and the male protagonist Van Veen write down their encounters and their biography as they remember them. The narrative process itself thus becomes a part of the novel. "Later" additions to the text, remarks written in the margin etc. connect the different levels of narrated events, retrospection, entries by the characters and reading. The illusionary process in the reader is permanently disturbed, the effect of the fiction subversed by itself.

In contrast to the principles of irritation in Nabokov's book the narrator's summary in John Barth's *Lost in the Funhouse* shows a resignation combined with self-reflecting irony regarding the application of traditional narrative components:

So far there's been no real dialogue, very little sensory detail, and nothing in the way of a *theme*. And a long time has gone by already without anything happening; it makes a person wonder. We haven't even reached Ocean City yet: (*Lost in the Funhouse*, p. 74)

The narrator who, as is done here, tries to reflect his own narrative and to consider it from a critical distance asks himself for whom his purpose to "trick this tale out" is so important:

For whom is the funhouse fun? Perhaps for lovers. For Ambrose [the vague protagonist] it is a place of *fear and confusion*. (p. 69)

The "funhouse", autoreflection and at the same time analysis of the narrative process, is a labyrinth all paths lead into; it is there only for those who share the secret, for lovers who want to devote themselves to its investigation - perhaps for literary scholars? For a non-professional reader with different expectations, suitable for mimetic fiction, this is indeed not a place of amusing entertainment, but of "fear and confusion". The reader of SF is rarely ever confronted with fears of *this* kind unless he wants to consider authors of innovative and experimental SF whom I propose to consider in the third chapter.

2.3 The Conception of the Protagonist and the Constellation of Characters

The central character in the stories by Borges was called "dreamer" and "phantom" ("Circular Ruins"). His hypothetical nature confirms the fantastic, imaginary essence of these examples from postmodern fiction. In a great number of contemporary American prose narratives the protagonist is not, as in Borges, separated from empirical reality, but he often sees himself in distance to it. The environment and the events taking place in it are reflected in the intramental processes of this character. Their reflections about themselves and their own narrower and wider frame of reference form the subject of the text.

The individual's quest for the self in the field of identity and environment is to be exemplified in the central characters of two novels which have often been ascribed a paradigmatic significance in the history of late modern American fiction. They are Ralph Ellison's *Invisible Man* (1952) and Saul Bellow's novel *Herzog* (1964). Ellison's novel, according to several literary critics, is

> far from being limited to an expression of an anguish and injustice experienced peculiarly by Negroes, [...] quite simply the most profound novel about American identity written since the war...
> a novel which in many ways is seminal for subsequent American fiction.[48]

The way of the nameless protagonist through the different stations of his biography is the story of a sorrowful process of development and growth. The central question of the book, "Who am I?" does not receive a positive answer, but instead is again and again revised, and in the end the narrator has to come to the conclusion that all the different roles and characters do not correspond to his own self. He arrives at the conclusion that for a long period of time he has confused a role forced upon him by others with his identity and his own self with the image others had drawn of him. As Tony Tanner says, the importance of this knowledge far exceeds the field of the historically and geographically identifiable race conflict; the colour of the protagonist's skin acquires a symbolic meaning, surpassing the concrete one:

> Why, if they follow this conformity business they'll end up by forcing me, an invisible man, to become white, which is not a colour but the lack of one. Must I strive towards colourlessness?[49]

The invisibility of Ellison's hero results from the loss of and liberation from social masks and behavioral patterns, serving not him, but others:

> I have also been called one thing and then another while no one really wished to hear what I called myself. So after years of trying to adopt the opinions of others I finally rebelled. I am an *invisible* man. (p. 462)

The question if and how an identity without the reference frame of the social environment is possible is asked but cannot be answered. Is the way into the outer and inner emigration, the "invisibility", perhaps also the way into losing the just discovered individuality and one's liberty to shape one's social roles autonomously? It is true that the narrator says "I am invisible, not blind" (p. 464), but this certainty about the existence of the self outside the social reference frame is almost immediately after this statement shaken again:

> Perhaps to lose a sense of *where* you are implies the danger of losing a sense of *who* you are. That must be it, I thought - to lose your direction is to lose your face. (p. 465)

Doubts and uncertainty are not eliminated or overcome. On the contrary, the novel points out the protagonist's way from security to insecurity, from action to reflection, from the belief in simple and stable structures to the defense of complexity and fluctuation. The result of the book is the refusal to say - and the impossibility of saying - anything precise and reliable:

> When one is invisible he finds such problems as good and evil, honesty and dishonesty, of such shifting shapes that he confuses one with the other, depending upon who happens to be looking through him at the time. (p. 461)

The slogan of the "unlimited possibilities" of America, which in relation to the protagonist's experience appears almost cynical, is at the end newly interpreted by him in an immaterial, non-conformist sense:

> my world has become one of infinite possibilities. What a phrase - still it's a good phrase and a good view of life, and a man shouldn't accept any other; that much I've learned underground. Until some gang succeeds in putting the world in a strait jacket, its definition is possibility. Step outside the narrow borders of what men call reality and you step into chaos - [...] or imagination. (p. 464)

The affirmation of the indeterminate nature of the world and of the concomitant insecurity of the individual is the result of a development that seems to lead from the manipulated individual to the autonomous differentiated self. But it seems questionable to the narrator whether with this separation from the usual context a final state is achieved or only a necessary temporary state.

In the opening sentences of the prologue Ellison's narrator wants to keep his distance from his autobiography, wants to avoid being a fantastic figure like the protagonist of H.G. Wells' novelette *The Invisible Man* (1897). In this contrast some of the fundamental positions important for our comparison are outlined:

> I am an invisible man. No, I am not a spook like those who haunted Edgar Allen Poe; nor am I one of your Hollywood-movie ectoplasms. I am a man of substance, of flesh and bone, fibre and liquids - and I might even be said to possess a mind. I am invisible, understand, simply because people refuse to see me. [...] That invisibility to which I refer occurs because of a peculiar disposition of the eyes of those with whom I come in contact. A matter of the construction of their *inner* eyes, those eyes with which they look through their physical eyes upon reality. (p. 7)

The invisiblity of Ellison's narrator is a metaphorical one which is intended to render an inner and immaterial fact visible and understandable. Griffin's - Wells' protagonist's - invisiblity is, in contrast to this, a literal, real invisibility. Yet it shatters the boundaries of the empirical reality of author and reader, in contrast to Ellison's novel, which interprets the empirical world of the coloured and the white Americans of our times.

The paradigm which reveals itself at this point if we compare Ellison's and Wells' protagonists, confirms and completes the chiastic relations of the signifying and the signified in SF and the chosen postmodern texts outlined at the end of the last part of chapter 2.2. Whereas Ellison presents empirical reality in an imaginary invisibility, Wells uses the motif of a material invisibility to describe an unreal non-empirical world. In other words, while Ellison proposes to write with mimetic intentions, Wells makes the imaginary his objective. The following diagram shows these relations:

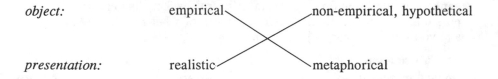

object: empirical   non-empirical, hypothetical

presentation: realistic   metaphorical

Warrick (1980) reaches the same conclusion when she mentions the "willing maintenance of disbelief" which for the reader of SF is as indispensable as - and must be a supplement to - the "suspension of disbelief every reader of fiction has to achieve. In her diagram she presents the complementary aspects of "real" and "unreal" in SF in a series of three binary oppositions, namely past vs. future, metaphor of present reality ("true") vs. metaphor of future possibility ("not true") and images in the reader's mind of the empirically verifiable world vs. images of alternative futures created by the writer's imagination. Thus the SF-reader's consciousness is not involved in a mimetic process - creating images of a determined world - but in a creative process directed towards a still indeterminate future. Warrick explains the reader's role in SF:

> The reader's consciousness moves between his present awareness of reality and the alternative reality the writer creates. [...] The SF creative process encompasses an element of indeterminacy. It assumes that the future has not been fixed by the past; the future is open. It assumes that the observer will alter reality. The future of man will be different [...]. (op.cit., p. 85f.)

The adolescent black anonymous protagonist in Ellison's *Invisible Man* is in most respects a contrast to the Jewish historian and college professor Moses E. Herzog, whose attempts to cope with his "midlife crisis" supply the subject matter for Bellow's novel. Yet the characteristics they share are stronger than their biographical differences. "I am the specialist in... in spiritual self-awareness; or emotionalism; or ideas; or nonsense", Herzog says about himself.[50] The rebel against social manipulation in Ellison's novel and the introverted and highly differentiated intellectual Herzog are variants of the same type of protagonist. As in Ellison's nameless hero, the introspection in Herzog, especially his memory, functions as a means of liberation from too much outside determination and from the compulsory premanufactured versions of reality, also liberation from standards and demands in regard to which he can only fail:

> Considering his entire life, he realized that he had mismanaged everything - everything. His life was, as the phrase goes, ruined. [...] [...] he admitted that he had been a bad husband - twice. [...] To his son and daughter he was a loving but bad father. To his own parents he had been an ungrateful child. To his country, an

indifferent citizen. To his brothers and his sister, affectionate but remote. With his friends, an egotist. With love, lazy. With brightness, dull. With power, passive. With his own soul, evasive. (p. 10-12)

In the end the question as to whether Herzog will succeed in finding a new beginning leading him away from his alienation and opening up to him a genuine relation to his environment is left open.

The protagonist's failure in coping with life is in Bellow's novel the result of a highly technological civilization which is too complex and at the same time too rigid to leave room for the realization of his own sensitivity. The self is paralyzed, it is asphyxiated by the mass of information and preconditioning of behavioral patterns.

The "invisible man" in Ellison succeeds by his reflections not in acquiring a new position but in keeping up with himself: his consciousness has arrived at a level from which he is able to see where he stands: "it placed me in a hole - or showed me the hole I was in, if you will - and I reluctantly accepted the fact." (*IM*, p. 461) His hope to find in the end a position that is equally far away from total determination (represented by Norton, Emerson, the Brotherhood) and from the social lack of contours (Rinehart) remains seminal - an occasional reader would perhaps say that it is nipped in the bud! It becomes a paradoxical promise: he will leave his hole and yet preserve his "invisibility".

Moses Herzog remembers - like Ellison's "Invisible Man" - for the whole length of the novel what so far has filled his life. His way is not the way from the naive to the enlightened individual; the book is not an *entwicklungsroman*. Herzog's awareness and intellectual reflectiveness are from the beginning far more developed than those of the young Negro. But Herzog's self-analysis serves the same purpose as Ellison's surrealistic imagery: to newly define the relationship between the self and the different patterns of relationships offered to each individual. In Bellow's case the ties that have to undergo new determinations and growth are primarily those to women, the family, the Jewish tradition, and to culture; in Ellison's novel the emphasis is on the relationship of the races and on the chance of the individual in the machinery of education, politics and labour. Both protagonists respond by their attempts to "hide" from the fact that the existence of the individual is determined by organized structures - a rebellion the outcome of which is uncertain, since it is impossible to see whether the self does perhaps not suffer more from the self-denial and refusal than from being organized and determined, because determination also means social security. Therefore Herzog has not yet found his place in the world by his emigration into the pastoral scenery of rural Massachusetts: "[...] a subtle, spoiled, loving man. Who can make use of him? He craves use. Where is he needed?" (p. 375) The novel ends on this note of lack of determination. "All this time he had no messages for anyone. Not a single word" (p. 416).

The type of protagonist here represented by Ellison's and Bellow's antihero belongs to a group of modern American novels. That this part is often considered the most promising and innovative line of mainstream fiction is also, if *ex negativo*, obvious in the comment of Robert A. Heinlein who can claim to have been one of the most celebrated authors of SF:

> But as for contemporary-scene literature, it is sick with a deep sickness - in its present state it cannot possibly interpret this fast-changing world. [...] Nor am I condemning every novel offered as a serious interpretation of the contemporary scene [...]. But I am condemning the overwhelming majority.
> A very large part of what is accepted as "serious" literature today represents nothing more than a cultural lag on the part of many authors, editors and critics - a retreat to the womb in the face of a world too complicated and too frightening for their immature spirits. A sick literature. What do we find so often today? Autobiographical novels centered around neurotics, even around sex maniacs [...]
> In my opinion a very large portion of what is now being offered the public as serious, contemporary-scene fiction is stuff that should not be printed, but told only privately - on a psychiatrist's couch. The world, the human race, is now faced with very real and pressing problems. They will not be solved by introverted neurotics intent on telling, in a tedious hundred thousand words, they hate their fathers and love their mothers.[51]

In spite of their vulgar anti-intellectualism and the outspoken *machismo* Heinlein's statements contain valuable information not only about the critic himself and his socio-psychological context,[52] but also for comparative literary analysis. Heinlein's aggressive rejection of that part of "serious contemporary-scene fiction" - the "novel of consciousness" and postmodern fiction -, is directed against certain forms of presentation. Especially the main characters of this type of fiction call forth Heinlein's criticism:

condemned to perpetual compulsive introspection, the victim of memories which refuse to be shut out, racked by endless, nagging cerebration.[53]

Needless to say not only the tough and brave heroes created by Heinlein, a John Wayne of SF, ostentatiously show that SF instead of an introverted character not sure of his own identity prefers the active and resolute protagonist. This contrast between hero in SF and antihero in postmodern fiction was already evident in the first comparison between the novels by Brunner and Pynchon. In SF the individual is given an extraordinary power of decision and action which contrasts not only with the reader's real situation but also with the reality of space travel, of a scientific discovery or an invasion from Mars.[54] In this point SF-heroes correspond with heroes from other branches of popular literature.

The preference for one central character who combines energy, will power, competence and stamina so effectively that he shapes events of world-wide importance can certainly be suspected of being derived from a desire for escapism. But how does it fit into the structural pattern of SF?

The intensity of action already noticed in SF fits the type of the active protagonist. He cannot be hindered by reflection to such an extent that he renounces action totally. His resolution and his energy only provide motivations for the events of the SF-tale with its episodes, its tension and its suggestive power which render SF so attractive for a great number of readers. The SF-protagonist, however, is not a mere activist and not a complete hero. He is equally prone to reflection, even resignation and self-doubts. But reflections are strictly directed towards aims and functions, and the feeling of insecurity is usually only temporary, the protagonist overcoming it after a short while, in order to influence the events once more. A lasting withdrawal is uncommon for an SF-character, the "Hamlet" in SF very rare.[55]

The protagonist's activity does not have to reveal itself in incredible heroic deeds. It may be primarily directed - as in "The Tunnel under the World", in *The Productions of Time* and in *Simulacron-3* - at the exploration of the unknown. The protagonist is among the characters of a text often the one whose curiosity remains unsatisfied. He distinguishes himself from his environment by a keener perception and the exploratory urge to find out himself in spite of conventional explanations what is going on. In this sense he is an "outsider", with less readiness to adapt and to conform than his average contemporaries usually represented by the other characters.[56]

Especially strong is the protagonist's exceptional position in texts whose central subject is the social collective, that is to say in the classical dystopia. In Huxley's *Brave New World*, Orwell's *1984* and Bradbury's *Fahrenheit 451* the central characters are rebels against the new order. It is true that the will power and scope of action of the individual are broken (John Savage, Winston Smith) or banished (Montag). But in spite of defeat the message of the antiutopian novel is the glorification of individualism; the world view of these authors exults in the revolt against conventional ideas (conventional if seen from the point-of-view of society in the novel) and against the passivity of the masses, thus making the novel a testimony of the human struggle for freedom.

The elitist type of protagonist is, however, in the majority of recent SF texts, less a result of ideology than of structure. The mutual dependence of the different narrative elements results in the fact that the resolute and active character remains a favorite with SF. This characteristic ostentatiously emerges in the texts which thematically offer possible intersections with the postmodern novel. This is the case where e.g. the SF text also questions identity or presents the exceptionality of the protagonist in his social and cultural framework.

These crises of identity are caused in SF especially by the motif of the simultaneous universe which often is called the motif of "parallel times".[57] Episodes in which the hero meets himself in an alternate world existing parallel to the empirically known world often merely serve as a riddle in which the expectation of the reader is primarily directed towards the external solution of a complicated situation by the active involvement of the protagonist.[58] This expectation is almost always fulfilled in SF texts. A text like Curt Siodmak's novel *Hauser's Memory*, which describes "memory implantation" and the resulting identity problems of the tested only superficially deals with the psychological and philosophical aspects included in the subject matter; the solution of the implied conflict potential is brought about by horror effects and action. The problem of identity occurs in the novel, but not in a dominant function. From the scale of possibilities included in the motif of biological manipulation mainly those are activated which are usually part of the pattern of the spy novel. For the SF genre this option is typical because of the long existing affinity to the spy thriller.[59]

The conception of the protagonist in SF in effect displays analogies to the previously explored components of the genre SF. These proved, for example, that SF texts lead to the confirmation of an objectively verifiable concept of reality, and this is also the case where this concept of reality had been questioned earlier. The acceptance of a reality definitely existing outside the individual was called a premise of the genre.

Crises and shocks related to the concepts of reality and identity in SF have only the value of temporary and tension-increasing stages. Present SF no longer excludes these thematic fields so familiar to the modern novel, but it does not focus on them. The treatment of the same or similar subject matters follows different rules of the game and leads to divergent results in effect. In addition to the activity and the typifying of the SF-hero he is also characterized by a specific relationship to his environment. The statement that he is an outsider only concerns him to a certain degree. As a rule his way leads out of isolation again, as he also finds his way out of doubts of his own mind. His insecurity in regard to his social ties remains an episode. It is true that in *Simulacron-3*, "The Tunnel under the World" and in *The Productions of Time* the protagonists are heroic fighters trying to escape manipulation and that they do not rest until the enigmatic events have been clarified. Yet they are supported by other people. Often women are assigned this role; there we find a possible functional explanation for the frequently criticized occurrence of trivial love stories in SF texts.[60]

The relation between the SF-protagonist and his social environment leads from participation to isolation (either geographically or by deviant behaviour) and back to reintegration in the old or the creation of a new social pattern.[61]

For the SF-protagonist this reference frame is indispensable for reasons inherent in the genre: otherwise he is lost. He cannot forego integration into a group - even if it is very small in number -, because such a situation would lead to extensive consequences which the SF-author does not strive for. The main character's exploration of territories which so far were considered non-existent or unreachable, needs the verification of a third party: the space team, another scientist (often a not very reliable witness), a woman, a friend. If this confirmation through the perception of other individuals is missing, the borderline towards a merely subjective concept of reality, a hallucination is blurred - as we have seen a generally unwelcome effect in SF.[62]

James Blish in his short story "Common Time" described the consequences of the hero's alienation from his social reference frame. Due to the loss of a common pattern, depicted in the example of a divergence of subjective and objective time (cf. title) conscious perception, maybe even physical existence is made impossible. The total individualization has as its last consequence the destruction of the individual:

> You and I are physical scientists [the protagonist Garrard tells a friend after his return to Earth], so we think about the world as being all outside our skins - something which is to be observed, but which doesn't alter the essential I. But evidently, that old solipsistic position isn't quite true. Our very personalities, really, depend in large part upon *all* the things in our environment, large and small, that exist outside our skins. If by some means you could cut a human being off from every sense-impression that comes to him from outside, he would cease to exist as a personality within two or three minutes. Probably he would die.[63]

Here Blish tries, with considerable success, not to exclude philosophical questions that are raised by the *plot* construction. In this tale the intellectual speculation indeed outweighs by far the action, and in the end it remains open whether Garrard will actually be reintegrated.[64]

The majority of SF texts, however, have a different attitude towards an activation of possible themes and the characterization of the protagonist, although these texts do not generally propose to make lesser demands on their audience. H. Harrison's novel *Captive Universe* and the short story "The Bliss of Solitude" by McIntosh are examples of a more conventional development inside SF.[65]

In the short story the narrative starts when the protagonist is already isolated inside the space ship. In the novel as the work with greater narrative extension a longer description of the gradual process of alienation precedes the state of isolation: the hero discovers an unknown world which literally includes the well-known, a *plot* like that of *Simulacron-3* and "The Tunnel under the World". As in Galouye and Pohl the stories by Harrison and McIntosh lead the protagonist out of isolation. His perception of reality is finally confirmed as true after several complications and crises.

The differences between *Captive Universe* and "The Bliss of Solitude" concerning the expansion of individual phases are chiefly conditioned by the choice of the long or the short form: Chimal, the protagonist in Harrison's text, after laborious efforts finally gains access to the primary world, after having discovered that his empirical reality is merely a "playworld" by nature. His former social environment is replaced by a new one. In the course of the novel it is described very extensively how Chimal qualifies for the position of chef-astronaut in a space ship diverted from its regular course, because in reality the "primary world" is only a space ship, and how he liberates the human beings from the "valley", that is the world he came from.

The short story "The Bliss of Solitude", however, condenses the story completely into the subject matter of isolation and makes the connection between the consciousness of reality and relations to the external world the focus of attention. The astronaut Ord, whose illness is called "Solitosis", looks for a possibility to discern imaginary characters from real visitors in his space ship.

> He could not say whether she existed subjectively or objectively - could he say whether the station existed, whether Earth existed, whether there was a Galaxy? Was there any essential difference between Una and his mother or sister? Were they all creatures of his mind?
> Life itself might be a thought in his mind. Matter could be merely a concept. *He* existed "*I think, therefore I am.*" He could accept that. Could he accept anything else?[66]

With the exception of the quotation from Descartes nothing seems logical to him. Only the presence of other people can protect one from the loss of a sense of reality. This is finally confirmed by a real visitor whose genuineness does not disclose itself by means of analytical thinking but by intuition and unselfish affection:

> "How did you avoid solitosis?" he asked.
> She smiled again. "The only way. There are fifty men and women in the *Lioness*, the relief ship. That number is well above the critical point. It will be still a while before they can land a big ship on this little world, but all the time while they're manoeuvring, they'll be keeping me sane by being there. I know they are, you see. When you do, you'll improve." (p. 171)

The concept of the protagonist in SF texts is, as shown in the different stages of the exploration, also an integral component of the genre. As long as this is not transcended completely each element obeys directions and regulations which to a large extent come from the system itself. Especially close is the correlation between the conception of the central character and the intensity of the action in the genre on the one hand and the conservation of a conventional, objective and idealistic notion of reality on the other hand, by which the fictional world claims the status of the real.

The type of the alienated, introverted loner as seen in the contemporary novel does not fit into these premises. Yet it is a grave misunderstanding, to say the least, if Heinlein believes that the insight into the inner self of a character could in a work of literature at best be of interest to a psychiatrist; for the literature of confession and introspection, which to him seems so private that it is totally uninteresting to everybody else, often claims to interpret the world by writing about the fate of an individual. The powerless and alienated individual is the representative of a part of mankind.

But SF-writers in general - not only Heinlein - do not approve of this type of person, partly because of their general world view. For SF-writing such a protagonist, an antihero, alienated from the established order, is downright dangerous, because he threatens the stability of the discourse typical of and until now necessary for the genre. As a prominent critic, C.S. Lewis, puts it, casually but precisely:

> To tell how odd things struck odd people is to have an oddity too
> much: he who is to see strange sights must not himself be strange.
> He ought to be as nearly as possible Everyman or Anyman.[67]

The credibility of the unheard-of has to be linked to a character who does not by his own insecurity and indeterminacy add further instability to the system and perhaps shock the conventional reader. An "alienated reader" is not intended in SF.

The qualities and the functional role of the SF-protagonist predetermine his effect on the reader. He can follow the perspective of the main character mainly because the protagonist in spite of his being average has idealistic traits. If this does not always lead to identification, it is for the reader at first not difficult to achieve an orientation with regard to the main character. His activism, his eagerness to make decisions, and his stability are clear signals: the reader knows what to think of him. Feelings of indeterminacy and ambivalence, even confusion such as Pynchon's, Bellow's or Barth's protagonists have and trigger in the audience do not correspond to the basic rules of SF, nor does the idea of a reader without illusions.

SF claims to be fictitious speculation about possible changes.[68] Yet the individual capable of making decisions and being active, the rational protagonist striving for more knowledge, whose scope of action and imagination is limited by the tension between the poles of individual autonomy and social integration by no means represents a brand-new type of person.

This model was rather coined by the past and by history, especially by the European Enlightenment and the beginnings of modern sciences in the late seventeenth century. In SF texts there are a striking number of reminiscences or explicit hints referring to historical concepts of the universe and to philosophical systems and relating them to SF's concept of an imaginary alternate reality, especially to the image of humanity in them; they reach from Descartes to German Idealism and Transcendentalism, to Darwinism and to the Phenomenological School of the early twentieth century.

In SF there seems to exist a general silent agreement that this image of human nature is so durable or unchangeable that it could also serve as a model in a different world. Some authors, however, seem to be aware that this attitude shows little reflection. Their intention of being innovative more often aims at the experimental design of a new, alternative man.[69]

Most rigorously this direction is chosen by J.G. Ballard in his novels and stories. But also Ursula LeGuin or Stanislaw Lem try to modify existing anthropological concepts. The effects of these experiments are to become the object of later detailed analysis. The preference of a number of authors for variations of exactly this partial aspect is explicable by fundamental considerations: if SF intends to be an exercise in "thinking the change", it cannot possibly restrict itself to variations of marginal details. Changes, however, that are so radical that they suspend the basis of SF will lead *ad absurdum*; this would be the case, as with all fiction, if the concept of language were to be changed fundamentally, not only to a fancy "Newspeak", followed by a glossary as in Orwell's *1984* or the likewise annotated "Nadsat Language" of Burgess' *Clockwork Orange*, but to a true New Language.[70]

For author and reader it is equally impossible to forego language or to introduce totally new concepts of communication. The traditional patterns of thinking and communicating are indispensable. For the change of the nature and concept of man, however, the limits are not so strict. Yet this aspect is also subject to restrictions; for the totally different, totally new lies outside human consciousness and outside language; therefore it also escapes representation. This difficulty is also the reason why only a minority of authors try to conceive the protagonist of an SF text in a fundamentally different way and why these experiments often meet with considerable resistance from the critics.

2.4 The Use of Time in Science Fiction

The discovery of time as an experimental area and its use as a substantial means of expression in modern prose fiction has become a widespread observation in the critical history of the contemporary novel.

The frequency of the time-travelling motif is one indication of the significance of time in Science Fiction.[71] The formerly most frequently used term in the German language, *Zukunftsroman* (novel of the future, futuristic fiction) even defines the whole genre by its relation to time.

SF uses time as a phenomenon in two different functions whose importance can vary from text to text. The first is the use of time as a topic or as the main reason for the evolutionary changes that are described. The SF texts discussed in this chapter are primarily those that are based on either the time-travel motif or the motif of parallel times.[72] When critical studies mention as one of their aspects "Time in SF" they almost always refer to its function as a theme in short stories or novels.

Besides, however, there is a second, much less thoroughly interpreted function of time in SF that is nevertheless very important for its profile as prose fiction: time as a structuring element of the narrative process. As can be supposed, this use is more implicit than the thematic employment, and its main effect is suggestive rather than designative.

The explicit, thematic function of time in this fiction is based on the assumption that a change in the imaginary world - compared to the world as known to the reader - is brought about by a changed structure of time. Time is declared a variable element of our reality concept, instead of being unchangeable. Based on this precondition the individual text shows the introduction and / or the effects of this manipulation.[73] In contrast to the rigid chronology of our sequential concept of time, a "leap" into the past, the future or into simultaneous time sequences are feasible in SF, as well as an inversion of the continuity of time. The generally accepted idea that history is irreversible as time is irreversible, is abandoned. Reversals of time are among the most interesting fictional experiments in SF texts based upon the concept of the variability of time structure: the idea that World War II was won by the Axis instead of the Allies[74], or that the American Civil War was won by the Confederacy instead of the Union;[75] that the Spanish Armada defeated the English in 1588,[76] or that the Native Indians were victorious over the European settlers in North America after a world desaster.[77] The radical change of reality in these novels is based on a change of history, on the realization of an alternative that from a historically verifiable point in time onwards was banished into the sphere of irreality. This is certainly also one of the main reasons why wars and battles as historical turning points are so very popular in SF: up to a certain point in time a different result was also possible, and this possibility is realized in an SF text.

Some authors make their games with time more intricate by using strategies of complication providing surprises and entertainment for readers. The theme of "interfering with history", which is a result of time-travelling and the irresponsibility of time-travellers: the assassination of his own ancestor, for example, could result in uncontrollable consequences for the protagonist.[78]

Another possibility of variation in the motif of the inversion of history that is very amusing for the reader is the exchange of fiction and reality in the two opposed worlds, so that from the reader's point-of-view the non-real world becomes the real and that world which for him is the real world becomes the fictional. In Disch's novel *The Man in the High Castle* ([1]1962) the population of the US - a country divided and occupied by the victorious Axis powers, German Nazis and the Japanese - are fascinated by a subversive and of course prohibited book with the fantastic title *The Grasshopper Lies Heavy*. In fictionalized form it describes the victory of the Allies over Nazi Germany and its consequences. The special interest and joke for the reader lies in the very intensive mixture of alienation and recognition of the world presented in the novel; imagination becomes reality, and the reality of the 'real' reader is imaginary for the fictional reader.

A concept of time that includes another paradox and has become popular in SF is the cyclic model of time. It is based upon the assumption very widespread in SF that everything will repeat itself, perhaps more than once. Under these conditions the idea to make time a variable element of reality leads to a special kind of immobility. Instead of the linear and evolutionary process we find a return to a former stage of development: a nuclear disaster being followed by the Middle Ages, as in Walter M. Miller's famous novel *A Canticle for Leibowitz* (1959), or once again by the colonisation of North America by Puritan settlers, as in Wyndham's novel *The Chrysalids* (1955). Authors who are especially bold write novels where several time cycles unfold simultaneously, but starting in different successive phases of time, either on this planet or in space. This is done in F. Hoyle's novel *October the First is Too Late* (1966). Robert Heinlein created an extreme example of the use of this motif, a so-called time-loop, in his story "All You Zombies".[79]

Beside these conceptions of the dynamics of time we also find the complete standstill of time in SF: in "The Tunnel under the World", by F. Pohl, one of the most important indications of a change in the known world is the constant repetition of the same and of the same date: every new morning is that of June 15; every morning brings an identical day.

The "freezing" of time is the core of the short story by Disch with the significant title "Now is Forever".[80] The one point that is so different in the New World is that it is completely static: there is never any change, never anything new. This immobilization becomes possible by one single interference with the axioms of our reality; a materializing of the author's idea is made effective, as often in SF, by the invention of one technical 'gadget': with a kind of super-xerox-machine everything, including people, can be copied at one's will, thus eternally repeating and conserving the present.

In comparison to the abundance of variations in SF - you could also say the frenzy for variation - in the sphere of a thematic use of time, its functions for narrative technique are less diverse. They differ especially in one point from every other type of narrative fiction: the future or the alternate reality that is only possible in the imagination is described in the past tense, as something in the past from the point-of-view of the narrator of the story.[81] Apart from this paradoxical trait SF uses the same narrative techniques as prose fiction in general, also in connection with the use of time. It is true once more, however, that here as with other components SF tends to experiment less where narrative techniques are concerned.

> Experiments with narrative time sequence, for example, are practically unheard of in science fiction, and yet the problems involved with time as an isolated *concept* are a staple of science fiction writing from Wells to Asimov.[82]

SF and the postmodern novel are both heading in the direction of the dissolution of an irreversible, continually progressing time concept. They differ, however, significantly in regard to their aims and methods of achievement. Modern novelists try to replace the usual, abstract model of time by the imitation of an individual, subjective, "experienced" time, that with Virginia Woolf's words can be called "the time of the mind". This "inner time" is formed in the minds of characters. Typical means of expression for these texts are therefore the flashbacks and chains of associations that connect the different levels of time.

It is the intention of the novel of consciousness to open up the reader's mind to the inner self of the characters and to make it appear as the "true" reality; postmodern fiction often leads to a mingling of 'fiction' and 'reality'. This is achieved - among other methods - by breaking through the conventional conception of time and replacing it by a subjective and psychologically "realistic" time. What counts is the intrasubjective time; it is the only significant experience of time. It becomes an integral part of the constitution of a text, either by the development of the individual (as in Ellison's *Invisible Man* or Nabokov's *Ada*), or by the individual's crisis (as in Bellow's *Herzog* or Pynchon's *The Crying of Lot 49*). The insight into the interior of a character is intended to reveal an interpretation of the present reality to the reader.[83]

This is different in SF. By an evaluation of numerous texts it becomes obvious that time as a component of the narrative is treated in SF in analogy to other components. This analogous procedure means, briefly, that in SF an externalization or materialization of structurally important elements is taking place - elements that in the postmodern novel are implicit and not part of the material of the story. Where in the postmodern novel the reader finds intrasubjective developments he may indulge in a series of actions instead in SF; in the place of an intrasubjective, metaphorical or fictional alternate reality of the mind SF describes a world that is supposedly real in the sense of an objective and material 'other' reality, thereby rendering the willing suspension of disbelief a necessity; instead of "leaps in time" through the consciousness of a character the reader is offered "real" time-travelling with the help of machines in SF. Finally, SF transposes the theme of variability of time from the sphere of narrative technique into the sphere of narrative subject matter.

This "transposing" of a theme is not to be understood as a genetic or hierarchical connection, as if the postmodern novel were the primary narrative from which SF is derived, or vice versa. They present themselves as two different discourses. The material and the representational methods of SF are integrated components of a narrative system, which results in producing mimetic literature. As far as the employment of the variable element "time" is concerned it changes its place as in an inverse function: whereas in the late modern and the postmodern novel "time" is mainly an instrument of narrative technique it is in SF primarily an element in the *plot* or material of the story.

The following survey gives an oversight of the results so far achieved by the exploration of SF and postmodern fiction. This outline demonstrates in a few words the juxtaposition of characteristics that were explained in the preceding interpretations. They result in the recognition that late modern and postmodern fiction in its last consequence is post-structuralist and non-mimetic, whereas SF epitomizes structuralist and mimetic literature.

Structural Pattern of Genre Conventions

postmodern novel	component	Science Fiction
emphasizing consciousness, non-teleological procedure, open-end structure; multivalent; deconstructive	*1. predominant structural element*	action-dominated, suspense-orientated, teleological development, *closure*
no clear borderline between fiction and reality; reality is subjective	*2. status of the fictional world*	postulate of reality; no questioning of axiomatic truth of an objective reality
narration is fictionalized auto-reflexive	*3. narrative situation and perspective*	narration is not thematic in the texts
introspective, reflective, disinterested in public issues, anti-hero, vague	*4. protagonist and constellation of characters*	active and rational character, knowledgeable, a leader and individualist, possesses integrating abilities
intra-subjective "experienced time"; emphasis on narrative techniques (flashbacks, citation)	*5. use of time and space*	time-travelling motif; emphasis on material of the *plot*
metaphors, connotations, parody, self-reflecting techniques or interior monologue, auto-referential	*6. narrative technique*	"conventional" presentation, relatively "straightforward" story, narrative sequence recognizable
reader is included, reflections on the reader and the audience; disruption of the reader's illusion	*7. conception of the reader and reader-response*	reader not reflected; autonomous fiction; willing suspension of disbelief
provocation and disorientation of the reader; highly intricate texts; ambiguities form the thematic focus; insecurity of the reader intended	*8. effect of text; objective of narrative process*	no lasting insecurity or disorientation of the reader; degree of sophistication not too high

2.5 Results of the Structural Pattern and Preliminary Evaluation

The results of the contrastive textual analysis show that between the individual elements of an SF text there are distinct interdependences. Only their sum and the combination of their functions form the structural pattern of SF. The catalogue of characteristics for SF does not contain items typical of SF alone. The priority of the *plot*, its development aiming at *closure*, the exclusion of reflections on the narrative situation and reader-response, in conjunction with narrative techniques aiming at unequivocation and fulfilling the readers' expectations - all these are characteristics used for the description of groups of texts in the different categories of popular literature. Indeed intersections between SF and the genre patterns of crime and adventure fiction, western novel and spy thriller are easily recognizable, so that occasionally critics have maintained that SF is a selection and new combination of elements from other generic patterns.[84] Yet this reduction means a neglect of several preconditions essential to SF.

Its specific component, the dominant, is first of all the relation of fictitious and empirical world. In this point the genre differs from other fiction, serious as well as popular.

> The dominant may be defined as the focusing component of a work of art: it rules, determines, and transforms the remaining components. It is the dominant which guarantees the integrity of the structure. (R. Jakobson, "The Dominant", p. 82)

The question "What if?" underlying SF not only renders a "willing suspension of disbelief" possible at some points while generally the ruling principles of the known reality retain their validity; it also makes these principles an indispensable premise. At the same time it applies strategies which make it easier for the reader to yield to the imaginary by encouraging the shaping of illusions.

The presumed suspension of the familiar concept of reality is - and this is a central paradox of the genre - linked to the preservation of a "realistic" and "rational" world concept. That means that the SF-reader has to accept the premise that in the world represented there he encounters a universe different from the one he knows, and he has to accept at the same time that this other world has the same status of reality as the empirical one.

It is not decisive whether the change concerns only one or several of the axioms which form the basis of our empirical world. It may well turn out that the change is more effectively indicated by a single interference with the structure of reality. To be successful it is important that the reader can accept a world where human beings are ambisexual, immortal or telepathic, a world ruled by women or by machines, as in the same way real as the one in which he lives.

The premise that the invention is easily recognizable as such and supposedly real is the crucial point and the touchstone of the text's belonging to SF. In the cooperation of this element with the other components of the system the possibilities of variation inside the genre are included. The abolishment of this precondition, however, has - in contrast to other deviations and infringements of rules - as a consequence a transcendence of limits. This provisional result is also confirmed and specified by the following analysis of experimental variations. Perhaps SF does not necessarily emphasize action - although it often does -, it may irritate the reader by its high degree of difficulty and abundance of connotations, but it cannot dispense with bestowing upon the fictional world the same axioms as the empirical world possesses.

A detailed analysis of the possibilities of variation inherent in the genre, of its effects on the entirety of the functional system and of its borders is chiefly the object of the following chapter.

But first I propose to interpret - in addition to the interim results - at this point the axiom of reality as an essential element of SF.

2.5.1 Functions of the Axiom of Reality in SF

The structural pattern of SF not only consists of different elements, but essentially also of their relations. On the occasion of the inquiry into the component "time" and "structure of time" a methodological analogy that is typical of the genre has already been explored. In relation to the strategies of the postmodern novel the methods typical of SF are generally to be described as "objectifying" or "substantiating".

In SF statements signalizing metaphorical use and subjective experience in other types of fiction acquire the status of empirical reality - a fictitious reality of course. That such a projection in the fields of the empirically real is characteristic of SF is founded upon the dialectic tension between the poles "real illusion" and "presumed reality"; this tension accounts for the special fascination inherent to the genre. SF is based upon the non-fictional, the merely imaginary; its representational intentions and methods all aim at the verification of a real material existence of the imaginary.

In contemporary postmodern fiction this relation is reversed: its primary world is - although exemplary and stylized - recognizably shaped according to empirical reality. It proposes to reveal a concealed reality behind the material and empirical which is represented in images and thoughts, generally in subjective experience, and is perceived as such.

SF is not by its nature, its narrative quality or its aims and intentions principally different from other narrative fiction. Like it SF stimulates new perspectives and insights into formerly unperceived relationships.

Especially its strategies are different:

1. It concentrates on the presentation of the "material" components of the fictitious reality: place, *plot*, protagonist.[85] The model organization of the world by narration is done in SF by presupposing both an objective reality and the coherence of what is represented - not by refractions, multivalidity, metaphors. If there are hints to be found in the SF-world - and it does include hints by the relation of parallels and oppositions to empirical reality - they are primarily located in *setting* and *plot* and in the characters. These are, as already stated in other contexts, so structured that they make orientation easier for the reader in the alien and strange world.

2. SF presents the image of a rationally explicable, empirically verifiable world. The SF text imitates an idealized experiment in the medium of narration.

As the SF-world is embedded in irreality, it has to be the more realistic, even naturalistic in narrative method. We can often recognize that procedures specific to SF operate against the background of and by means of associations with existing verbal and literary conventions of other prose fiction - , intertextuality becoming for the "literary" reader one of its most striking characteristics. For this reader a surprising point may also lie in the fact that the literal instead of the figurative understanding of a text is confirmed during the course of narration.

An SF text exemplifying the association with other literary processes and showing clearly how parallelism and opposition are created by a systematic de-metaphorization of the established pattern is Brian Aldiss' novel *Report on Probability A* (1968).[86] It reveals a method called by Brian McHale (1987) "the postmodernization of science fiction".

Critics point to the close link from this work and Aldiss' later novel *Barefoot in the Head* (1969) to the French *Nouveau Roman*.[87] Unfortunately they usually do not give reasons for this similarity or the existing differences which account for their categorization as SF; for they are counted among SF.

Report on Probability A is a radical SF counterpart to the *Nouveau Roman*, and is intended to be. The most obvious parallels are to Alain Robbe-Grillet's novels *Le Voyeur* and in particular to *La Jalousie*.[88]

If Aldiss' novel is being selected as the exemplification of an SF-procedure this is done because it illustrates this procedure in a paradigmatic, even exaggerated way. Doubtless *Report on Probability A* is an extremely ostentatious "reference text" (*roman à clef*) in which the specific literary model largely determines the novel, as is also the case in Aldiss' *Frankenstein Unbound* in connection with Mary Shelley's novel. Aldiss' profile as SF-writer is shaped by these experiments with the SF structural pattern modeled on concrete literary texts.

Although the novels *Report on Probability A* and *La Jalousie* obviously refer to each other and Aldiss adapts numerous characteristics of Robbe-Grillet's narrative techniques, this is not sufficient evidence for a convergence of SF and modern and postmodern mainstream fiction, as Aldiss postulates in his history of the SF genre *Billion Year Spree* (p. 257 and 307). Nevertheless a distinct relation of parallels and contrasts of these two texts is very suitable, in my opinion, to discriminate the scale of arbitrary and individually applicable inherent processes belonging to prose fiction in general from one or several phenomena that are typical of the SF genre. In spite of the didactic value it is doubtful that an innovative impulse for SF can generally be derived from the *Nouveau Roman*; for, as S. Kohl states, the *Nouveau Roman* has different aims: "The history of realism repeats itself with the *Nouveau Roman* and its renewed reference to reality on another level: by questioning reality an antinovel is conceived, directed against the conventionalised and apparently unrealistic novel types of the past and the present" (my translation).[89]

Report on Probality A shows similarities to Robbe-Grillet's novel by its disorientation of the reader, its lack of action, but especially by its minute descriptions of objects. The main emphasis is on visual observation, dissociated from emotional or intellectual implications in *Le Voyeur* and *La Jalousie* as well as in *Report on Probability A*. The represented reality thereby assumes the character of a still life. Almost no action occurs in these novels and the details that are being observed allow quite different conclusions. Thus no cohesion of the action - let alone a *plot* with causality and precisely built patterns of tension - is made visible, not in Aldiss' novel either; the central characters also never engage in introspection. The characters appear less in the role of actors than as onlookers; at the same time they are the objects of a clandestine observation; they are seemingly passive and lacking emotions. They resemble puppets on a string, moved invisibly, without revealing anything about their consciousness and motivation. The novel becomes a "laboratory of report" (Kohl, p. 182; my translation).

Robbe-Grillet uses this technique to liberate the perception of reality for the time of narrating from the omnipresent anthropomorphous metaphorical language, metaphors that have long escaped the awareness of narrator and reader. Objects regain their autonomous existence in the narrative and are no longer only reference points and reflections of psychological processes. The information they give away about events and characters is equivocal; several versions are imaginable. For each of the interpretations it has to be considered that the process of being observed has itself a structuring effect on the object of observation. Emotions and events cannot be revealed by an insight into the inner life of the characters, but rather the reader has to (re-)construct thoughts and emotions from the communicated observations, to which his projection as a share in the result contributes considerably. The reader thereby represents a further step in a relativistic process, as to what is communicated to him in the story; and he becomes a copy of the central character of the novel who is merely presented as audience of the spectacle.

Robbe-Grillet's narrative technique aims at a disclosure of unusual vision. "While seemingly devoted to factual views, realism reveals itself as a subjective design" (my translation).[90]

In contrast to the *Nouveau Roman Report on Probability A* describes a world that is being observed by characters who also provide the point-of-view; they do not behave *like* voyeurs, passively watching from outside, but rather they *are* voyeurs in the literal sense, watching from a post outside our space-time correlatives. They do not live the life of alienated strangers because of their social and psychological situation in the fictional world - they *are* aliens.

Our empirical world is in Aldiss' novel only one in a series of simultaneous universes; as "Probability A" it is one of a number of space-time systems, "a world within a world within...".

*And there were watchers watching them, and they too had watchers,
who also had watchers, and so on, and so on, in an almost infinite
series.* (p. 153)

None of these probabilities has ontological preference over another one.
Each is as little or as much real as each of the others.[91] We see external
processes that are pedantically registered: the coming and going of Mr. Mary
and his wife, of G. and S. and C. What is the meaning of these visual
perceptions - are all three Mrs. Mary's lovers? did Mr. Mary notice anything?
do the three men hide from him? - only suppositions can be made:

*Every stage of watcher had a theory about the watched; every stage
put something of its own passions into the watching.* (p. 153)

Aldiss restricts himself to the representation of three simultaneous
universes arranged in a row: each subsequent one observing the "lower" one.
For the reader this "Chinese box"- world is made relatively clear by different
types of print and by attempts at individualization by naming some of the
"spies". However, a precise geographical location or ontological determination
of the different worlds is ostentatiously avoided:

*it so happens that the first group of inhabitants we come across is
studying another world they have discovered - a world in which the
inhabitants they watch are studying a report they have obtained from
another world.*
[...]
*Suppose that report comes from the real world! Suppose the guys
reading it, and the guys on the hillside watching them, and us
watching THEM, are FALSE worlds, phase echoes. ... Makes your
flesh creep, doesn't it?"*
*The Congressman said, "All we are after is facts. We don't have to
decide what reality is, thank God!"* (p. 96)

It is also Aldiss' intention to break the anthropocentric and
anthropomorphous image of reality in his readers, thereby for the first time
making them aware of it. He succeeds by reporting with accuracy the
narrator's perceptions of the external world while at the same time refraining
from interpreting it. The matrix of the perceived reality is largely unknown to
the voyeurs in the novel, this being the reason for a merely tentative evaluation
of what is investigated. The equivocal subjective status of observations and
consequences ("probabilities") has its basis not only in the consciousness of the
characters and in their subjectivity, but also in diverse realities.

For the turning of the *Nouveau Roman* into an SF novel Aldiss uses the artistic device of a simple inversion, which as a consequence is followed by a change in paradigm. Instead of an alienating representation of the accustomed world as in Robbe-Grillet - that is to say an implied metaphor and a perspective capable of interpretation - Aldiss' novel deals with several objectively different alternate realities, each of which is as real as the others. The voyeur in *Report on Probability A* not only feels like and regards himself as an observer, as does Robbe-Grillet's protagonist, - he really *is* a spy watching through a telescope and at the same time the object of observations from other worlds. Instead of a modal difference the SF novel describes an "objective" difference between the known and the unknown world. The metaphor is materialized in SF. Apparently the figurative character is missing from the language, making its use denotative instead of connotative; everything has to be taken literally. Nevertheless the effect is very similar to that of the *Nouveau Roman*: both make the reader aware of the anthropomorphous perspective by abolishing it or making it relative: Robbe-Grillet by the exclusion of the person involved, Aldiss by contrasting the anthropocentric world view with that of remote strange worlds. The reader only notices the lack of something which on account of his literary and extra-literary experience he is used to expecting: the well-known matrix, the perspective of twentieth century *Homo Sapiens*. Both types of novel present the attempt to divest oneself of this omnipresent but rarely perceived perspective for the time being.

The alienating distance, the awareness of the unknown in the supposedly well-known, presents itself in SF through the acceptance of an objectively different fictitious reality. In the postmodern novel and in the *Nouveau Roman* this distance is produced by different forms of modalization. In *Le Voyeur* and *La Jalousie* there is no doubt for the reader in spite of all conjecture and all gaps in information that the events of the novel are of this world and not "of worlds beyond", not "about the other worlds out among the stars - the other kinds of men, the other lives", as one of the most popular SF novels of recent years concisely phrases it.[92]

In *Report on Probability A* the SF-reader is confronted with a novel which in different respects is more similar to its postmodern model than to other works of SF; in regard to its lack of action and suspense, its verbally demanding narrative methods concerning changes in point-of-view and irritation of its readers. But it turns out to be only the more distinctly in this one respect a part of the SF genre: by pointing out an objective difference, a difference in the identity of the worlds, where the *Nouveau Roman* uses the deviation of its perspective from an anthropocentric standard in order to communicate connotations.

But *Report on Probability A* not only converts its literary model into something quite different. One of the characters reflects upon the narrated events in the following manner:

> He was trying to puzzle out [...] how the events were interfered by reason of their being observed. Others, too, felt the sense of mystery. [...] Every stage of watchers had a theory about the watched; every stage put something of its own passions into the watching. (p. 152f.)

The main concern of a character of this novel, namely the question of how an object that is being observed changes ("how the events were interfered with by reason of their being observed") and whether the created picture partly reflects the image of the observer ("every stage put something of its own passions into the watching"), is a reminiscence in literary form of Heisenberg's uncertainty principle and relativistic quantum mechanics.[93] SF which, as we have seen, - itself cannot transcend certain limits of imagination because of its links to language and the human consciousness, in this passage recalls a fundamental problem of the natural sciences, especially of the theory of postmodern physics.[94] There doubts are often expressed nowadays as to whether nature is truly comprehended by our knowledge, or whether perhaps we achieve instead of a picture of nature "as it really is" only a speculative and anthropomorphous reflection of the relations between the observer and nature as the sole result of all our efforts.

It is true, nevertheless, that usually - in spite of the above quotations - contemporary inquiries and ideas now widespread in the sciences are rare in SF. The comparatively few exceptions of the avantgarde in SF - among them Aldiss, Lem, M. Frayn, and J. Brunner as well as the authors in chapter 3 - are to be evaluated later in this book.

To the reader *Report on Probability A* offers an interesting and in my opinion rare example of an appropriation in recent SF of patterns of imagination that are transformed into new representational conventions. Its approach derives from two opposed directions: the *Nouveau Roman* on the one hand, and the postclassical theory of physics on the other. The text becomes an

SF novel only by using general strategies of fictionalization common in narrative prose - this distinguishes it from scientific research -, and by postulating an objectively different, materially existing reality in addition to the reader's empirical world - this being the main difference to its literary models of the *Nouveau Roman*.

Notes Chapter 2

[1] T. Tanner, *City of Words. American Fiction 1950-1970.* (1971), p. 180.

[2] For this cf. in particular *The Crying of Lot 49* and J.P. Leland, "Pynchon's Linguistic Demon: *The Crying of Lot 49*", in: *Critique* 16 (1974/75), p. 45-53; P.L. Abernethy, "Entropy of Pynchon's *The Crying of Lot 49*", in: *Critique* 14/2 (1972/73), p. 18-33 and A. Mangel, "Maxwell's Demon, Entropy, Information: *The Crying of Lot 49*, in: G. Levine / D. Leverenz (edd.), *Mindful Pleasures. Essays on Thomas Pynchon.* (1976), p. 87-100. Robert Newmann, *Understanding Thomas Pynchon* (1986), p. 67-88.
Whereas Mangel pays great attention to the scientific concepts (thermodynamics, "Maxwell's Demon", informatics) in Pynchon's work, other critics predominantly regard them as metaphors of the "human condition" (J.W. Slade, *Thomas Pynchon*, 1974, p. 151) and primarily try "[to] translate its thermodynamic and information science senses into social terms" (Abernethy, op.cit., p. 20).- Tanner (op.cit.), p. 141-152 convincingly proves the multiple integration of the concept of entropy in the contemporary, especially the postmodern American novel.

[3] Quotations follow the Bantam edition, New York 1967.

[4] Slade (op.cit., p. 128f.) rightly points to the frequency of religious terminology in Pynchon's novel.

[5] The sentence "the tapestry was the world" by the equation of artefact and reality moves the novel close to Borges' *Ficciones*, e.g. of "Tlön, Uqbar, Orbis Tertius" (Cf. chap. 2.2.1.1 and 2.2.1.2). Leland also mentions this relation (op.cit., p. 47).

[6] James Clerk Maxwell is the name of a Scottish physicist, born in 1871, who invented a hypothetical construction which under the name of "Maxwell's Demon" was introduced into the laws of thermodynamics. This imaginary demon would be capable, according to Maxwell, of suspending the second law of thermodynamics on the entropy of the universe.

[7] See especially Slade, op.cit., p. 152f. and C.B. Harris, *Contemporary American Novelists of the Absurd* (1971), p. 26-28. Harris proves that a number of American authors of the sixties create characters with *telling names*, e.g. "Billy Pilgrim" in Vonnegut's novel *Slaughterhouse-Five* (see chap. 4.1). A famous example of the use of *comics* for American postmodern fiction is of course Italo Calvino's *Cosmicomics*.

[8] Several critics draw these parallels, e.g. R.M. Olderman, *Beyond the Waste Land. A Study of the American Novel in the Nineteen-Sixties* (1972); C.B. Harris, op.cit. (1971) and T. Tanner (1971). Pynchon, Barth, Borges,

Burroughs, and Vonnegut are the authors most often cited for their cross references, e.g. M.F. Schulz, *Black Humor Fiction of the Sixties* (1973).

[9] Quotations follow the Penguin Edition (Harmondsworth 1970).

[10] In a brief passage Pynchon exemplifies the interdependence of the two worlds in his novel when the protagonist is once addressed as "Mrs. Edna Mosh" over the intercom. When she asks why her name is so distorted, the answer is: "It'll come out the right way [...]. I was allowing for the distortion" (p. 103f.). Edna Mosh and Oedipa Maas are one and the same person; the first name is the superficial obvious one, the second the underlying deeper meaning.

[11] I know only one SF novel which has no *closure* and where the most important questions are ostentatiously left open: *Rendezvous with Rama* by Arthur C. Clarke (1973). Clarke's inclination towards mystical and speculative endings (*Childhood's End, 2001*) is here obviously modified to an affirmation of human ignorance (chap. 3.1.2).

[12] J.L. Borges, *Ficciones* (1962; original Spanish publication 1959).

[13] E.g. "The Library of Babel", in: R. Silverberg (ed.), *The Mirror of Infinity* (1970).

[14] "[...] the impingement of an imaginary real upon our world of secure reality" writes Leland (op.cit., p. 47). He links this story thematically closely to Pynchon's novel *The Crying*.

[15] The part of *Ficciones* which includes "Tlön..." was originally published in 1941. The time in which parts I and II of the story take place reaches from 1935 to 1938; late in 1937 or early in 1938 - shortly after its owner's death in September 1937 - the narrator finds the *First Encyclopaedia of Tlön*; the first meeting with Uqbar at this time is about two years previously (p. 21). The time of narrating parts I and II supposedly is 1940 (p. 30 and 17). These dates exactly fit the pattern of time of the real writing and production of the story, while the postscript is inscribed "1947". - The reconstruction of a precise chronological sequence is really possible then, although laborious. Playing tricks on the reader with fiction and reality corresponds to the author's playing with the process of narrating itself.

[16] T. Todorov (1972) uses for this technique the term *modalisation*. It consists in introductory phrases which modify the relation between the subject of the statement and the statement itself, without change of meaning (p. 37).

[17] "Although it has not been adequately commented on, the narrative voice of the story is perhaps the most significant indication of the importance of the

'revelations' which it contains." (D.W. Foster, "Borges and Structuralism: Toward an Implied Poetics", in: *MFS* 19 (1973/74), p. 347); cf. also: 'Despite the nearly 1500 critical studies on Borges, not one has dealt convincingly or even directly with the role and function of the narrator in his prose'. (T.E. Lyon, "Borges and the (somewhat) Personal Narrator", in: *MFS* 19 (1973/74), p. 363).

[18] Significantly Vonnegut defines the narrator according to this:

> To say that he was a writer is to say that the demands of art alone were enough to make him lie, and to lie without seeing any harm in it.
> *Mother Night*, "Editor's Note", p. IX.

[19] In contrast to Pynchon's *Crying* the role of the protagonist who in Borges is identical with the narrator is so constructed that its divergence from the role of the reader becomes increasingly stronger; the last stage of knowledge of the narrator, who claims that all the others live in a world of fantasy, cannot be understood by the reader. An identification with the narrator is prevented.

[20] The close connections to a number of postmodern American authors are to be mentioned here; this aspect, however, will be focused upon in the following analyses, e.g. on Barth and Nabokov. Barth writes on Borges' work: "it illustrates how an artist may paradoxically turn the last ultimacies of our time into material and means for his work." (quoted from Tanner, op.cit. p. 47). This problem of the impossibility of narrating is also Barth's concern as his novels and his fiction "Lost in the Funhouse" illustrate.

[21] Cf. the results of the comparative analysis between Pynchon and Brunner. The problem of a solipsistic world view in this comparative analysis again turned out to be a significant detail of postmodern fiction.

[22] M. Moorcock, Behold the Man ([3]1972).

[23] F. Pohl, "The Tunnel under the World", in: *The Penguin Science Fiction Omnibus* (ed. B. Aldiss, p. 337-369).

[24] The short story "Jokester" by I. Asimov is a variation on the same motif: it is found out that the jokes that are stored in a super-computer are in reality a testing program by means of which aliens can investigate human reactions.

[25] A pointed ending of a short story which implicitly opens up new questions which are no longer the subject of the narrative is widespread in SF. Thus the problems of identity, consciousness and especially the change of the narrative by this *closure* are not made thematic. Seen from the dynamics of the short story that is hardly possible and at any rate unnecessary; from the standpoint of intellectual consistency it would be possible to argue that with the climax

the foundation of the whole text gets lost and the story would have to start all over again! Thus the very last part is not in coherence with the rest.

[26] The terms "teleological development" and "predictability" do not exclude surprises and turns. The predominant impression of the SF texts, however, is usually only a straightforward development in single steps, which resembles the deductive principles of the sciences. This characteristic contrasts with the seemingly open-end structure of texts like *The Crying*. Of course such a fictional text also realizes a plan, but in a more sophisticated and less obvious sense.

[27] Instead of "metafiction" R. Federman uses the term "Surfiction" (1975).

[28] Here "fictitious universe" has the meaning "a world in fiction", not a "simulated world". An SF story of this type presents what McHale (1987) calls "Chinese-box worlds", "abysmal fictions", inclined "toward infinite regress".

[29] *Plot* includes not only action but thought processes and events.

[30] The following textual analyses which prove this tendency to an abstract and objective presentation are all taken from the first part of "The Tunnel under the World" (p. 337-343):

> It was more real than any dream he had ever had in his life. He could still hear and feel the sharp, ripping-metal explosion [...]
> He [...] stared, not believing what he saw [...]
> Burckhardt said suspiciously [...]
> Burckhardt hesitated.
> Burckhard shrugged.
> No, not the *usual* commercials, Burckhardt realized. [...]
> It left him a little uneasy. The commercials were not for familiar brands; there was no feeling of use and custom to them.
> [...] it had been a confusing and, in a way, a frightening experience.
> It was an unpleasant thought [...]
> But they made Burckhardt uncomfortable all the same.
> He didn't like nightmares.
> [...] it was that the *wrong* things were wrong.
> [...] he was strangely *aware* of it happening [...]

The protagonist here evaluates the narrative himself.

[31] In the definitions known to me of SF it has been usual to consider the aspect "science" as a content of SF. It seems much more important to me to explore the mimetic presentation of structural patterns taken from science as they occur in these fictions. As subject matter technology is much less important

now for SF - the question is whether it is as a method. In a later chapter this question is discussed at greater length.

[32] Research as a metaphor used in SF is also hypothetically stated by U. Suerbaum (1973, also in Suerbaum / Borgmeier / Broich 1981, p. 29f.).

[33] Warrick in a very concise remark states this (1980):

> Along with the willing suspension of disbelief, the reader of SF also practices a willing maintenance of disbelief. This complementary mode is essential to the function of the fiction. Grounded in the present reality of this world, the reader must know that the imaginary world is not true. But grounded in the reality of the world he enters with his imagination, the reader must know that world is true - for the duration of his reading of the work. Thus the creation of a credible alternative setting becomes one of the major tasks of the writer.

(Op.cit. p. 85, see also her footnote 10 there with Asimov's remark).

[34] The analogies to *Frankenstein* are obvious in the description of the creative process in "Circular Ruins":

> Within a year he had come to the skeleton and the eyelids. The innumerable hair was perhaps the most difficult task. (p.60)
> He also remade the right shoulder, which was somewhat defective. At times, he was disturbed by the impression that all this had already happened (p. 61).
> Gradually, he began accustoming him to reality. Once he ordered him to place a flag on a faraway peak [...]
> With a certain bitterness, he understood that his son was ready to be born - and perhaps impatient. That night he kissed him for the first time and sent him off to the other temple (p. 61).

[35] The problem of amnesia is also important in SF texts whose subject is a simulated world. This act removes the link between the new and the original reality and thereby abolishes the distinction. In "The Tunnel under the World" the complete action is based on the assumption that in the protagonist Burckhardt the cancellation of his memory is imperfect.

[36] New York 1964 (Bantam Books).

[37] The topic "advertising, polls, manipulation" is very common and popular in SF (see Pohl, "The Tunnel under the World"). The most well-known example is probably the novel *The Space Merchants* by Pohl and Kornbluth. But also J.G. Ballard, whose SF works mostly exemplify the experimental *New Wave*

of SF, chooses in his tale "Subliminal Man" the theme of compulsory consumption by manipulative advertisement.

[38] The motif of an antagonism between "pure science" (represented by Hall and his predecessor Fuller) and the power and greed of politicians and capitalists can be encountered frequently (see also "The Tunnel...", where Burckhardt does not represent academic scholarship but the urge to explore which is typical of common sense, his opponent Dorchin being the unscrupulous businessman). - In some cases this constellation leads to SF texts that come close to spy novels (e.g. Curt Siodmak's novel *Hauser's Memory*, 1968).

[39] A critical situation during the quest for a solution which covers all incongruences is shared by all the texts so far discussed here, SF as well as postmodern.

[40] SF texts illustrating in different ways this principle of the genre are e.g. H. Harrison's novel *Captive Universe* and *Do Androids dream of Electric Sheep?* by Ph.K. Dick.

[41] Examples of this tendency are also to be found in the SF texts already discussed, that is mainly where the literal meaning of a text proves to be the really intended meaning (cf. e.g. "The Tunnel under the World": "It was more real than any dream he had ever had in his life.").

[42] There are indeed a few - in my opinion unsuitable - allegorical interpretations of SF texts. The most well-known to me are an interpretation of Lem's novel *Solaris* in David Ketterer's book *New Worlds for Old* (1974), p. 189-199 and Damon Knight's interpretation of Blish's story "Common Time" in his volume *In Search of Wonder* (1967), p. 265ff.; both try a psycho-analytical word-by-word translation from the fictional to the abstract sphere; especially Ketterer's interpretation is almost grotesque sometimes. There are, however, less forced applications of psycho-analysis (Barmeyer, p. 133-163), but they also give evidence an allegorical interpretation of SF. I object to an arbitrary allegorical interpretation of SF. There are some works of SF, especially among the *New Wave* authors, which invite allegorical understanding, e.g. S.R. Delany *The Einstein Intersection* where relativity theory is allegorised, further R. Zelazny, "For a Breath I Tarry", H. Ellison, "I Have No Mouth, And I Must Scream", P.A. Zonine, "The Heat Death of the Universe", where already the title announces the allegory of the 2nd law of thermodynamics.
For psychoanalytical concepts in SF see chap. 3. See also the interpretation of Aldiss' novel *Report on Probability A* with its processing of Heisenberg's concept of indeterminacy principle. More on SF's treatment of modern sciences in Warrick (1980), p. 5-8 and 85-88.

[43] J. Barth, "The Literature of Exhaustion", in: *On Contemporary Literature* (ed. R. Kostelanetz); also in Federman (ed., 1975), p. 19-33.

[44] For the term "postmodernism" see Ihab Hassan (1971 and 1982), who claims that innovation is the characteristic of these literary products (see also M.H. Abrams, *A Glossary of Literary Terms*, 5th edition, on "Modernism and Postmodernism", and compare G. Ahrends' discussion in *Die amerikanische Kurzgeschichte*, p. 212).

[45] J. Barth, *Lost in the Funhouse*, (1968), p. 152.

[46] V. Nabokov, *Pale Fire*, (1962).

The title "Pale Fire" is from Shakespeare's *Timon of Athens*:
    The sun's a thief, and with his great attraction
    Robs the vast sea; the moon's an arrant thief,
    And her pale fire she snatches from the sun;
    The sea's a thief [...]
    (IV,3, l. 434-37).

"Editor" Kinbote quotes the passage in his "commentary", but by a translation "from a Zimblian poetical version" it is so "alienated" that it is hardly recognizable:
    The sun's a thief: she lures the sea
    and robs it. The moon is a thief:
    he steals his silvery light from the sun.
    The sea [...]
    (*Pale Fire*, p. 58).

[47] *Ada, or Ardor: A Family Chronicle* (1969).

[48] T. Tanner, *City of Words*, p. 51.

[49] R. Ellison, *Invisible Man* (1952) 1970 (repr.), here p. 465.

[50] S. Bellow, *Herzog* (1961) 1964, here p. 374.

[51] R.A. Heinlein, "Science Fiction: its Nature, Faults and Virtues", in: Davenport et al., *The Science Fiction Novel. Imagination and Social Criticism* (1969), p. 41-43. Heinlein imagines an "all-American" SF-hero with the masculine qualities of a frontier pioneer, as is clearly shown in most of his own novels, for example *Farmer in the Sky*, *Methuselah's Children* and *The Day after Tomorrow* (the original title was *The Sixth Column*). The most violent Heinlein controversy developed over the publication of *Starship Troopers*, for which the author won the 1960 Hugo Award for the best SF novel; because of the author's obvious chauvinist attitude the novel as well as the award were harshly criticised by many readers. Nevertheless his novel

Stranger in a Strange Land made him a few years later one of the most celebrated gurus of the American hippie-scene - an astonishing problem only for somebody who has not yet got used to the attractiveness of such radical changes in trend in the American public. Heinlein is to many a kind of catalyst for attitudes that are *en vogue* in the US.

[52] This aspect has mainly been dealt with by critics of ideology in SF, cf. Pehlke / Lingfeld (1970), for criticism on Heinlein p. 70-75, also Nagl (1972).

[53] T. Tanner, *Saul Bellow* (1965), p. 87.

[54] German newspaper reports said that in 1966 the TV-audience of a US SF-series were greatly annoyed when the broadcast was interrupted by the coverage of the accident of the spaceship Gemini-8 (quoted according to J. Hienger, "Abenteuer und Gedankenspiel", in: Rucktäschel / Zimmermann (1976), p. 339).

[55] Where we find him will be explored in chap. 3. For the traditional character of the protagonist in SF see Suerbaum (1978), p. 23 and 55.

[56] As in "The Tunnel under the World" his lack of adaptation may be caused by material reasons: imperfect conditioning by the manipulators. It is a material-physical variety of a lack of psychological and social adaptation which characterizes the protagonists of Ellison's and Bellow's novels.

[57] Cf. P.K. Dick's *The Crack in Space* (1966) and J. Wyndham's humorous story "Opposite Number" in his anthology *The Seeds of Time* (1956). The same motif is at the centre of his short stories "Chronoclasm" and "Pawley's Peepholes" in the same anthology.

[58] In more average works the reader can clearly recognize "avoiding strategies". When the author reaches a field of themes by the use of specific motifs which he is unable to cope with by his narrative means or believes it is too abstract to confront his readers with, he tries to evade these themes by escaping to other motifs - a frequent solution in novels because of their expansion, e.g. H. Harrison in *Captive Universe* - or he ignores a difficult subject matter by simply dropping a motif without being able to conceal his embarrassment through the use of alternative suspense-creating techniques (thus D. Masson, "A Two-Timer" with the motif of parallel times, in: M. Moorcock (ed.), *The Best SF Stories from New Worlds* (1967).

[59] That the entry into the problems of identity crisis caused by biological or behavioristic manipulation could lead away from SF into social satire is well demonstrated by A. Burgess' novel *Clockwork Orange*, a borderline case of SF ([7]1972).

60 In *Simulacron-3* the protagonist receives physical and psychological support from Jinx Fuller, his contact unit from the other world. - Murray Douglas in *The Productions of Time* finds support in a girl who like himself has fallen into the hands of the *aliens*. - In "The Tunnel under the World" Swanson, whom Burckhardt knows superficially, supplies the necessary confirmation of what Burckhard perceives.

61 The latter is again one of the special characteristics of the antiutopian novel: the protagonist and his followers unite to a counterworld - usually supported by the sympathies of the author (Orwell, Huxley, Bradbury, Samjatin). Yet the model *world vs. alternate world* is not restricted to antiutopia; it is one of the basic models of SF in general. Its presentation is triggered by the motif of telepathic communication: the mutants and the "standards" unite in a front together (see for example J. Wyndham, *The Chrysalids* (1955), 1973 (repr.), also the conclusive part of A.C. Clarke's novel *Childhood's End* (1953), where no war conflict takes place between the mutants and their world of origin but instead a peaceful process of detachment.
Generally it can be said that the SF texts influenced by Darwinistic evolutionary ideas that focus thematically on the "survival of the fittest" are especially dependent on a bipolar structure of the society in the novel. This is true of Wyndham, Heinlein et.al. and also of the SF ancestor H.G. Wells in "The Time Machine".

62 Walter M. Miller in his short story "Command Performance" tells about the dramatic conflict of a telepathic woman, who made her contact partner commit suicide, because she felt driven into the corner and placed outside normal standards by him. Too late, after his death, she realizes that she has completely isolated herself only by her desperate act which nobody except herself can understand in its true nature (in: Aldiss, *SF Omnibus*, p. 107-125).

63 James Blish, "Common Time", in: *SF Omnibus*, p. 566-587, here p. 584f.

64 A variation of this solution lies in S. Lem's novel *Transfer* (1961): the first-person narrator, the astronaut Hal Bregg, returns from an expedition into space which according to (subjective) time on board the space ship lasted ten years but in terrestrial time 127 years. On Earth he meets a reality whose anthropological and technological preconditions have changed so deeply that communication and social integration have become impossible to the protagonist. It is true that Lem in spite of the isolation of his protagonist knows how to prevent the impression that he is talking only about fantasies: Bregg's memory of the world before his departure is identical with the essentials of the reader's world. However, a woman, Bregg's girl friend Eri, is able to convince the protagonist of the material changes that have taken place in the meantime.

[65] H. Harrison, *Captive Universe* (1969) 1976; J.T. McIntosh, "The Bliss of Solitude", in: *Best SF 4* (ed. E. Crispin) (1960), 1970 (repr.), p. 152-172.

[66] "The Bliss of Solitude", p. 170f.

[67] C.S. Lewis, "On Science Fiction", in: *Of Other Worlds. Essays and Stories* (ed. W. Hooper) (1966), p. 65.

[68] It is more precise not to call it "fiction of the future", but layout of an "alternate reality" or "alternate presents" (see Ballard, in: *The Coming*, p. 140).

[69] That this cannot be done in a mere historical retrospection (Stone Age Men or the first settlers in North America) is as obvious as the fact that the description of biological or genetic manipulation alone does not achieve a change in the concept of man; the theme of physiological conditioning is often used to defend the ideal of a rational, autonomous and freedom-seeking individual.

[70] In S. Delany's novel *Babel 17* (1966) language and its significance are the main theme. The decoding of the aliens' language is the key for an insight into their "thinking". Delany's novel is certainly an experimental borderline case of recent SF.

[71] See the catalogue of motifs in Hienger's *Literarische Zukunftsphantastik* and the typology of the "Ultimate Science Fiction Anthology" *Final Stage* (1975; ed. E. Ferman / B. Malzberg).

[72] An analysis of the functional displacement between the fields "motif" and "theme" will follow later.

[73] The above-mentioned SF texts "Common Time" and *Transfer* are examples of the focusing on time as an element of change.

[74] P.K. Dick, *The Man in the High Castle* ([1]1962), 1974.

[75] W. Moore, *Bring the Jubilee* (1955).

[76] J. Brunner, *Times without Number* (1969).

[77] W. Tenn, "Eastward Ho!", in: *SF Omnibus*, p. 536-552.

[78] The question, arising from a "time loop", as to how the chronological sequence of time can be protected from the interference by time-travellers is extensively dealt with in Brunner's novel *Times without Number* and especially pointedly in the short story "The Rescuer" by A. Porges, where Christ's salvation from death on the cross is prevented at the last minute, because it has

catastrophic consequences for the "future" (in: *SF Omnibus*, p. 478-484). For this subject which often leads to paradoxes see also Lem, "The Time-Travel Story".

[79] In: *Survival Printout* (1973), p. 295-308. (Cf. Lem, "Time Travel", p. 74-76).

[80] T.M. Disch, "Now is Forever", in: *World's Best Science Fiction*, 1st series (edd. Wollheim / Carr) (1965), p. 235-251).

[81] For this observation cf. also Suerbaum, *Studienbrief*, p. 16-18.
There are very few exceptions to the rule that stories from the future are told in the past: an article by B. Schleussner (1975) mentions an SF novel by Michael Frayn, *A Very Private Life* (1968), that is not available any longer, because there was too little demand. We can see the fact that a narrative technique difficult to read is hardly accepted in SF in spite of its logic. Cf. also the analysis of Moorcock, *Breakfast in the Ruins*. - Another exception is the extrapolating type of SF, which is far less frequent than many readers believe, Jules Verne being its main representative. In more recent SF it can also happen that the reader's presence already surpasses the imaginary future of the author, for example in John Brunner's novels *Stand on Zanzibar* (1969) and *The Sheep Look Up* (1972), which both focus on the idea of entropy. In the latter novel Brunner depicts a world polluted and destroyed by chemicals produced by industry. At times the book reads like a superficially fictionalized report on the chlorid gas catastrophe at Seveso or the cadmium and mercury poisoning on the Japanese coast. The often rightly denied prognostic quality of SF here for once seems to be confirmed.
In this novel the "alienation" in style is much more intensive than in the subject matter. Brunner here continues a tendency which he had begun with *Stand on Zanzibar* - with the topic of overpopulation; instead of evolution these texts exemplify entropy as a concept for the history of Earth. Interior monologue and close-up become the main instruments of representation; they also provide a stylistic alienation for the reader.

[82] G.K. Wolfe, "The Limits of Science Fiction", in: *Extrapolation* 14 (1972), pp. 30-38, here p. 34.

[83] Postmodern fiction does not use stream-of-consciousness, as the late modern novel frequently does. Intertextuality, citation and referentiality are common instead.

[84] "Not only did SF especially after 1950 assimilate thematic as well as structural conventions of the detective story, the western novel and the *Robinsonade*; it also borrowed in many instances the political and social

themes of the utopian and anti-utopian fiction." (Broich, *Gattungen*, p. 126; my translation).

[85] Scholes refers to exactly this characteristic of SF when mentioning "representational discontinuity" as typical of SF (in contrast to a mere "narrational difference from life" which characterizes all fiction (Scholes, *Structural Fabulation*, 1975, p. 62). Suvin's term of "conceptual estrangement" aims at the same phenomenon: "In SF, the attitude of estrangement [...] has grown into the *formal framework* of the genre. [...] *SF is, then, a literary genre [...] whose main formal device is an imaginative framework alternative to the author's empirical environment.*" (Suvin, "Poetics", in: *College English* 34 (1973), p. 375). The physical details of the imaginary reality with their material attributes - especially *setting* and *plot* - are ingredients of the dynamics of the text and in this sense a "formal device".

[86] Quoted edition: London: Sphere Books 1973 (repr.).

[87] E.g. Ketterer, *New Worlds for Old*, p. 255.

[88] In *La Jalousie* the protagonist is called "A". The constellation of characters - one woman and several competing lovers - has a parallel in Aldiss as does the motif of distrustful observation. Even some small details like the painting on the wall of the room are an imitation or reminiscence from Robbe-Grillet's spot on the wallpaper.

[89] Cf. S. Kohl, *Realismus: Theorie und Geschichte* (1977), p. 182.

[90] Cf. Kohl (1977) on the *Nouveau Roman*, p. 181.

[91] This is an important difference from the system of "Chinese box worlds" in Pohl's and Galouye's SF (see above).

[92] U. LeGuin, *The Left Hand of Darkness*, p. 283.- *Of Worlds Beyond* is the title of a collection of essays edited by L.A. Eshbach in 1964, in which the self-presentation of SF in the forties is discussed.

[93] It says, in short, that it is impossible to absolutely define place and velocity of an electron simultaneously - or, more generally: the fact that an experiment takes place alters its result. The Newtonian world-view, which is deterministic, is thus replaced by a probabilistic and relativistic conception.

[94] For this compare also Warrick, op.cit., chap. 1 and 4. Her results are also supported by postmodern theories of physics.

3. VARIATIONS AND VARIABILITY
OF THE STRUCTURAL PATTERN IN SCIENCE FICTION
AND THE TRANSCENDENCE OF THIS PATTERN

This chapter investigates to what extent SF has to be defined as "the genre of variation". Doubtless the principle of variation is of great importance here: SF is founded upon a tension between the repetition of the same phenomenon and the transition into something new. It shares this characteristic with other types of popular literature. U. Suerbaum in his analysis of detective fiction defines the detective novel as "the genre of variation" and is of the opinion that its peculiarities contribute to rendering detective fiction a "closed genre" in comparison to other types of fiction:

> Genres based on variation are always inclined to a formation of their own conventions which distinguish them from neighbouring literary forms; and after a system of peculiar conventions has once been introduced, it often results in a rigid conservatism which offers resistance to any change of its structure and any inclusion of new themes and which often also forces the genre involuntarily to assume the character of a game following artificial rules that has its purpose in itself.[1] (my translation)

According to an often cited argument SF is a literary genre in which everything is possible. This judgement can at this point of our investigation be confirmed only with considerable restrictions. SF is unlimited insofar as it can supersede axioms of our reality, but it can be debated in which way and to what degree its structuring principles are changeable. Especially after the end of the fifties considerable attempts at innovation emerge among SF-authors.

It is the aim of the following textual analysis to find out the types of variation that can be integrated into the system, those that contribute to its evolution, and those transcending its boundaries. I take issue with the above-quoted hypothesis by Suerbaum of the "rigid conservatism" and the isolation of SF and propose the counter-thesis of an extension of the genre and a criss-crossing especially between postmodern fiction and SF.

The genre's "resistance to structural changes" stated by Suerbaum about detective fiction immediately leads to the more general question of the "structurally determining antagonism of the formal characteristics of a genre and the content of a literary work, in other words the generic affinity of the subject-matter or topic and the material predisposition of each particular 'genre'", - a problem which has been extensively dealt with by research on the history of literary themes and motifs.[2] Especially in genres characterized by "variation of the same" like crime fiction and SF thematics are without doubt to a high degree "a structurally determining part of the literary work of art" (Beller, op.cit., p. 2; my translation).

The predisposition for variations in the subject matter of SF is most obvious in the scope of its motifs. The catalogue of SF-motifs has become one of the most popular fields of research; the function and significance of the motif, of its connection with the themes and the typology of *plots* in SF has nevertheless not been clarified so far.[3]

Although this study does not aim at a fundamental discussion of this connection I want to point out here a gap in the research on SF. I propose to explain briefly the terminology and different concepts of subject matter, themes and motifs, before turning again to interpretations of the literary texts. An extensive comment on the relationship of motif and subject-matter based upon former research on fairy-tales is authored by Victor Šklovskij, who regards subject-matter and theme as identical:

> The ethnographic school [...] tried to create a poetics of subject matters and reached the following result: first, one ought to distinguish between the terms subject and motif.
> a) A motif is the simplest narrative *unit* which figuratively corresponds to the different needs of primitive knowledge or the observation of the environment.
> [...]
> b) Subject matter I define as a literary theme, in which different situations and motifs are included. (V. Šklovskij, "Sujetfügung, p. 39; my translation from the German edition).

Lotman refers to Veselovskij's definition of motif as a situation of reality, not only of literature:

> The event is considered as the smallest unit of a construction of subject matter, which A.N. Veselovskij defines by the term *motif*. In search of a distinctive characteristic of the motif he turned to a semantic aspect: a motif is an elementary indivisible narrative unit which is related to a typical unified event on the external everyday level: "By motif I mean a formula which originally answered the questions of society about the nature of man wherever it emerged: a formula which either conserved especially impressive, apparently important or recurring impressions of reality. The characteristic of a motif is its metaphorical unified pattern" (J.M. Lotmann, *Die Struktur literarischer Texte*, p. 330f.; my translation).

The figurative character and structural unity of the motif is also underlined in an article by W. Freedman. He defines the literary motif as a combination of literal and figurative elements, which are mingled.[4] The decisive function of the motif lies in its symbolic meaning in the widest sense, which is created by recurrence and "improbability"; that is to say in passages where it appears it has to be striking, not commonplace, and the whole context has to stand at a decisive point in the work. Finally the motif can only be effectively displayed in a text if it is appropriate to what it symbolizes, that is to say that the signifier and the signified have to be recognized as corresponding.

In contrast to Lotman W. Freedman does not restrict the term "motif" to events and as a consequence his definition lends itself more easily to an application in SF-analysis:

> A motif, then, is a recurrent theme, character, or verbal pattern, but it may also be a family or associational cluster of literal or figurative references to a given class of concepts or objects, whether it be animals, machines, circles, music, or whatever. It is generally symbolic - that is, it can be seen to carry a meaning beyond the literal or immediately apparent; it represents on the verbal level something characteristic of the structure of the work, the events, the characters, the emotional effects or the moral or cognitive content. [...] it indispensably requires a certain minimal frequency of recurrence and improbability of appearance in order both to make itself at least subconsciously felt and to indicate its purposiveness. (p. 127f.)

In SF the stock of motifs typical of the genre falls into quite disparate categories: qualities of the characters, like telepathy, extrapolation of socio-political problems, e.g. overpopulation on earth, triggers for *plot* and action, like nuclear disaster, types of protagonists, for example mutants, places of action like an alien planet, philosophical and anthropological premises, e.g. Darwin's theory of the survival of the fittest. Although the range of motif is broad it is a common characteristic of all these elements that they are materialized in the *plot* of the text. SF-authors vary familiar elements by new combinations, multiplication and transference of motifs. The corresponding criticism examines the motifs and their widespread and conventional variations or it analyzes possibilities of variations and varieties of a field of motifs. Yet the kind of SF-variations since 1950 has changed considerably.

3.1 Transmission in the Relation Motif vs. Theme

Consistency, recurrence and symbolic content are the characteristics of the motif shared by its otherwise different definitions. The literary motif receives its special value only by its function in the text. For Freedman a relatively high degree of complexity is the main source of the literary quality of the text, because it results in a stronger involvement of the reader. He feels the appeal of the anthropomorphic characteristics of art, and among them are "symmetry", "richness", and "complexity" (op.cit., p. 130). As an instrument of the novelist the motif contributes considerably to this amplification of the narrative. Finally Freedman reverts to Veselovskij's and Šklovskij's hypothesis of the analogy between external and narrated world, which reveals itself in the motif. "A motif, then, is a recurrent theme...", Freedman introduced a concise definition, and he thereby establishes ranking of the two phenomena: a theme can become a literary motif on account of certain functional characteristics, which means for him it can gain value and significance.

As with other components of the text SF, especially the SF written after 1950, also displays a contrasting tendency: traditional SF-motifs sometimes form only the meaningless vehicle for the presentation of a theme alien to the genre. Themes so to speak grow into the genre, authors availing themselves of the catalogue of literary motifs typical of the genre.

Free play in the variability of SF was also a component in the author's turning to other factors than the "material" ones, especially narrative strategies. Recent SF has proved that its experimental field can be extended and transmitted to virtually all textual components. The following part of the study is concerned with variations of different single aspects. It first examines the already mentioned shift between motifs and themes in SF since 1950.

In a series of textual analyses from contemporary SF I will exemplify the different principles of variation of the genre. It is based upon the pattern of conventions already worked out in the exemplary comparative analyses of SF and postmodern fiction, on one hand, and on the other hand upon a selection of texts which in spite of an inevitable limitation can also claim to be representative.

It has to be admitted that the experimental tendency and the trend towards a deep-rooted innovation did not extend to all SF of the fifties and sixties. The following part of the study focuses on an interpretation of its bolder efforts.

3.1.1 The Significance of Literary Motifs in SF

The shift of emphasis in conventional motifs has to be regarded as a trend in SF after approximately 1965. In order to pin down the changes in this segment one has to consider the importance of the motifs for SF and its criticism. The most frequent categorization of SF texts is that according to motifs. Whereas criticism has very thoroughly explored some particular motifs, its attitude towards the significance of a motif or the decline in significance is totally unreflected. Yet also the fact that single motifs in SF texts receive different emphases and functions has not been considered so far. The analysis of structure and function of a motif is based upon examples where a motif dominates. Texts where it only fulfils marginal functions or is applied in combination with other motifs remain usually disregarded, although this is typical of a large part of SF. Especially the long forms, novella and novel, often use clusters of motifs, the emphasis shifting from one motif to the other. It is, however, a characteristic of short SF that one single motif may stay central to the text from beginning to end and does not decrease in intensity, which is comprehensible in regard to the greater narrative expansion of the novel.

3.1.2 Combinations of Motifs

This chapter therefore proposes to explore texts which combine different motifs and display their different significance.

Since the systematic analysis of this aspect would result in a book-length study of its own I do not propose to pursue this here much further. Instead the presentation of three exemplary novels by one specific SF-author is the aim of this study, where combinations of motifs can be investigated - an author who achieved a high degree of fame and popularity: Arthur C. Clarke's *Childhood's End* (1953), *2001: A Space Odyssey* (1968), and *Rendezvous with Rama* (1973).[5] Apart from the merger and combinations of motifs typical of the genre and with varying significance this textual comparison displays some of the characteristics typical of the author Clarke. In his novels *Childhood's End* and *2001* Clarke applies a technique of dividing up the text which is suitable for our method of *close reading* in dealing with examples of combinations of motifs.

Childhood's End is divided up into three large sections, entitled "Earth and the Overlords", "The Golden Age", and "The Last Generation". Part I is dominated by the motif of invasion of the earth: huge space ships of extra-terrestrial intelligences approach the earth, but instead of landing they hover above capitals and metropolitan areas. From there their crew members start to communicate with the human world, which is represented by UN-General Secretary Stormgren. The so-called "Overlords" - this is the new name for the invaders - rule the Earth without violence or force, only by means of reason, and lead mankind to unknown peace and prosperity. - The first part of the novel has an open-end structure, resulting in the question of the identity and shape of the extra-terrestrial visitors, who have remained an enigma.

Part II starts with the solution of this riddle. The speaker of the Overlords reveals his outward appearance: it resembles the Devil to the last detail as fairy-tales and myths from millenia of the human past describe him. The era of the Overlords is the beginning of a Golden Age without wars, without predicaments or destitution, without pain and great effort. Mankind, however, is also threatened by an intellectual devolution.

Generally this part fulfils the function of a transition to a new *plot*. The motif of mutants, which is unravelled in Part III, is announced at the end of the second part.

The concluding section shows the greatest accumulation of motifs. Children of the "Golden Age"-generation become mutants by telepathy and carriers of an evolution which finally unites mankind with the highest form of cosmic intelligence, the "Overmind", an obvious reminiscence of Ralph Waldo Emerson's Over-Soul. This apotheosis takes the shape of a cosmic catastrophe; that is to say, the earth is destroyed, but this appears less as a disaster than as the beginning of a new era. Everything imperfect disappears, a metamorphosis of mankind has taken place. The relation this ending bears to Transcendentalist philosphy is undeniable.

If we consider this novel under the aspect of its motifs, the significance of the divisions is evident. In the field of motifs the novel shows less continuity than transition and shift, either gradual or abrupt as after the end of a sequence of events and actions like the revelation of the identity of the Overlords. - The peaceful invasion is the motif determining the action in the first part; the quickly emerging riddle of the invaders' origin, species and objectives soon starts to contribute to the structuring of action and narrative procedure. After the transitory second part the third "The Last Generation" is finally dominated by the motif of evolution. Mutants, telepathy and world catastrophe fulfil supplementary functions in the description of an evolutionary climax that governs the action of the novel.

Clarke's novel *2001 - A Space Odyssey*, written in 1968, is based upon the film script written in conjunction with the director Kubrick. Similar to the composition of *Childhood's End* its division into six segments is mainly founded on a change of motifs, by which each time new sequences of events are put into motion. Part I describes the genesis of the human species. This is done through the use of the motif of colonisation by superior extraterrestrial intelligences. They initiate the evolution of one primate into the species *Homo Sapiens* by means of a monolith left behind on earth. Human evolution makes such rapid progress that the leap from prehistoric times into the year 2001, when astronauts from earth discover an identical monolith on the moon, seems plausible. As before the mysterious object offers a stimulation for development: it motivates mankind to further interplanetary voyages which are intended to clarify their origin and message.

Consequently, Part III describes the flight of the spaceship "Discovery I" in the direction of Jupiter and Saturn. Besides the astronauts the super-computer Hal is on board the capsule; "his" malfunctioning in Part IV causes a fight between man and machine, which the astronaut Borman alone survives. Part V continues the motif of space travelling with its adventures and tests and peaks in the discovery of a third monolith on Japetus, one of the moons of Saturn, which is similar to the one found on the Moon and to the prehistoric one on Earth.

Part VI, "Through the Star-Gate", concludes the spaceflight and ends in a world-catastrophe which for the protagonist, however, means unification with the super-mind - a kind of *unio mystica* of the space age.

The time-travelling motif underlies the whole novel, because, - as the movie demonstrates very emphatically, - the space travel is a journey back to the origins, for the human species as well as for the individual.

Rendezvous with Rama dispenses with the division into major sections and instead has a *plot* which compared to the two earlier novels is relatively homogeneous, being a series of episodes inside the framing action. The whole story deals with the adventure of space travel, a great number of small adventures mirroring this great enterprise.

Compared to the conventions of the genre the specialty of this novel lies in the fact that riddles remain unresolved at the end and that the primary pragmatic aim of space travelling, which is to clarify the origin and significance of the extraterrestrial huge flying machine "Rama", is not achieved. The protagonist Norton, captain of the spaceship "Enterprise" and provider of the narrative perspective for most of the novel, has to draw the conclusion at the end that "for the rest of his life he would be haunted by a sense of anticlimax and the knowledge of opportunities missed." (p. 273f.)

The example of this novel clearly shows a displacement in the relation between theme and motif. The typical SF-motifs - adventures of spacetravelling, alien encounter, and communication with aliens - are instrumentalized for the *plot* of *Rendezvous with Rama*, but they all three turn out to be merely loose ends in comparison to their conventional use in SF, including Clarke's own novels. For not only the mere existence of a motif, but also its procedures and development structures are ruled by the expectations of the reader, which are based on the conventions of the genre. Exactly this dynamism traditionally inherent in these motifs is changed in Clarke's *Rendezvous with Rama*: the purpose of the space travel is not achieved. The project "Enterprise" ends without scientific results, but it has its meaning in itself. The alien encounter with extraterrestrial intelligences does not take place; only its traces and requisites are to be found in the huge spaceship. Communication finally is tried from one side only, but no interaction takes place.

The theme and result of the novel are not new for the reader of Clarke's books, but their anticlimactic effect is stronger here than in *Childhood's End* or *2001*. The fundamental questions as to purpose and meaning - also of spacetravelling - are elusive to the human or the rational approach. Indeed the highest precision in scientific technology reaches insurmountable limits. In this collision of the scientific and the mysterious, as Clarke demonstrates, there also lies a convergence between rationality and mysticism, or religion, between physics and metaphysics.

The parallelism between a scientific project and the SF-novel is maintained until the end; idealizing traits, however, decrease. The sense of anticlimax is for the reader as for the astronaut and protagonist Norton the most forceful impression at the end of the space travelling adventure. Shorter units of suspense are resolved in the course of the action, but not the ultimate suspense.

3.1.3 Expansion of Themes while Conserving Conventional Motifs

Numerous SF-authors strive to revive the potential of possible themes. They do not think it desirable or feasible to comply with the obligation of variation, which is so typical of the genre, and on the other hand try to evade the process of automation innate in the traditional SF-motifs. Therefore they avail themselves of the usual SF-motif, which goes beyond its traditionally inherent structure by association with a new thematic idea.[6] The argument of a text may therefore be new to the scope of SF, while its motif remains conventional.

Such a divergence characterizes especially the products of the *New Wave*, but not only authors like Moorcock and Ballard who are to be dealt with at a later point. It is also recognizable and innovative in effect, as for example in James Blish's short story "Common Time" (1960), where behind the motif space-travel the wider questions of consciousness and reality, relativism and objectivity and the effects of isolation emerge.[7]

In Ursula LeGuin's famous *The Left Hand of Darkness* (1969) the choice of the SF-motifs *alien planet* and *alien encounter* is quite conservative, whereas their thematic and intellectual context is unusual, as we shall see.

The novel *Do Androids Dream of Electric Sheep?*[8] is about an Earth declining into entropy, most of whose inhabitants have already fled to other planets. Those staying behind have to do so because they are harmed by radiation or are for other reasons a liability to the emigrated colonists, for example, because they are mentally retarded, or because professional obligations prevent them from leaving. Among the latter are especially the so-called "bounty hunters", policemen hunting androids, robots equipped with human shape and human psychology who infiltrate the Earth. One of these policemen is the protagonist Rick Deckard. His task is to expose and then kill the androids living under the disguise of the shapes and identities of emigrants they killed. As their most effective means of exposing these androids, the so-called "empathy test" is used, by which emotions and spontaneous reactions of a person are examined for their human nature, in order to exclude the artificial creatures who only copy human characteristics.

This turns out to be increasingly difficult in the novel, finally impossible. What is "genuine", what "artificial" is no longer to be clearly distinguished, certainly not by means of the "empathy test".

On another level the result is manipulated by the difficulties of the android-hunters themselves: each of the remaining inhabitants on Earth strives for his supreme happiness, which is to possess something "genuine", something "living". But artificial and real animals are also not immediately to be distinguished any longer; this is only possible by lengthy experiments.

The perfectioning of the technique and the process of degeneration in nature are so far developed that they become interchangeable at the point of their convergence. An "absolute, utter, completely real illusion" (p. 153) possesses all the qualities of reality - and that means that for empirical experience it is nothing but reality: "[This] 'isn't a fake', he said. 'Unless reality is a fake.'" (p. 153)

With the acceptance of this possibility the novel reaches areas that formerly were reserved to philosophical speculation and that remind the reader vividly of postmodern fiction by Pynchon and Borges. In this text Dick succeeds in transforming the limits of reality and illusion into an SF-theme, which can be presented in the pattern and with the instruments of the genre.[9]

The linking of the motif "man vs. machine" (= android)" with the theme of identity is also varied in a comparatively early short story that is effectively designed in narrative technique: in Alfred Bester's "Fondly Fahrenheit" (1954).[10] The protagonist, a highly developed "multiple aptitude" - android, suffers from a functional disorder which causes him to kill at temperatures above 90° Fahrenheit. His human owner Vandaleur changes his place of dwelling and his name to avoid an arrest of the android, but does not leave him. The apparently plausible, though unusual explanation for the behaviour of the "machine" is at the end surpassed by an even more unusual, seemingly paradoxical, but in *plot* structure and narrative perspective clearly outlined climax: the technological "disorder" of the android is in reality a disorder in his human master. Both are *doppelgaenger* or multiple selves, in reality halves of the same identity, as well-concealed narrative techniques make increasingly visible. By means of empathy the android knows what Vandaleur secretly desires, and he realizes his wishful thinking.

The communicative strategies of the author are indirect and are very skillfully handled. The first sign of the close relationship between android and human is the constant shift of the perspective and of the first-person point-of-view between the two, often abruptly in the middle of a sentence:

> My android entered the room, home from its tour of duty at the university power plant. It was not introduced. *I* motioned to it / and *I* immediately responded to the command and went to the beer keg and took over Vandaleur's job of serving the guests. / Its accomplished fingers writhed [...] (p. 54; my emphasis and division).

While in the first two sentences of the quotation Vandaleur is the speaker and the provider of the narrative perspective, there is a change of the grammatical subject in the middle of the sentence: "I [Vandaleur] motioned to it [Android] and I [Android] immediately responded [...]." In the following sentence the exchange is taken back again, which is indicated by the possessive pronoun "it".

> Vandaleur bruised my [the android's] forehead again and sent me out to find work,/ and while the android worked, I [Vandaleur] consulted with Blenheim. (p. 58; my division).

In this passage the division of the sentence imitates the split personality of the first-person narrator - one is reminded of the literary model of Dr. Jekyll and Mr. Hyde - thereby making evident the android's function as a *doppelgaenger*.

Finally the author uses the progress of action for the unravelling of the *plot*: the concluding paragraph of the short story relates that after the final destruction of the murderous android by fire, a much simpler specimen which Vandaleur has acquired develops the same aggressive impulses as the first one did at 90° Fahrenheit.

The traditional conflict between man and machine that helped to create innumerable SF-variations of the sorcerer's apprentice-motif is transformed into a symbiotic relation. One identity splits into two agents.

Telepathy and the problem of identity are linked in John Brunner's story "The Last Lonely Man" (1964).[11] The change of the known world here is brought about by the world-wide introduction of an obligation to establish contacts. These telepathic contacts achieve by means of metempsychosis the practical immortality of each individual; if he has a fatal accident his identity parasitically joins the mind of one of his contacts, ideally persons close to him. Of course for this reason everybody tries to have a great number of stable contacts which are not broken off, in order to secure his survival. A complete industrial branch blossoms on this contact business.

The first-person narrator, while intoxicated, is recruited as a contact by a complete stranger. This relationship, however, the narrator discovers too late, proves extremely burdensome, since the contact person is paranoid, living in constant fear of loss of love and contact. The narrator threatens him with breach of contract because of his paranoid jealousy; as it turns out this is a capital mistake, because his partner commits suicide as an act of revenge, unites his own identity with that of the narrator and controls this union to such a degree that he reproduces the paranoia of the "dead".

Both Bester's and Brunner's short stories use traditional SF-motifs, but then bring something surprisingly new to light, so that the conventions of the genre, in so far as the themes presented are concerned, are considerably extended. Unmistakable to both is also the tendency to stretch the scope of the sciences considered as the basis of SF, in this case the knowledge of modern psychology. Ideas like "projection" (Bester), "separation anxiety" and "overprotection" (Brunner) emerge in the short stories either explicitly as topics (Bester) or in implied form in the action (Brunner). At the same time both texts have satirical characteristics, which become effective especially by the author's contrasting real theory and SF-reality. In both stories the characters possess knowledge of the basic psychological contexts, but this knowledge and intelligent speeches are useless; for as the processes of actions' prove they cannot influence the fatal effects.[12]

From the scale of methods of variations the shift in the relation of motif and theme has turned out to be one of the most important and fruitful for SF after 1950. It opens the possibility of underlining new thoughts and theoretical concepts and yet not to disturb the balance of the different functional elements of the texts so deeply that the identity of the genre becomes uncertain. The structurally shaping principles - prevalence of action, autonomy of the fictional world, stances in regard to the reader, and narrative conventions - remain intact and specific to the genre. This, however, is the most important precondition for the preservation of continuity in the genre. If this rule is strictly followed, the fact that several of the newly introduced thematic fields - identity, communication, reality vs. illusion - show clear parallels in the area of postmodern and modern fiction does not generally lead in the end to an abolition of the autonomy of the genre or to a change of paradigm. Rather, it contributes to poetic evolution as defined by structuralism:

> Poetic evolution is a shift in this hierarchy [of artistic devices]. The hierarchy of artistic devices changes within the framework of a given poetic genre. (R. Jakobson, "The Dominant", p. 85)

In the field of re-structuring and re-definition of the possibilities which the SF-motifs contain, the system of rules of genre conventions remains intact. The most capable of the authors avoid a radical breaking through of the SF-structures as well as a pedantic exclusion of every unorthodox thought or action, practices which often characterize the weaker products of a genre.

The possibility of a thematic expansion lies in the promising opportunities of innovation for the genre, under the condition that the author succeeds in integrating the theme into the functions typical of the genre SF.

3.2 The Transformation of Individual Elements of Composition

3.2.1 The Change in the Concept of Man

As early as the thirties and forties SF texts made the mutant one of their *topoi*. He exists in various forms: as superman and subman, has telepathic abilities or an extremely long life, or is a participant in a superhuman "overmind". The positive mutations of the human species surpass the negative ones; the thankless role of disgusting "bug-eyed monsters" is usually transferred to extraterrestrial monsters.

Most of these fictitious mutations are closely connected to the concept of evolution and the future. Generally, however, they stay inside the possibilities of perfecting the familiar: the mutants are human beings with still greater life expectancy, still better control of disease, with a higher IQ or greater strength, of a more tolerant, more altruistic, more adaptable nature than is known in empirical reality; we are therefore dealing with mere extrapolations.

For the investigation of innovative or experimental forces inside the genre these examples are only of limited interest, because they mostly proceed according to a pattern of linear continuation of the empirically known. The *plot* of such texts is often exhausted by the conflict between mutants and 'normal' men, after the discovery of the mutations; the mutants form a minority, but frequently the superior and forward-looking variation of the species.

This analysis deals with texts whose conception of man diverges from the well-known and is not restricted to an elevation of the empirical to the ideal. We are primarily interested in the question: What is to be done with the structural pattern of the genre when the element "man" (which the fictional text identifies with the characters of the action) is made changeable and unstable?

The chief example chosen for an investigation of this question is Ursula LeGuin's novel *The Left Hand of Darkness*,[13] which has become one of the most widely-read SF novels since 1970, especially in the US. Several reasons which can be summarized under the common denominator "joining current fashionable trends in and outside literature" account for this fact:

1. a general popularity of mythological and fantastic literature - Tolkien's *Lord of the Rings* being the most famous example; in contrast to more experimental SF novels concerned with mythology this one is easier to read and therefore read by a larger audience than, for example, Zelazny,[14]

2. the text of *The Left Hand* contains long passages of an adventurous character (the journey through the ice, the labour camp, fight for survival against the elements),

3. the novel contributed greatly to feminist discussions of the late sixties and seventies - these were discussions outside the field of literature, which interested an even larger audience,

4. structurally the novel is based on juxtapositions (binary oppositions) like warm vs. cold, male vs. female, black vs. white, life vs. death, light vs. darkness, left vs. right, separateness vs. togetherness. *Duality* is revealed as the most outstanding characteristic of *homo sapiens*. Models from structuralism were transferred into literature - when structuralism was a widespread method in anthropology and literary criticism.[15]

The reasons for the novel's popularity therefore lie partly outside literature in feminism, anthropology, structuralism. It was a fashionable topic, fashionably dealt with, and its popularity continues. Science and criticism contributed to a fictional text that made these ideas popular with a wider audience. The fictionalized form is more appealing, more exciting and easier to read for a wider audience than non-fiction.

The novel is based on the Alien-encounter motif.

Genly Ai (I; eye) the protagonist, is an envoy to Gethen (Winter), an extremely cold planet. Ai is human, male, black. The inhabitants of Gethen are mutations, the result of an experiment abandoned thousands of years ago. They are androgynous, with a latent sexuality that is activated only at certain regular times - like that of many mammals; the sexually active time is called "kemmer". Each individual is free to choose his sexual role each time he / she enters "kemmer". For the rest of the time these beings are androgynous.[16] The main purpose of this "new species" of humans on Gethen is, of course, to underline the specific qualities and special handicaps of *homo sapiens* by providing a contrast. The reader - following Genly Ai's perspective - becomes aware of the peculiarities of his own species by learning about another. Genly - as a black man - also provides a contrast to most of his readers, who thereby can only partly identify with him. A former investigator, who earlier reported about Gethen, was a woman, and the most detailed report about the Gethenians in the exact centre of the book was written by her. Genly Ai is an astronaut, a black man, and the messenger of the space colonists.[17] The intention of the "witnesses' reports" betrays the main purpose of the changes:

> What is very hard for us to understand is that, four-fifths of the time, these people are not sexually motivated at all. [...] The society of Gethen [...] is without sex.
> Consider: Anyone can turn his hand to anything [...]; everybody has the same risk to run or choice to make.
> Consider: A child has no psycho-sexual relationship to his mother and father. [...]
> Consider: There is no division of humanity into strong and weak halves [...]. In fact the whole tendency to dualism that pervades human thinking may be found to be lessened, or changed, on Winter. (p. 93f.)

It is not only to arouse our curiosity or provide thrilling adventures, but to question the principle of our reality - to demonstrate that our whole perception of reality is anthropomorphic as a result of a pervading and predominant binary structure in ourselves. The fact that sexuality in *homo sapiens* is definite and unchangeable provides frustrations, tensions and actions that are absent from this culture. What is 'normal' to us is 'abnormal' to Gethenians - thereby showing that our standards and perceptions are only relative and caused by a set of preconditions:

there is less coding, channeling, and repressing of sex there than in any bisexual society I know of. [...] it produced not frustration, but something more ominous, in the long run: passivity. (p. 170)[18]

LeGuin's model is not utopian, nor is it a perfect world. The readers are led by the protagonists and by the author beyond the usual limits of our imagination and begin to realize that we belong to a certain biological and cultural pattern which is one possibility among a variety of other possibilities. The contrast that is provided by Gethen and the Gethenians makes us aware of a set of expectations and preconceptions that has usually escaped our consciousness. The sexual and social roles are suspended on Gethen, thereby making the readership aware of the fact that they exist. For the representative of the species we - the readers - belong to, this observation becomes an appalling and almost disturbing experience. The suspension of sexual definiteness and of the specifically human characteristic that in an adult person sexuality is not latent but potentially always present leads to a radical change in behaviour patterns, psychological structure and cultural framework.

Expressions like "discontinuity" (Lem), "distortion" (Scholes) and "estrangement" (Suvin), the creation of "alternate presents, alternate realities" by SF[19] are used by critics to characterize LeGuin's - certainly highly successful - attempt to arouse awareness of the reality we live in. SF then is about *us* and about reality; in other words, it is mimetic and referential - and conducts its examination "from outside".

Our entire pattern of socio-sexual interaction is nonexistent here. [...] This is almost impossible for our imagination to accept. (p. 94)

Archetypes and mythological environments make the novel outstanding: the journey through the ice, the fight against the elements, the archaic culture with a feudal society on Gethen, oracles, myths, monastic communities, feuds and fraternal or friendship ties, legends about heroic deeds, tragic love encounters etc. dominate the life and culture on Gethen and the novel.[20]

This, of course, is a strong contrast to the norms of the ambassador's own technological world. In this novel a degree of change is achieved that goes far beyond that of many SF texts. At the same time, however, the pattern of genre conventions is not given up; the goals of SF are achieved and also one of its functions is to make the axioms and problems of reality evident by creating a new perspective. This is also the aim of the narrative strategies. If measured by the conventional pattern of SF the protagonist is no longer the dominating figure. His part is divided, according to the principle of dualism dealt with in the novel, into Genly Ai and the Gethenian Therem Estraven. The point-of-view technique is highly developed for an SF novel and used in a sophisticated and functional way: the identity and the perspective of the narrator change often without transition or commentary. In verbal expression imagery predominates. This method is made especially forceful through the setting of the narrative, which is an archaic, terrifying environment controlled by the unmitigated power of the elements. This enhances the effect of the *plot* and the new world view of the novel. However, in spite of these significant alterations in a few structural components of the subject-matter the whole pattern of the genre model is only moderately affected.

The works to be dealt with now leave a quite different impression on the SF-reader.

3.2.2 *The Relativity of the Narrator*

The SF short story "MS Found in a Chinese Fortune Cookie" by C.M. Kornbluth (first published in 1957)[21] is unconventional in different respects. It consists of two interfering narratives distinguished by the printing type: the first-person narrative by the writer Corwin, who from a lunatic asylum writes letters which he smuggles outside through the institution's bakery; and a second narrative sequence - in italics - which is the commentary by the editor C.M. Kornbluth accompanying the story itself.

In addition to this curiosity the course of the story culminates in an anticlimax. The riddle, the discovery which Corwin allegedly has made and on account of which he has been brought to the lunatic asylum by malicious contemporaries, remains unknown to the editor and to the reader since the manuscript remained incomplete.

The *plot* of the story itself obviously bears the author's - Kornbluth's - signature known to SF-readers from his novel *The Space Merchants* (1952) written in cooperation with Frederick Pohl. His chief topic is the mystery of advertising and marketing: How does one stimulate the consumer's needs? This question is of vital interest for an author - as it is for everybody who wants to promote his product. Corwin is sure he has found *The Answer*, but does not want to disclose it. But he is forced to discover that others also know about his secret: the nation's writers of bestsellers who owe fame and money to their discovery. When Corwin is not ready to cooperate with them, they have him institutionalized for insanity.

The riddle can be solved by the reader, even if the climax does not come at the point prescribed for it in the story. The sales promotion of an article that can also be immaterial by its nature - as for example a desirable opinion or a political decision - is induced by means of a combination of the mechanism of a self-fulfilling prophecy and the snowball system. A certain need is suggested to the victim of manipulation from all sides until he believes that it is his own and acts accordingly. How this automatically controlled reaction functions with writers is explained to Corwin by the ambassadors of the mafia of authors:

> You get to be a best-seller. We review your books, you review ours. We tell your publisher: 'Corwin's hot - promote him.' And he does, because we're good properties and he doesn't want to annoy us. (p. 520)

The charm of the narrative lies in the relationship of the story itself and the frame narrative. By fictionalizing the "real", biographical author of the text in the text itself - not only does he make comments in the first person singular but he also signs each inserted passage with his initials "C.M.K." - the reader is dragged into the merry-go-round of the story's narrative functions. Kornbluth's parodistic abilities render not only the narrator, but also the reader relativistic, and not in this short story alone, but in the whole genre SF, when for instance, the first-person narrator says:

> I was quite sure I had turned paranoid, because I've seen so much of that kind of thing in science fiction. (p. 513)

He continues:

> Anybody can name a dozen writers, editors, and fans who have suddenly seen the light and determined to lead the human race onward and upward out of the old slough. Of course The Answer looked logical and unassailable, but so no doubt did poor Charlie McGandress's project to unite mankind through science fiction fandom, at least to him. (p. 513)

The ironic treatment of SF in an SF story is intensified by the intrusion of the author at this point:

> (I have here omitted several briefly sketched case histories of science fiction personalities as yet uncommitted. The reason will be obvious to anyone familiar with the law of libel. Suffice it to say that Corwin argues that science fiction attracts an unstable type of mind and

sometimes insidiously undermines its foundations in reality. C.M.K.)
(p. 513)

The SF-reader will feel himself to be the victim of a practical joke while reading this story; this is made possible by the connection of SF and SF-criticism in one and the same short story. The *doppelgaenger*-role of the third-person narrator Corwin - Kornbluth turns the story into a game of vexation, in which absurdity and knowledge, play and seriousness mix. Corwin's self-presentation as an author reads like the instructions for the writing of an SF short story - but C.M.K. violently denies its authenticity; through the ironical refraction the denial - as in the passage quoted above - is rather reinforced than diminished:

> I'm a writer. There's a touch of intellectual sadism in us. We like to dominate the reader as a matador dominates the bull; we like to tease and mystify and at last show what great souls we are by generously flipping up the shade and letting the sunshine in. Don't worry. Read on. You will come to The Answer in the proper artistic place for it.
> *(At this point I wish fervently to dissociate myself from the attitudes Corwin attributes to our profession. [...] The only reason apparent for this, as for so many of his traits, seemed to be a wish to annoy as many people as possible. C.M.K.)*
> Yes; I am a writer. A matador does not show up in the bullring with a tommy gun and a writer doesn't do things the simple, direct way. He makes the people writhe a little first. (p. 515)

The most obvious intrusion into the structural pattern of genre conventions is in this story the duplication of the narrator by the fictitious editor. By doing this the "real" author assigns a role to himself and thereby also has his own identity stylized as fiction. But this self-dramatization, which renders a gradual transition between fiction and reality possible, is not restricted to the narrator. It turns out, quite to the contrary, that the connection of reader and subject with reality is also fragile. Introducing into the story the *doppelgaenger*-motif has as a consequence that the reader and the intended message are also duplicated: the real reader meets his own fictionalized self (see quote), and the SF story is framed and intruded upon by a meta-story: the history of its publication.

By these characteristics "Ms Found in a Chinese Fortune Cookie" comes close to some features of avantgarde prose fiction.[22] The parodistic self-reflexion of SF as an art product in an SF text is a serious violation of the rules. The inclusion of analysis in fiction undermines the structural pattern of the genre conventions realized in fiction.

Ten years later Thomas M. Disch in his SF short story "The Squirrel Cage"[23] also questions the role of the first-person narrator; confronting his reader with different versions of his story he leaves to him the decision about the credibility of the different interpretations:

1. The narrator is the only survivor of the human kind and is kept by aliens in a cage for the purpose of close observation;
2. the narrator is mad and serves as a test person or "guinea pig" for M.I.T. psychologists;
3. the last version, especially favoured by the author: "It's only a story, after all." (p. 158)

Only the first possibility would be an SF story in the proper sense; the third transcends the genre and creates a meta-story. The second solution chooses a way which leads away from the field of SF into that of fantasy or allegory: the world as a laboratory and the individual as an isolated guinea pig. The narrator wants to exclude this interpretation without quite being able to achieve this, according to his own opinion.

The reader is offered no aids to orientation as to which version to believe. The manner of publication in an SF-journal or anthology is conducive to choosing the first option (= aliens), but the author is so opposed to the acceptance of a fictitious alternate reality that on the side of the reader the "willing suspension of disbelief" on the part of the reader is prevented. Disch undermines - like most of the *New Wave*-authors - the conditions which he himself still wants to use. He suspends what must be regarded as the foundations of SF primarily by questioning and dismissing the reality-axiom of the genre. By including the author and the narrative process in the story he deeply interferes with the mechanisms of the genre. The naive and not further reflected concept of reality is suspended, and the addressee - the reader - is granted a role which is as iridescent and prone to interpretation as that of the narrator; action and *plot* are minimal, there is no suspense connected to *plot* or theme. Intrasubjective and empirical, "objective" reality are mixed. Lastly, the protagonist is a man in a locked room who is sitting on a stool in front of a typewriter.

As the reader may see from this enumeration this short story disproves almost all the constant elements of the system of genre conventions. It is even impossible to say any longer that change, the main characteristic of SF, is realised in "The Squirrel Cage".

The example of a relativistic narrator as in this story shows two essential functional principles of SF:

1. Even if an alteration primarily concerns one compository element, the other elements are generally also affected by the change.
2. The effect which more than other infringements leads to a breach of the literary pattern of the genre is brought about by a change in narrative conventions and the concept of reality.

Disch's short story is fundamentally different from a "classical" SF story and undermines its principles. The self-exclusion from the SF-genre is achieved solely by the references to editing and publishing.

3.2.3 The Inversion of the Time Sequence

The texts that have so far been dealt with vary the pattern of conventions of SF by innovations of a few individual elements. In Disch's story it shows, nevertheless, that interventions at single points, if they affect a vital structural principle, can have far-reaching consequences; for in such cases it has to be concluded that the genre SF is present only in its vestiges. The text merely reflects the concept of SF, but does not realize it any more. Instead of being a medium SF has become the object of the short story.

In the following examples we are dealing with texts which radically change different elements and thereby lead to a change in paradigm.

Michael Moorcock's novel *Breakfast in the Ruins*[24] could also be discussed with reference to different structural components other than the concern with a time sequence. Since this aspect, however, represents the most conspicuous violation of the rules, it is chosen here as the starting-point for the analysis.

It is important to see that the most widespread paperback edition of the novel - that published in The New English Library - is not labeled SF. Only very vague phrases on the book cover, "A startling novel of inhumanity - past, present and to come...", "his quest through time and space" point at a link with the genre SF.

It will be our aim to see what the criteria are that distinguish Moorcock's novel from the genre SF.

The chapter headlines of the contents make it clear that this text is not an SF novel; seen from the standpoint of the reader, it takes place in the present and in the past. The first and the last chapters allegedly take place in 1971, the year of the copyright; in the intervening chapters a period of exactly one hundred years - from 1871 - is covered. Only chapter 18, the last but one chapter, is an exception. It takes place in London in 1990 and is mainly narrated in the future tense - something almost unique in SF.

In parallel narrative sequences the novel develops four narrations that are continued in turns throughout the nineteen chapters. They are distinguished by print, verbal strategies, *setting* and level of time. Primarily they are linked by the character - or rather the name of the protagonist - Karl Glogauer, who was also the central character in Moorcock's novel *Behold the Man*.

With the exception of the first and the last chapters each chapter consists of four parts: First, the frame story that takes up chapters 1 and 19 completely and is continued in 2 to 18 in italics. This foreground-story describes the meeting between young Karl Glogauer and an artificially coloured homosexual in the roof garden of a London Hotel. They pass the rest of the day and the night together and separate the next morning at the same place where they met.

Second: A short quotation from a newspaper or a contemporary document precedes each of the fragments of this foreground-narrative; it somehow relates to the third chapter. - The third, usually most extensive part of each chapter is a *flash-back* to the different historical stages between 1871 and 1971. The moments fixed are usually riots, upheavals, wars and revolutions - from the Paris Commune (1871) to the Vietnam War. Fourth: Added to the close-up of a historic moment is the direct address to the reader which each time bears the headline "What would you do?". It contains descriptions of a series of hopeless situations that have to be solved by the individual but are not solvable. Usually the protagonist has to choose between several equally terrible or inhuman options. Their significance lies in proving to the addressee his weakness, especially the powerlessness of rationality. He is the victim of a force which cannot be defined.

The different parts of the narrative are conceived so that they can mutually complement and clarify each other. This is not always achieved in a manner satisfactory for the reader. Yet the function of the different texts and their coordination is fairly evident in most cases. That this is made possible is to a great extent a result of the continuity provided by the protagonist.

Segments II and III of each chapter show him as the responsible agent. Glogauer, however, is not a protagonist in the usual sense, that is to say a fictitious character, who in spite of being stylized is generally shaped according to the characteristics of a real person; he is not even an antihero. As the concept of the text is not linear, but similar to a collage and fragmentary, its central character is also a name with different identities, an anonymous synthetic construct. In the second part of each chapter, the section that in each case belongs to the frame story, the author gives to Glogauer always the same identity existing in a continuous sequence of time and space: he is twenty-one years old and meets a homosexual; the *plot* consists of the conversations and descriptions of the sexual activities of the two men. - In the historical retrospects Karl Glogauer is never the same person. He remains a Jew - this is his one continuous characteristic -, but he is successively victim and victimizer, thereby incorporating the explicit principle of the novel "We are all victims". Glogauer is first a seven-year-old boy, finally a young man; one time a dissenter, another time an opportunist.

If the construction of the central character is already quite unusual in the field of SF - his identity is dissolved, as is the fictitious sequence of time, space and action, the structural effects and the method of reception are directly opposed to the SF earlier examined. At times the reader is invited to identify or sympathize with Glogauer; a short time later it is made impossible for him to do this. The protagonist becomes in turn the object of compassion and loathing. It is not possible to define him: he is victim, aggressor, persecutor and persecuted.

The constant change of roles in the protagonist and the changing direction of sympathy manipulated by the author have the effect of a constant cynical provocation of the reader. This effect is neither desirable nor meaningful in the pattern of SF-conventions. But here these techniques are employed to convey a "message" which the novel rehearses and displays in different narrative sequences on several levels; each individual is manipulator and manipulated, powerful and powerless, suppressor and suppressed, the world is irrational and chaotic.

With this novel Moorcock leaves the SF-pattern[25]; its presence is almost magically recalled by some reminiscences. In his later novels published after 1970 even this is no longer true. *Breakfast in the Ruins* forms the transition from the novelette *Behold the Man* where the variations altering the conventions are already announced, to the hallucinatory fantasies of the later years.[26]

3.2.4 The Transformation of Plot Structures

Like Moorcock Ballard is one of those SF-authors who want to radically change the genre. He is considered one of the chief representatives of the *New Wave* by SF-authors and critics.

The slogans coined by Ballard that "The only truly alien planet is Earth" and of "inner space" as the place for New SF point to a reversal of principal genre characteristics. But in contrast to Borges or Vonnegut, for example, Ballard regards himself as a reformer of SF, and by his critics he is also classed with the SF-genre, although, like Moorcock, as an eccentric marginal figure.

The following interpretations also start from the premise that Ballard is experimenting with SF and has to be numbered among SF-authors. The examination of two texts serves to find out how he actually deals with the conventions of SF and whether he manages to achieve an innovation of the genre by his attempts, which is what the *New Wave* proclaims as its aims.

The transformation of *plot* patterns is in the foreground of these interpretations because it is a striking feature of Ballard's art of fiction. Other compository elements of the SF pattern are also affected by this change, on account of the interdependence of the components.

The novel *The Drowned World* (1962) indicates by its title one of Ballard's predilections: the function of natural forces as a trigger of the action presented and at the same time as a means of expression for the message of texts (other titles of his novels are *The Crystal World* where the gradual fossilisation of the earth is described, and *The Wind from Nowhere*). Water as the fundamental element of life assumes a place of special priority in these texts.[27]

More than all the other SF-authors Ballard applies the art of variation. The reader who is familiar with a great number of texts by Ballard can reduce his message as well as his expressive imagery to a few recurring constituents. His work is not so much characterized by development as by recurrences and new combinations.

The Drowned World[28] tells about the devolution of the earth into a tropical wasteland of water and jungle, like the one that characterized the Mesozoic. The change of climate affects all living creatures and vegetation, but most of all human civilization. Where the city of London had been situated there are only few remains of constructions in the fictitious future, and huge lagoons and tropical primeval forests. The inhabitants have fled to zones of moderate climate or have been evacuated. Some scientists who have remained in the ruins, among them the biologist Robert Kerans, regard this metamorphosis as the gradual return to the past of the earth. Climate, flora and fauna step by step reassume the shape that they had possessed during the Triassic. Only a few more organisms of high order, among them man, have survived as anachronistic remnants in the ancient-new situation.

At a very early point the action of the novel is interpreted by the main characters, giving the understanding of the text a decisive turn. In view of the further developing catastrophic situation - catastrophic because of the danger resulting from it for human civilisation and the continuation of the species *Homo Sapiens* - Kerans and his colleague scholar Bodkin exchange their thoughts and feelings:

> Is it only the external landscape which is altering? How often recently most of us have had the feeling of déjà vu, of having seen all this before, in fact of remembering these swamps and lagoons all too well. However selective the conscious mind may be, most biological memories are unpleasant ones, echoes of danger and terror. (p. 42)

The archetypal impression of prehistoric and evolutionary phases in the collective subconscious of mankind has a parallel in the history of individual development. The earliest stages of biological development not only of the species, but also of the individual, emerge from the unconscious, provoked by a changing environment; for the individual carries the stamp of each of the evolutionary stages which its species has gone through in the course of millions of years:

> These are the oldest memories on Earth, the time-codes carried in every chromosome and gene. Every step we've taken in our evolution is a milestone inscribed with organic memories [...]. The brief span of an individual life is misleading. Each one of us is as old as the entire biological kingdom, and our bloodstreams are tributaries of the great sea of its total memory. The uterine odyssey of the growing foetus recapitulates the entire evolutionary past, and

its central nervous system is a coded time-scale, each nexus of neurones and each spinal level marking a symbolic station, a unit of neuronic time. (p. 42f.)

The characters become aware of the implications of such a devolution for mankind:

[...] this is [...] a total reorientation of the personality. (p. 43)

This reorganisation of the human individual becomes evident and concrete in the *plot* structures of the novel. Kerans, the scientist, remains in the devastated city, at first allegedly for research purposes; but gradually his true motivation is revealed: an inexplicable, irresistible fascination. He destroys attempts of a bunch of plunderers and gangsters headed by their seemingly demoniac leader Strangman to block the advancing waters and to keep them under control with technical means; he bombards the dams and floods the hated civilization once more. He flees from all survivors into the jungle to the south, towards the deadly sun, the waters, and towards the dissolution of his identity and his physical existence.[29]

Kerans follows an inward urge which had announced itself in dreams a long time before: the urge to self-destruction and dissolution into warmth, water and emptiness. With his long march towards the south he brings the "inner landscape" of his dreams into accordance with the outside world. He returns to a primeval stage, because he is no longer afraid of this return but longs for it as a redemption.

The symbolic content of the events around the central character Keran is enhanced by the effective use of imagery. Surrealist paintings by Dali, Delvaux and Max Ernst, used as symbols in other texts, also reflect the action of the novel by Ballard.

The descriptions of landscapes, interiors and often also of people form a setting of irreality, but at the same time also evoke an immaterial reality behind the real, which has great suggestive power. Ballard does not avoid morbid visions in his descriptions. The character of Strangman - the name alone ("hangman", "strange") evokes associations that are confirmed by his appearance - incorporates in *The Drowned World* demoniac uncanniness with partly grotesque horror effects: a figure from another world who seems to know the secrets of the unconscious.

The transformation of *plot* structures is at first achieved by the predominant role of the action, which has been defined as an essential characteristic of the pattern of composition for the whole genre. Suspense directed towards the development of the action is replaced by suggestive imagery in Ballard's SF. This displacement of emphasis is made possible by Ballard's sacrifice of the reality axiom typical of SF. He leaves no doubt about the fact that the symbolic contents of events, persons and landscapes in his stories is meant to signal the only true purpose of physical reality, which is - according to him - to reveal and represent the inner and immaterial reality.[30]

Instead of the change of reality as the basic principle of SF we are dealing here with the extension and change of consciousness. To disengage the phenomena of reality from their associations - "de-identify" is Ballard's expression for this development -, to systematically dismiss every acquired interpretation of the world and to reduce one's own existence as well as the existence of others to a mere physical perception, is the aim of the protagonists in almost all of Ballard's fiction. They achieve it by the dissolution of the individual rational existence, an event that is not experienced as a catastrophe but predominantly as a liberation.[31]

The transformation of the type of protagonist in Ballard is closely linked to the suspension of the predominance of the *plot* and of the reality axiom, which postulates the illusion of reality in the text, and to the sacrifice of the concept of a linear time-sequence, which is replaced by a cyclical model. Though mostly scientists, Ballard's protagonists in the course of the novels turn their backs on rationality and the will to action so typical of SF, and become suffering heroes almost obsessed by a death-wish. The giving up of intellectual, emotional and physical identity does not seem too high a price to any of them, compared to the aim of the "return to the womb". To Ballard the future man is a being whose activity is directed solely towards a return to his origins.

Thus Ballard gives up the concept of world and man and its corresponding narrative structures typical of SF. In contrast to Moorcock, however, he does not simply destroy this system of conventions, but rather transforms it. Therefore he is certainly the more interesting author of the two.

Ballard's short story "A Question of Re-Entry"[32] starts with a traditional SF-motif: space travel. A group of UN scientists searches the virgin forests of the Amazon for a lost astronaut who has probably crashed, failing to reach the anticipated destination. Their search leads to primitive Indian tribes with dark and possibly cannibalistic cultural traditions. It is supposed that they know something about the lost astronaut but that they keep this knowledge a secret.

The scientific expedition in the hands of the author becomes a kind of search for the Holy Grail. It is a search with an only superficially rational character which moreover gradually decreases in importance in the consciousness of the central character. His true aim is to discover the meaning of his existence. Space travel has assumed the character of a metaphor; the failure of the expedition first brings forth immense feelings of guilt and the experience of total failure:

> If the sea was a symbol of the unconscious, was space perhaps an image of unfettered time, and the inability to penetrate it a tragic exile to one of the limbos of eternity, a symbolic death in life? (p. 9)

As in *The Drowned World* the protagonist very soon also loses in "A Question of Re-Entry" the awareness of reality and purpose even the will to survive which are so characteristic of the SF-hero. He begins to get lost in the depths of the subconscious, which are awakened by the pre-historical setting.

> His close escape [from a dangerous situation] had left him feeling curiously calm and emotionless, and he looked back on his possible death with fatalistic detachment, identifying it with the total ebb and flow of life in the Amazon forests, with its myriad unremembered deaths, and with the endless vistas of dead trees leaning across the jungle paths radiating from the campong. After only two days the jungle had begun to invest his mind with its own logic, and the possibility of the space-craft landing there seemed more and more remote. The two elements belonged to different systems of natural order, and he found it increasingly difficult to visualize them overlapping. (p. 32)

The duality between the two worlds of the jungle and highly technological civilization, between biological and civilized forms of life seems unsolvable; both areas have become more and more diverse in modern times. But the extremes in the end will meet again in a mystical *coincidentia oppositorum*, which unites technology and magic, pragmatism and instinct. This symbolic unification is incarnated in space travelling:

> The implication was that the entire space programme was a symptom of some inner unconscious malaise afflicting mankind, and in particular the western technocracies, and that the space-craft and satellites had been launched because their flights satisfied certain buried compulsions and desires. By contrast, in the jungle, where the

unconscious was manifest and exposed, there was no need for these insane projections [...]. (p. 32)

The mystic return to the origin coincides with the peak of scientific research and technological precision. This is not only true of one story; Ballard's short stories are all variations of this topos: space travel becomes pointless, as soon as the "landscape of the unconscious" has been reached. In "The Reptile Enclosure" masses of human beings throw themselves like lemmings into the waters at the very moment a new satellite takes off. The protagonist in "The Cage of Sand" wants to remain at the site of the failed space travel enterprise, awaiting certain death, but still in that situation closer to the remote unreachable aim than by a return to civilization.[33] As in numerous other examples the salvation of the protagonist planned from outside is real death from his perspective; he is indifferent to physical destruction or even longs for it, because it leads to the real origins of life.[34]

Ballard's SF constantly varies the same fundamental idea and the same images. In addition to the forming principles of surrealism it is primarily the contents of his texts, strongly influenced by Freud's and C.G. Jung's psychoanalytical approach, which distinguish them from other SF texts. In this sense, and in this sense alone the element of science is still present in his works. The scientific contents which many readers still expect from the genre, in the sense of inventing new technological developments does not play a part here any longer.

The displacement of real events into an inner space, into the consciousness of the characters, gives a different function to the setting of place and time; they become the mere correlatives of subjective experience and lose more and more the status of autonomous reality. In a series of texts Ballard goes to the extreme of giving the status of reality at the end only to the subjective, inner development.[35] Apparently he thus takes up one of the characteristics of postmodern literature; it is at any rate clear that he moves away from traditional SF.

SF structures are pierced in his texts and their motifs now assume explicitly symbolic functions.[36] It is, however, Ballard's aim to extend the possibilities of SF and to measure their significance and not to fit into the traditional pattern of the modern mainstream novel.[37] This, it is true, leads to a paradoxical situation: since the author supplies an interpretation of SF in the fictional text SF is no longer able to preserve its autonomy to the full extent.[38]

If SF primarily serves the purpose of being a plain of projection for subconscious drives, as Ballard believes, then its effect evaporates when this character of allegory is made evident; the effect is similar to that of the catharsis which fairy-tales allegedly have on children as psychoanalysts claim, and which is blocked as soon as one explains to them the reason for their fascination - to cope with the child's conflicts and fears by the contents of fairy-tales.[39]

Measured by Ballard's own aims, therefore, the method he uses seems at least contradictory. But he is not the first author in whose work the programmatic declaration of intention and the real effect differ.

Ballard tries - by the use of SF-motifs as a mere vehicle - to interpret[40], and the constant attempts at interpretation obstruct what according to the opinion of many readers is the core of SF: the design of an *alternate* reality, whose axioms certainly point to empirical reality - otherwise an alteration would not be noticed as such - but which presents something different, non-identical with the self and the well-known, and not, as Ballard himself proclaims, the same, namely the human mind.[41] If the difference between the well-known and the alien described in the text is suspended by the text's own revelation of their identical nature - that of the setting and the "inner landscape", the search for the dead astronaut and the search for the origins of life, space travel and death-wish - then fiction lacks that structural asymmetry between empirical reality and imaginary irreality, which alone makes possible suspense and the reader's purpose-directed expectation; but it also loses the perception of sameness and difference, to say nothing of the aim of entertainment, which is probably uppermost in the minds of most SF-readers during their reading.[42]

It is true that Moorcock enthusiastically celebrates Ballard as "revolutionary" and as the forerunner of those who "introduced a new era of SF - an age which was no longer equaled with space and technological progress, but with time and the human psyche, and with the philosophy of the Sciences."[43]

Yet Moorcock avoids the impression that the authors of the *New Wave* only tried to approach the conventional novel. The reverse, however, is true: mainstream fiction is rejected by them as is traditional SF with its conventions. He claims for the products of the *New Wave* the label "New Literature", not "New Science Fiction".

According to the conclusions which can be drawn after a thorough analysis of the texts this claim cannot be fulfilled by Ballard and it seems that it might be simply too high. His fiction has the charm of the experimental, but in regard to the continuity of the genre or its renewal its result strongly resembles the "dead end" outlined and violently rejected by Moorcock: "to take away from Science Fiction its proper nature and to transform it into a half-breed that ceases to be truly speculative fiction without fulfilling the purpose of the traditional mainstream novel either." (op.cit. p. 8)

In considering Moorcock's and Ballard's SF this study comes to the conclusion that a very rigid genre model is indeed an obstacle for SF-criticism and -interpretation, but that "the conventions [...] usually considered necessary for the preservation of SF's identity" (Moorcock, p. 7) cannot altogether be thrown overboard, because this would result in blurred borderlines of the genre and a disappointment of the reader. How robust or sensitive the genre's identity is and how it can be influenced by modifications can only be studied by the analysis of infringements of conventions.

In the texts by Moorcock and Ballard that have been dealt with this identity is easily lost. The connection with the structural pattern of the genre is fundamentally established by the conservation of SF-motifs. That such continuity is only in the foreground and is filled with new functions and meanings is made evident through the examples by Ballard dealt with in this chapter. SF-motifs merely introduce the presentation of ideas which are mainly developed by psychoanalysis and surrealism.

The following summary of the results achieved in chapter 3 completes the structural model of the comparison between the genres in some points:

1. SF displays its potential which is particular to the genre especially in the fields of *plot*, motifs, and setting. Imagery and metaphorical expression which dominate in the compared texts from postmodern fiction are often "materialized" or "objectified" in SF.[44]

2. SF imitates scientific principles; this is one of its mimetic functions. Scientific thinking, research and experimentation express themselves in contemporary SF mainly as representational principles; for the contents or message, however, the sciences are far less relevant now than numerous definitions claim.[45]

3. SF creates alienation in regard to the familiar by creating an imaginary but decidedly realistic world thus opening up new perspectives for the

knowledge and interpretation of empirical reality. This function does not distinguish itself principally from that of other fiction; it makes SF an extreme variation.

4. Intrusions into the narrative structures of SF usually are of greater impact in regard to the continuity of the genre than thematic innovations. This is mostly the case if they result in a shift of emphasis to the reflexion of a medium and its conventions in the text.

5. SF is a genre whose variability is limited. Apart from the principle of redundancy the desire for innovation of and experimentation with the well-known patterns is undeniable.

Notes Chapter 3

[1] U. Suerbaum, "Der gefesselte Detektivroman", in: *Poetica* 1 H. 3 (1967), p. 365; see also U. Suerbaum, *Krimi. Eine Analyse der Gattung* (1984).

[2] Manfred Beller, "Von der Stoffgeschichte zur Thematologie. Ein Beitrag zur komparatistischen Methodenlehre", in: *Arcadia* 5 (1970), p. 2. For current research see there, p. 1-3.

[3] Vladimir Propp's studies of the fairy-tale (*Morphologie des Märchens*, ed. K. Eimermacher, 1972) with their structural analysis of *plot* developments and their functions inspire reflections about the appropriability of the same model for SF, since SF also frequently uses recurrent motifs and interdependent genre characteristics. Moreover one part of SF- criticism has repeatedly called it a fairy-tale or mythology in modern disguise.
That Propp's method can in principle be transferred to other genres is demonstrated by I. Nolting-Hauff in her article "Märchen und Märchenroman. Zur Beziehung zwischen einfacher Form und narrativer Großform in der Literatur" (part 1 in *Poetica* 6 H. 2 (1974) and part 2 in H. 4 (1974)). The author at the beginning points to the affinity of fairy-tale and so-called trivial fiction, which she accounts for by "the fact that they are easy to read, a result of the redundancy of fairy-tale *plots* as well as trivial *plots*, 'unlimited repetitions of *settings*, characters, motifs, and props.'" (p. 129, n. 3; my translation)
Propp's analysis of the magic fairy-tale seems applicable to SF at first sight, because he formalizes recurring elements, primarily *plots* and characters. By determining the invariables of the magic fairy-tale and their interdependences he can analyze the conditions and results of its composition. This logic is convincing, but the situation of SF is much more complex. Propp introduces such a large number of categories and subcategories, which only serve to analyze one single type of fairy-tale, that an application of his approach to SF short stories and novels seems impracticable even for the conventional examples.

[4] William Freedman, "The Literary Motif: A Definition and Evaluation", in: *Novel 4* (1971), N. 2, p. 123-131; here p. 131.

[5] Texts used were: *Childhood's End* (1953), 1974 (repr.); *2001 - A Space Odyssey* (1968); *Rendezvous with Rama* (1973), 1974.

[6] It has already been mentioned that SF-authors tend to avoid very often a thematic expansion, even if motif and *plot* development make this possible.

[7] *Ex negativo* the necessity of this distinction becomes visible to the reader when he considers the summaries of a number of SF texts in reference works

166

or textbooks: they usually focus on the motif or motifs of a text. Little is said about the thematic scope of a work or its main ideas. This leads to an incongruence between the story and its abstract summary which can give to the reader the impression of distortion (cf. e.g. D. Tuck, *The Encyclopedia of Science Fiction and Fantasy*, vol. 1, 1974).

8 Edition of 1969 ([1]1968).

9 The reality axiom of the SF-world remains unaffected, in spite of the uncertainty concerning a definition of reality that exists for the protagonist. This is the chief difference in comparison to the texts by Pynchon, Borges and Barth discussed above whose effect on the reader is totally different in spite of the existing overlapping in thematic scope.

10 Edition used: A. Bester, "Fondly Fahrenheit", in: *Survival Printout* (ed. by Total Effect), *Science Fact: Science Fiction* (1973), p. 45-67.

11 J. Brunner, "The Last Lonely Man", in: Wollheim/Carr (edd.), *World's Best Science Fiction*, First Series (1965), p. 142-159.

12 This ironic skepticism distinguishes these two short stories clearly from Ballard for example, who reduces SF in a moralising and unreflected way to a tool of expression for the psychology of the unconscious. - A satirical treatment of modern psychology and psychotherapy is to be found in P.K. Dick's "Oh, To Be a Blobel!" (1964) and Zelazny's short story "He Who Shapes" (1965).

13 U. LeGuin, *The Left Hand of Darkness* ([1]1969), [7]1974.

14 Ketterer judges the book only according to his mythological contents which he criticizes because of its "overly conscious use of mythic material" (p. 90).

> That an 'intelligible' summary of the often arbitrary action of LeGuin's novel is possible without any mention of what it is that makes the Gethenians especially distinctive, especially alien - namely their unique form of bisexuality - argues against the book's structural integrity.
> *(New Worlds for Old*, p. 79f.)

This criticism appears to me rather as an argument against the quality of Ketterer's own summary. The reason for this analytical lack of focus lies in the tendency inherent in his book to project his own preferences for a methodology of American literary criticism based upon the tracing of literary archetypes (N. Frye, L. Fiedler) into the objects of his study. Here the background of Ketterer's approach is evident.

[15] Robert Scholes' hypothetical statement that SF is "Structural Fabulation" is largely based upon *The Left Hand of Darkness*. He considers this type of speculative fiction topical, since it is more adequate to contemporary man who regards himself as "part of a patterned universe" than other, more traditional fictional forms (R. Scholes, *Structural Fabulation. An Essay on the Fiction of the Future* (1975), p. 38).

[16] "The Question of Sex", an exploration of the sexual nature of Gethenians, is dealt with in detail and precedes the beginning of the main *plot* (p. 89-96). The *plot* exemplifies among other things these theoretical debates by the friendship between Genly Ai and the Gethenian Therem Estraven (p. 220-224).

[17] The inhabitants of the planet Earth, of Hain, where Genly came from, and Chiffewar, the place of origin of the scientist who wrote the first report on Gethen, are similar.

[18] S. Lem deals with the connection between aggression and activity in his novel *Transfer* and equally reaches the conclusion that prestabilised harmony caused by the elimination of aggressiveness (in *Transfer* this is called "betrification") does not only have desirable consequences:

> It was half as bad as long as only half-truths were spread to judge about numerous characteristics of the past, as for example wars - I could accept that, as well as the total (!) absence of politics, quarrels, tension, international conflicts [...] which I had to consider a gain, not a loss. But it was worse if this reversal of all values closely touched my most private affairs.
>
> (*Transfer*, p. 219; my translation)

For it turns out that the human race as a consequence of this intrusion into its nature has also given up spacetravel and the exploration of the universe - a fact which is inexplicable and inacceptable to the protagonist.

[19] Scholes outlines this concept tentatively in the epilogue of his book *Structural Fabulation*, p. 104.
Michel Butor comments very critically on the thesis that SF has an alienation effect: "The doors have been opened widely to go for adventures, and then it turns out that we have only walked around the house" (M. Butor, "The crisis of SF", in: Barmeyer, p. 76-85, here p. 84). This criticism is justified under the condition that it refers to the very simplistic and cliché use of space as setting for horse operas or frontier mythology, which, of course, is not a very promising and speculative interpretation of the genre SF (see also Vera Graaf's comments on American SF in her book *Homo Futurus*). Nevertheless it seems beside the point to consider every reference to reality a flaw of SF and to demand from this genre that it should only deal with what is *totaliter aliter* -

which would turn out to be impossible, by the way (Butor, also Lem in his essay "On the Structural Analysis of SF").

[20] The conception of the androgynous shape of man and his undivided sexuality recalls the speech of Aristophanes in Plato's *Symposion*. The Gethenian Estraven represents the "man with the two faces": "And I saw then again, and for good, what I had always been afraid to see, and had pretended not to see in him: that he was a woman as well as a man." (*Left Hand*, p. 234).

[21] Aldiss (ed.), *SF Omnibus*, p. 512-522.

[22] See also John Barth, *Lost in the Funhouse*, where especially in the parts "Title", "Life-Story" and "Lost in the Funhouse" the effects of literary prose are mirrored and commented on by the medium of fiction itself. This self-reflectiveness results in a dissolution of so-called realistic narrative conventions and a continuous prevention or destruction of the creation of illusion in fiction.

[23] T.M. Disch, "The Squirrel Cage", in: Moorcock (ed.), *The Best SF Stories from New Worlds*, p. 143-158.

[24] M. Moorcock, *Breakfast in the Ruins. A Novel of Inhumanity* (1972).

[25] This is not yet characteristic of his novelette *Behold the Man* which still proved him an experimental SF-author (see chap. 2.2.1.1).

[26] The novels by Moorcock *A Cure for Cancer* (1971) and *An Alien Heat* (1972) are - as tentatively also *Breakfast in the Ruins* - collages of texts; moreover their hallucinatory character and the surrealistic imagery connects them to purely fantastic literature. These texts are so different from SF that they cannot innovate the genre any more. Cf. C. Pawling (ed.), *Popular Fiction and Social Change* (1984), p. 200-203.

[27] Short stories whose title and contents also reflect Ballard's interest in the oppositions culture vs. nature, rational vs. subconscious and moreover make use of the sea metaphor are "The Delta at Sunset", "The Drowned Giant", "Now Wakes the Sea", "Prisoner of the Coral Deep" and the wellknown title story "Terminal Beach".

[28] *The Drowned World* (1962), 1965 (Penguin).

[29] The act of self-destruction is a recurrent motif in Ballard's texts: the hero in *The Crystal World* finally returns to the fossilized forests; in "Terminal Beach" the protagonist voluntarily stays behind on Eniwetok and awaits his doom; "The Overloaded Man" ends with the protagonist's drowning himself; in "The Voices of Time" he sinks into total apathy and a sleep which paralyzes all

activity and finally leads to death. The most powerful emblematic expression of the death-wish is the really existing, but hyperbolically raised place of action Eniwetok (in "Terminal Beach"), the testing ground where the first hydrogen bomb exploded. Beside the transposition of real places and real points in time into the metonymic and symbolic Ballard chooses instruments from didactic literature, as in his story "The Reptile Enclosure", where the protagonist tries to explain why the people bathing on the beach throw themselves like lemmings into the water as if at a secret command:

> The tide-line is a particularly significant area, a penumbral zone that is both of the sea and above it, forever half-immersed in the great time-womb. If you accept the sea as an image of the unconscious, then this beachward urge might be seen as an attempt to escape from the existential role of ordinary life and return to the universal time-sea.
>
> (*Terminal Beach* (1966), p. 113)

[30] Cf. "The Coming of the Unconscious", an essay inserted into the short story anthology *The Overloaded Man* (1967) in which he deals with surrealistic art:

> The real landscapes of our world are seen for what they are - the palaces of flesh and bone that are the living façades enclosing our own subliminal consciousness. As Dali has remarked, after Freud's explorations within the psyche it is now the *outer* world which will have to be eroticized and quantified. The mimetizing of past traumas and experiences, the discharging of fears and obsessions through states of landscape, architectural portraits of individuals - [...].
>
> (p. 145)

[31] The process of "emptying consciousness" is impressively demonstrated in the short story "The Overloaded Man". The protagonist Faulkner suddenly sees his wife standing before him while he wants to sink into his day-dreams:

> For a few minutes Faulkner examined the discrete entity she familiarly presented, the proportions of her legs and arms, the planes of her face. Then, without moving, he began to dismantle her mentally, obliterating her literally limb by limb. First he forgot her hands, forever snapping and twisting like frenzied birds, then her arms and shoulders, erasing all his memories of their energy and motion. Finally, as it pressed closer to him, mouth working wildly, he forgot her face, so that it presented nothing more than a blunted wedge of pink-grey dough, deformed by various ridges and grooves, split by apertures that opened and closed like the vents of some curious bellows.
>
> (*The Overloaded Man*, p. 157)

These pictures of a "decoded" and deconstructed, that is an autonomous physical reality robbed of every kind of meaning and connotation as well as the accompanying reactions of the protagonist - fear and disgust - correspond to the last detail to descriptions in Jean-Paul Sartre's novel *La Nausée* [*Nausea*]. Significantly, Ballard is discussed under the headline "The postmodernization of science fiction" by B. McHale in *Postmodernist Fiction* (1987), p. 69f.

[32] "A Question of Re-Entry", in: J.G. Ballard, *Terminal Beach* (1966), S.7-39.

[33] Ballard's mythological overloading of the space travel motif is becoming evident here in a scenery transferred from empirical reality: near Cape Canaveral sand from Mars has been unloaded before, which turns out to be contaminated by a virus; the area is therefore cordoned off hermetically. Three people, among them the protagonist, return there. - This planet Mars literally lies on Earth: the aim of his wishes is not extraterrestrial, but an enclave - instead of a jungle or the sea a sand desert - inside the technological world. The conquering of an alien planet is revealed as an "insane projection" (see quotation from "A Question of Re-Entry", p. 161) which the protagonist at the end of this story can cancel, because he has reached his aim on Earth.

[34] Ballard uses several times the same constellation of characters to grasp this dualism in the *plot* development: the protagonists, mostly scientists and exponents of a rational world view that is tired of its own statements, become "renegades of the unconscious". Their forced return to civilization is to be realized by members of the army or the government forces, to whom the mystical experiences of the anti-heroes are concealed because they are representatives of a pragmatic narrow-minded way of thinking.

[35] E.g. in "The Time Tombs", "Minus One", "The Last World of Mr. Goddard" and "Watch Towers".

[36] "just as the sea was a universal image of the unconscious, so space was nothing less than an image of psychosis and death" ("The Venus Hunters", p. 99).

[37] J.G. Ballard, "Notizen vom Nullpunkt", in: *Koitus 80. Neue Science Fiction* (ed. F.R. Scheck), 1970 (in English "Notes from Nowhere" in *New Worlds* Nr. 167). Cf. Ballard, "The Coming of the Unconscious", in: *The Overloaded Man*, p. 140-145. In both these essays Ballard coined his well-known phrase of the "inner space".

[38] An explicit commentary on the function of the genre SF is given by one of the characters in "The Venus Hunters":

It's unfortunate for Kandinski [an outsider at Mount Vernon Observatory, who claims to have met Venusians], and for the writers of Science Fiction for that matter, that they have to perform their task of describing the symbols of transformation in a so-called rationalist society, where a scientific, or at least a pseudo-scientific explanation is required *a priori*. And because the true prophet never deals in what may be rationally deduced, people such as Charles Kandinski are ignored or derided today.

(*Terminal Beach*, 1964, p. 108)

[39] Concerning this thesis see B. Bettelheim, *Kinder brauchen Märchen* (1975), 1977 (*The Uses of Enchantment*); here p. 47-54.

[40] "At present I am working on a story of an accident in space which - even if it turns out so poorly - for the first time tries to find out what space means to us. [...] In my story a catastrophe in space is translated into the terms of our inner and outer environment" (J.G. Ballard, "Notizen vom Nullpunkt", p. 43). Here the author explicitly describes what the purpose of his SF is and what the texts are repeatedly doing: they *explain* what SF is about.

[41] This connection explains again the previously maintained thesis that in SF we are dealing with an extreme model variation of literary fiction by which its characteristics, especially the intention to describe what is not empirical reality, is more clearly outlined.

[42] "The aesthetic effect [is based] actually upon the fact that recognition and denial of these elements are both present. This presence of contrasts, this recognition as well as denial of the already well-known in characters and actions is one of the most significant preconditions of aesthetic pleasure; because the simply denotated, the unambiguous would irritate the reader or leave him unmoved." This effect of "irritation" of the reader is therefore frequent in Ballard's work.
(J. Schulte-Sasse, "Karl Mays Amerika-Exotik und deutsche Wirklichkeit", in: Kreuzer (ed.), *Literatur für viele* 1, p. 131; my translation.)

[43] Moorcock, "Eine neue Literatur". In: Scheck (ed.), op.cit., p. 7.
That time as "time of the mind" (V. Woolf) takes up an eminent position in Ballard's work is proved by the already cited texts as well as in his short stories "The Day of Forever", "The Waiting Grounds", "The Voices of Time", "Tomorrow is a Million Years", "The Time Tombs", "The Garden of Time" and "Chronopolis".

[44] Terms, which label the French *Nouveau Roman* in literary criticism, like "objective" or "objectifying" literature (R. Barthes, B. Dort), "roman descriptif" (B. Pingaud) and "Dingroman" - "object-fiction" (G. Zeltner-

Neukomm) can also be applied to SF in a modified sense in order to describe the prevalence of thematic components so typical of SF. About the *Nouveau Romanciers* S. Kohl writes in a quotation: "Their novel becomes research, a 'laboratory of reporting'" (op.cit. p. 182 and n. 189).

[45] Compare for the relation of SF and science Suerbaum in Suerbaum / Borgmeier / Broich, op.cit., p. 30; "procedures of science are so altered, simplified and deformed" that SF often conserves an outdated image of scientific operations. SF does not clearly show this metaphorisation, which is only revealed by literary criticism, whose purpose is often to arouse the reader's awareness for otherwise unconsciously operating strategies of fiction (see also Schulte-Sasse, op.cit., p. 131). Compare for this "metaphorization" my discussion of Aldiss' novel, *Report on Probability A*. By their function as a mimetic representation of reality the SF texts do not only point beyond the limits of the genre but also beyond the realm of fiction.

4. BORDERLINE AREAS BETWEEN SCIENCE FICTION AND EXPERIMENTAL FICTION: THE WORKS OF KURT VONNEGUT AND WILLIAM BURROUGHS

Introduction

In this chapter two contemporary American authors are explored whose works have aroused much controversy, concerning the purpose, the literary value, and especially the affiliation of their works. Against the background of the knowledge so far achieved their works are used for further analysis of forms of presentation specific to the genre or transcending it.

4.1 Kurt Vonnegut, jr.

Vonnegut's popularity and the enthusiastic reception of his works have been noted by literary criticism at a comparatively late point in time. There are hints that the attention he has received is already past its peak.

Vonnegut can serve as an instructive example of the history of reception and effects of the contemporary novel. Publishing strategies, existing trends and fashions in the American cultural scene, the development of extra-literary topicality and the competition of critics all brought about a pattern of mutually enhancing elements and led to a real boom in Vonnegut's works, in addition to celebrating him as a guru of the '68 generation. Seen from the viewpoint of the eighties the reception of his works appears as a rapidly rising movement between 1965 and 1975; they then reached a high level of popularity and finally lost their appeal. Vonnegut is now something like a classic of popular culture.

The upswing for Vonnegut began with a few reviews by literary scholars, the first ones by C.B. Bryans and Robert Scholes appearing as early as 1966.[1] It was their special merit that they took an author seriously who had not been paid much attention to either by academic literary criticism or by a wider audience and decided to analyze his novels. Vonnegut's breakthrough as an author of bestselling novels was achieved with the publication of *Slaughterhouse-Five* in 1969 and the paperback edition of all the novels published so far and of his short stories by Dell (starting in January 1970). Thus *Cat's Cradle* saw thirty (!) editions during the following four years. The novels *The Sirens of Titan, God Bless You Mr. Rosewater* and the short story anthology *Welcome to the Monkey House* followed, whereas *Player Piano* and *Mother Night* were published again after 1974.

A real flood of criticism on Vonnegut started, at first mainly in articles for journals or collections of essays. The greatest number was probably published between 1971 and 1974, partly in publications of literary criticism, partly also in journals and magazines with a wider editorial concept and readership suited to exert a significant influence on the general intellectual climate in the US. Vonnegut reviews and interviews appeared, for example, in *Esquire, The New Republic, The New Yorker, New York Times Book Review* and *Playboy*. Leslie Fiedler's article "The Divine Stupidity of Kurt Vonnegut", which appeared in *Esquire* in September 1970, especially contributed, because of its famous author, to free Vonnegut's name from the notoriety of being just a pop-artist.

More important than Fiedler's article were, as a critical analysis, the chapter on Vonnegut in Tony Tanner's book on modern American fiction, which appeared in 1971[2], and the publication of two book-length studies on Vonnegut in 1972[3], which in 1973 were followed by a collection of essays on different aspects of the "Vonnegut phenomenon" partly making previously published articles available to a great number of readers.[4]

With these publications the preconditions had been created for a very high degree of popularity of the author and a great availability of his works for a mass audience. Interviews, lectures everywhere in the country and TV-promotion further contributed to his enormous success and popularity with the readers.

In American Studies and American Literary Criticism in Germany the reputation of Vonnegut began hesitantly to gain ground, generally after 1973. Then, however, articles on him appeared in rapid succession in different collections of essays on contemporary American fiction - a certain indication of the fact that the author had been canonized as the representative of one section of Anglo-American mainstream fiction.[5]

Vonnegut's role as a prophet of "subculture" was thereby over. He had been the mouth-piece of a counterculture, especially among college students and teachers, in the late sixties and early seventies, with a political and ideological position and commitment that questioned existing standards and established norms. His works used the vernacular of the times, which secured him additional interest from the young generation.

The most scholarly monographs on Vonnegut in the seventies are by P. Reed (1972) and Stanley Schatt (1976.)[6] Regarding his relation to SF the discussion of Vonnegut is characterized by gaps and contradictions.[7] On the one hand almost no critic fails to mention Vonnegut's past as an SF-author and to make it responsible for the fact that his work was not taken seriously for a long time: "Vonnegut was dismissed for so long with the disreputable title of science fiction-writer", the author of one study states with overtones of embarrassment.[8] Usually the authors do little more than mention Vonnegut's SF-"origins".

Professional SF-critics, on the other hand, frequently blame Vonnegut for being a renegade and deserter whose literary fame made him so lightheaded that his "origins" did not seem adequate to him any more.[9] Very seldom has the question been asked how it could happen that Vonnegut was in turn either ignored by the literary *mainstream* as well as SF or claimed as one of their own.[10]

This study will therefore try to clarify what Vonnegut's relation to the genre SF is, what the differences are and what led to his recognition as an author of contemporary mainstream fiction.

The selective approach which focuses on the SF-aspects necessarily leads to a certain neglect of other elements in Vonnegut's work. A comprehensive interpretation of more general aspects is not the aim of this study.

The relation between Vonnegut's novels and SF is especially obscure because critics often confuse comment on SF in a fictional work and the use of SF-elements. Because of this indistinct interpretation the explanations often lack precision. It is not sufficient to say that SF "is present" in Vonnegut, without exploring its functions and effects.

In order to clarify the role of SF in Vonnegut's work the following chapter does not discuss his novels exactly in their chronological order. The first novel to be analyzed is *Player Piano* (1952), followed by *The Sirens of Titan* (1959) and *Cat's Cradle* (1963); these novels are most often named in connection with SF. The novel *Mother Night* was also published during this early period of Vonnegut's writing (1961).

In the debate on the three novels mentioned the ambivalence of the critics is evident. Differing according to their viewpoint the critics tend to either see in them the climax of Vonnegut's literary career or merely a preliminary phase - often misunderstood - for his "better, serious" novels.[11]

The following part of my examination is based on the novels *Mother Night* (1961), *God Bless You Mr. Rosewater* (1965), *Slaughterhouse-Five* (1969), and *Breakfast of Champions* (1972).[12]

The first aim of this analysis is to try and clarify Vonnegut's borderline position between SF and other types of fiction today. It makes use in doing this of the list of characteristics developed in the preceding chapters. A further aim is to interpret the development of his fiction in connection with his use of SF and to distinguish modifications from innovations and permanent from changing elements.

Player Piano (1952)

More than any other of Vonnegut's novels *Player Piano* corresponds to the conventions of SF, to be more precise, of the anti-utopian novel.[13] The novel is a fictional extrapolation of the future from trends of the present, thus satisfying one of the most common conditions of SF-theory.[14] Its satirical criticism is especially directed against the omnipotence of technology. The dichotomy of technology and nature, the social oppositions and contrasts, the outsider as the hero of rebellion, the caricature of the American Way of Life, the guided tour for the unfamiliar visitor around this Brave New World - all these are elements which are well-known from other dystopian novels of the twentieth century. A detailed comparison with Huxley's novel *Brave New World* would reveal a number of similarities, including the above-mentioned factors but also a number of differences.[15]

The dystopian character of this novel has also been discussed repeatedly in SF-criticism. *Player Piano* shows more conformity with SF than the other novels and therefore has been less controversial in regard to its genre affiliation. Only a diachronic comparison with Vonnegut's later novels reveals that *Player Piano* touches upon themes and techniques which later on increase continually or move from the fringes to the centre of the narration.

The determination from outside and the concomitant loss of identity of the individual bear a significance typical of the anti-utopian novel, but with a special twist. The determination is not exercised by physical influence, but rather the protagonist is made the pawn of rival parties to such an extent that it is impossible for him to keep up autonomy and identity.[16] He is used like a tool, so that not only the success of technology but also the fight against it become absurd.

Paul Proteus whose initials are identical, also with those of the novel's title, which in itself is a reversal of the normal usage "Piano Player" - is already labeled by his last name as a non-identity, changing his shape and colour like the Grecian Sea-God. Yet nothing is more important to him than to prove his identity to himself and to his environment. All that he does only leads to the reverse of his desired effects: the more he tries to get out the deeper he gets into the network of manipulation. When he tries to achieve the final proof of his autonomous personality the situation develops into a farce.

The theme of such tragi-comical attempts and their absurd results is brought forward several times in the novel. The first anti-climax of this kind is described by the author in chapter 23 of the novel. Proteus wants to give up his position as a top manager after long inward struggles, since he believes that he does not want to bear any longer the responsibility for an inhuman technology. But his intention is undermined by the leaders of the system. At the moment when Proteus tries to escape from their control they expel him from the system - whether only for appearances as they say, or in earnest is impossible to tell - only to let him infiltrate the forces of the enemy as an *agent provocateur*.[17] Proteus' helpless anger, his desperate attempts at being an autonomous person are greeted with hilarity and applause, since they are categorized as role-playing only. Perfect play and the authentic expression of his own will can no longer be distinguished.

Proteus meets the fate of the "plotted plotter" who wants to be a rebel but can only be a puppet on a string. The leaders of the revolution also use him as an instrument for purposes of their own. Without his knowledge and against his will he is turned, as later happens to the protagonist Campbell in *Mother Night*, into the mouthpiece for the ideas of others. But the revolutionaries in the end all meet their defeat when they become witnesses for the victory announcing only a new round in the cyclical return of the same. The rebels are more than happy after the destruction of all the machines to prove their usefulness and competence by repairing the machines which in a short time will again render men superfluous.

Tanner has already pointed out that Vonnegut by the example of Proteus describes a dilemma which characterizes the anti-hero of a whole type of fiction and, we have to add, which is quite unusual for the protagonist of an SF novel: in order not to succumb to a huge mechanism the central character wants to withdraw:

> wanting to find a place beyond all plots and systems, some private space, of "border area" - a house by the side of the road of history and society. (Tanner, *City*, p. 182)

Proteus' development and fate would fit the protagonists of mainstream novels, e.g. those by Ellison or Bellow, much better than an SF-hero. This rebellion is not a way out for the individual; whether the withdrawal into the self can be realized is unclear.

If in *Player Piano* we are dealing with a work that preserves in a rather conventional manner the norms and traditions of the genre SF and dystopia,[18] Vonnegut's next novel *The Sirens of Titan* already reveals a specific and unorthodox use of SF and its elements.

The Sirens of Titan (1959)

Determination and manipulation in *The Sirens of Titan* become the central themes: the course of the action exemplifies by the changeable fate of the characters the predominance of these themes. For the characters the action culminates in the central knowledge that the human condition is governed by a combination of arbitrariness and determinism. This recognition recurs as a theme in the other novels by Vonnegut. But *Sirens* also recreates in the guise of the novel the contingency which is so characteristic of life and imitates by its structure the topic it deals with. The text describes a universe which is "plotless" as well as "plotted". The *plot* of the novel partly appears erratic, like a loosely connected series of episodes which can only be kept together by the main characters Constant and Rumfoord. Thus it becomes the equivalent of the interplanetary odyssey of the protagonist Malachi Constant.

The reader's impression of being tied up into permanent narrative digressions is equally true and false. On the one hand it turns out that the different parts and their themes have clearly a place in the total plan of the novel. Yet at the same time the individual sequences, which are linked together by the unaltered setting, preserve their episodic structures. Each serves the development of a *sub-plot* loosely connected with the rest of the action and illustrating a single aspect of the general topic.

This chief topic is the existence of a system which manipulates the whole of the history of the planet Earth and of mankind. The Tralfamadorian Salo reveals shortly before the end that evolution merely served the purpose of helping the courier of the planet Tralfamadore on his intergalactic travel.

Moreover, *Sirens* also discloses a number of other themes, each of which is significant not only in this novel but also in Vonnegut's other novels:

a) the search of the human species for purpose and explanation, "how to find the meaning of life", incorporated in the character of Malachi Constant:

> Constant pined for just one thing - a single message that was sufficiently dignified and important to merit his carrying it humbly between two points. (p. 17)

The quest for the meaning of life is answered at the end in a way justifying Reed's headline "Existential Science Fiction" for *Sirens*. For Chrono, Constant's son, all meaning is enclosed in the moment and in existence itself.

b) The American Way of Life, a parody of its ideologies, which are illustrated in the biography of Malachi's father "from rags to riches" and their self-presentation in language, social conventions, life style etc.

c) The problems of partnerships, friendship and love, varied in the failed and only partially successful examples. The failure of partnerships is variously exemplified in the motif of rejection, desertion, the killing of a friend by a friend. By means of this theme Vonnegut also displays his representation of lack of human freedom and misguided intention, which does not lack a certain tragic or tragi-comical element. Consequently Unk-Malachi kills his best and only friend Stony Stevenson; but Béatrice Rumfoord becomes Malachi's girlfriend, although she has sworn sacred vows never to stay in the same time-zone with him.

d) The authenticity of feelings, their devastation and elimination by the total planning of the individual. While men are turned into automatons the machine Salo from Tralfamadore has developed human qualities.

e) Finally there is the war topic (Mars vs. Terra), whose cynical presentation in chapters 6 and 7 anticipates the pacifist and didactic element in Vonnegut's later novels.[19] Militarism appears as the hyperbolic variation of the theme of the manipulation and dehumanizing of the individual.

The motifs by which the author introduces the themes into this novel are in *Sirens* mainly interplanetary travelling, invasion, aliens, robots. They are traditional SF-motifs.

The key for the answer to the question of Vonnegut's special relation to SF lies, as far as *Sirens* is concerned, especially in this combination of themes and motifs.

In a first opposition of a catalogue of themes and motifs a certain incongruence is striking which as an impression also accompanies the reading of the novel. The few motifs seem overloaded by the amount of ideological aphorisms and satirical and didactic intentions.

All the themes of this novel are widespread in modern and postmodern American fiction. All the motifs come from the repertory of SF. For *Sirens* therefore the strict division into themes and techniques as Goldsmith proposes it, seems understandable:

> At any rate, neither Vonnegut's motifs nor techniques need be defended in a discussion of his themes, which are without doubt as respectable a collection as could be found anywhere in the modern American novel.[20]

It would have been more meaningful for the critic if he had paid less attention to defensive strategies and the proof of "respectability" and had instead more thoroughly looked into the function of the incongruence of themes and motifs.

The overriding theme of the novel, which is the omnipresence of a controlling system that as a *leitmotiv* can be traced in all of Vonnegut's novels,[21] was also to be found in other fictional works, e.g. Pynchon's *The Crying of Lot 49.*[22]

The linking of the theme with SF-motifs is achieved in a very characteristic way as early as Vonnegut's second novel. The SF-motifs in *Siren* are little more than mere vehicles. The author uses these as suitable means by which he can represent his themes.

The motifs he uses, however, change with the influence of superior themes. They assume the function of metaphors. The narrator leaves no doubt for his reader that the fictitious world is only *prima facie* a different one and that his statements really aim at an empirical reality. The unreal character of Vonnegut's fictitious world is correctly characterized by a critic with the phrase "parodies of realism".[23]

The metaphorical use of SF-elements by Vonnegut, however, violates the dominant of SF, because we had stated that traditionally it is fundamental for the genre to bestow all the elements of the real world on the fictitious one and to present the SF-world as ontologically different from ours. Indeed in this novel the author's distance from the genre SF first reveals itself. Whereas *Player Piano* could still be seen as an extrapolating vision of the future *and* as social criticism of existing trends *Sirens* obviously aims at epistemological and philosophical questions, besides being a social satire.

The fact that the novel employs motifs of SF as explicit metaphors, namely the consciously coded and visibly intended transformation of a phenomenon the reader is familiar with, is revealed in a number of other passages and also in Malachi's identification as a figure symbolic of the human race. When after his episodes on Mars and Mercury he has landed on Earth once more, he describes his biography in a nutshell:

I was a victim of a series of accidents, as are we all. (p. 229)

An ancient literary *topos* is ostentatiously employed here, stressed by the printing: the (space-)journey has become an allegory for the odyssey of human life.

The use which the author in *Sirens* makes of the SF-motif "aliens" is another indication of the functional change of SF in this novel. The two extraterrestrial species the author creates are the "harmoniums" on the planet Mercury and the inhabitants of the planet Tralfamadore. Both represent contrasting alternatives to *homo sapiens*. But their only purpose is the ironical and remote characterization of the human race by the author. The myth of the planet Tralfamadore tells of the creation of its first inhabitant, a machine, and about its creators:

> These creatures spent most of their time trying to find out what their purpose was. And every time they found out what seemed to be a purpose of themselves, the purpose seemed so low that the creatures were filled with disgust and shame. And, rather than serve such a low purpose, the creatures would make a machine to serve it. This left the creatures free to serve higher purposes. But whenever they found a higher purpose, the purpose still wasn't high enough. (p. 274)

Here Vonnegut once again plays with an SF-convention: the alienation of the well-known. In this case, however, he presents only a parodistic as-if-alienation, and the process of codification is all too obvious. Not the "estranged" as a contrasting parallel is the centre of attention, but the well-known. In contrast to LeGuin's *The Left Hand of Darkness*, for example, where the description of another species makes the anthropomorphic structures of our mind more clearly visible, Vonnegut describes the empirical and real *as if* it were something alien. And although Clarke's *Space Odyssey* is a space journey and at the same time a symbolic journey through the individual and collective history of mankind with a clearly visible purpose of initiation, this remains only one of the aspects that become significant in the novel. Clarke still exemplifies the genre SF as "a literature of change", which he postulated as an essayist "In Defense of Science Fiction".[24] In Vonnegut's novel, however, the main accent is on the symbolic function of SF.

With *Sirens* Vonnegut has reached a turning point in regard to the use he makes of SF-elements. As a system of rules the genre and its structural pattern are no longer effective in this novel.

The elements that he isolates from the SF-system of conventions are put to a new kind of use. The "representational discontinuity" that can be considered typical of SF becomes in his hands a merely modal alienation.[25] In contrast to the narrative conventions of SF Vonnegut makes evident that he is talking exclusively about the Here and Now. The printed revelation of the metaphorical character puts this novel outside the genre SF.

Apart from the philosophical themes of *Sirens* it is primarily the structure of the *plot* that is not typical of SF. The action does not proceed teleologically, but in episodes; Freese concisely uses the image of the spiral to define its movement. The suspense of the novel's action is rather weak. The imitation of the scientific experimental progress frequently realized in SF texts, and both pragmatic and purposeful, because of the *plot* of the novel, is not to be found here.[26] In contrast to, for example, *Player Piano* and *Cat's Cradle Sirens* is not even based upon essential technological changes and scientific developments. Instead of the imitation of the scientific formal principle *Titan* often uses aphorisms which are sometimes full of sentimental pathos.

And the antihero is a creation of postmodern fiction rather than SF. Vonnegut's protagonists are primarily suffering heroes; that as victims they are at the same time "outrageous fortune's cruelest agents" (p. 162) they are only able to recognize at a late stage or not at all; and then this fact seems grotesque, because the predominant sensation of the characters is always the helplessness in regard to the action.

Sirens is a novel that in the criticism on Vonnegut's works remains in the background. This lesser degree of popularity with critics and readers is understandable if we consider the reduced suspense and the lack of historical intertextuality which characterizes *Slaughterhouse-Five*.

I therefore conclude that fans of "SF proper" will possibly feel duped by this novel, because Vonnegut plays with SF-conventions. The non-message of the Tralfamadorians, which is "dot = greetings" presents certainly an anti-climax even for the expectations of an SF-reader. The way in which the author solves the tension in a *closure* is a practical joke - not only at the cost of the human race and their culture but also at the cost of SF.

What has to be examined in the following interpretations is which of the characteristics of *Titan* are preserved and how Vonnegut further uses elements from SF.

Cat's Cradle (1963)

The topic 'science' and the prototype of the scientist as the central character seem to place *Cat's Cradle* more than any other of Vonnegut's novels in the neighbourhood of SF.

The first part describes the attempt of the first-person narrator Jonah (John) to collect as many facts as possible about the "father of the atom bomb", Dr. Felix Hoenikker. Finally the narrator travels to the island San Lorenzo in the Caribbean to visit Hoenikker's eldest son, Franklin, after having interviewed a number of persons in the USA. Franklin lives on San Lorenzo as the closest adviser and deputy of the dictator Papa Monzano.[27] While the narrator is there the world-catastrophe "Ice-Nine", Hoenikker's last discovery, takes place and paralyzes everything. Only a few individuals survive the end, among them Jonah and Bokonon, who is the founder of the religion "Bokononism".

The examination of this novel will also be limited to those aspects that are significant for the use of SF-elements characteristic in Vonnegut. Therefore other components like the role of the narrator in *Cat's Cradle* and its function as satire of the American Way of Life remain in the background. The role of religious beliefs and Bokononism, although a central theme of the novel, is also only interpreted as an aspect of its relation to SF.[28]

Bokononism, the world view and philosophy named after its founder, which is prohibited on San Lorenzo but whose rites are practised by all the inhabitants of the island - even the narrator converts on account of the events described in the novel - stands in sharp contrast, on the one hand, to every institutionalized denomination based on dogma and theological teaching, especially Christianity, and on the other hand in opposition to the sciences.[29] In contrast to both, Bokonon's doctrine focuses on man and his pursuit of happiness.

On the level of the constellation of characters this contrast is reflected in the characters of Hoenikker and Bokonon. Felix Hoenikker as the spiritual father of the nuclear bomb represents the character of science and technology, which is hostile towards man. Because of the hypertrophical rational thinking and experimenting and the connected schizoid dissociation of all emotions his mind and his actions have lost all moral orientation. Hoenikker is, as is underlined several times in the novel, "innocent": "he'd never hurt a fly [...], he was so innocent he was practically a Jesus - except for the son of God part" (p. 52). Yet this "innocence" is a crime, since it does not precede the original sin, but is its effect. Newton Hoenikker, the youngest son of the scientist, reports to the narrator that on the day of the first nuclear test a colleague told his father: "'Science has now known sin.' And do you know what Father said? He said, 'What is sin?'" (p. 21).

Felix Hoenikker is psychologically invulnerable, even towards his own children:

> He was one of the best-protected human beings who ever lived. People couldn't get at him because he just wasn't interested in people. (p. 19)

This invulnerability in him corresponds to his incapacity for empathy.[30] Hoenikker is psychologically dead. "I wonder if he wasn't born dead", one of the interviewed persons says about him (p. 53).

In one point *Cat's Cradle* meets the usual understanding of SF more than other novels by Vonnegut: the topical character of the "mad scientist" is revived - modified - in Felix Hoenikker, and science is a main issue. It is true, however, that the author is not concerned with extrapolation plans of the future or speculations on the basis of presumed technological and social developments. Science is exclusively dealt with from the point-of-view of ethical aspects. Research and technological evolution as having their end in themselves, as "pure science", are, - as Vonnegut makes clear to his readers, - immoral, because they are inhuman. Scientific research and experimentation have lost their ideal character. Hoenikker's 'innocence' is the most serious guilt that he can be reproached with, because he ignores the category of a human sense of responsibility and of humanity in general.

For Hoenikker scientific and exploratory activity has the character of an intellectual game:

> Why should I bother with made-up games when there are so many real ones going on?

he says about himself (p. 17). The experiment of the nuclear bomb explosion finally is one of the "real games".

The pair of contrasts "made-up game vs. real game" has its correspondence in the dualism of faith vs. science and illusion vs. truth. As in the binary oppositions past vs. present and atom bomb vs. Ice-Nine these are only apparently contrasts. In reality they merely occur in combinations.

The category of the future is fundamentally irrelevant for *Cat's Cradle*. The aim of the novel is the interpretation of the past and the present, not the invention of presumably real future worlds. This is here obvious to the reader, in contrast to traditional SF texts. The widespread view that SF is about the future, should be modified to the statement that it is a hypothetical, not a prognostic type of literature. This also does not concern *Cat's Cradle*: what *might* be is not the question here.

The opposition on which the structure of *Cat's Cradle* is based and which is symbolized by atomic bomb and Ice-Nine is actually not past vs. future but reality vs. fantasy, fact vs. fiction. These two poles are symbolized by Hiroshima and Ice-Nine.

"The book was to be factual", says Jonah about his planned report on August 5, 1945 (p. 11). But as the sentence already suggests, it turned out differently: the resulting book is not a report. *Fact* and *fiction* are combined and mingle in the novel. The two central events, the nuclear bomb explosion and the freezing of the world, reflect each other. The second is created to mirror and explain the first. This turns the divided narrative into an allegory of the role of fiction: to be an interpretation of reality and to reveal reality by coding and decoding.

The relation fact / fiction seems reversed: the historical facts which the narrative wants to describe, that is to say the dropping of the nuclear bomb and the life of its inventor, are only indirectly accessible to the narrator. He has to rely on the reports of other witnesses. Selection and perspective thus undergo a multiple reflection through the different narrators who serve as media. The fictitious event, on the other hand, the world catastrophe Ice-Nine, appears as a factual report and direct description by the eye witness Jonah.

The most important reason for the selection of this form of representation lies in the subject-matter of the book. There is, according to Vonnegut, a category of facts whose reality can only be worked out and grasped by the medium of fantastic fiction.[31] One of these facts is the dropping of the atom bomb.[32]

Instead of suspended SF-characteristics Vonnegut here focuses on moralistic, didactic and poetological statements. In *Cat's Cradle*, the author eliminates fundamental rules of SF and dissociates the novel from the genre. The most significant are the category "future", "change of the world", the power of rationality as principle of perception and formation, and the reality axiom as a necessity for the fictitious world of the narrative. The remnants of SF which link *Cat's Cradle* to the genre, are inherent in the topic of science and its historical landmarks, by which the narrator introduces his themes; in the scientist as the protagonist of the novel and in the traditional SF-motif of a world catastrophe as a dominant motif of the action.

The interdependence of fact and fiction is to become the main theme in *Mother Night*. But on the whole *Slaughterhouse-Five* can be more easily compared to *Cat's Cradle* than *Mother Night*. As Reed emphasizes, *Slaughterhouse-Five* contains numerous parallels and allusions to *Cat's Cradle*.[33] As he correctly remarks the reflection of the real catastrophe in an imaginary end of the world is imperfect, as opposed to *Slaughterhouse-Five* which was written later:

> The final catastrophe by ice-nine [...] does not become a dominating event in itself. The Dresden raid does achieve such centrality in *Slaughterhouse-Five*. (p. 186)

In *Cat's Cradle* the integration of fantasy and reality is not yet successful. The novel has still something of the loose and episodic structure which flawed the narrative effectiveness in *The Sirens of Titan*. Thus *Cat's Cradle* seems a final rehearsal for *Slaughterhouse-Five*.

We are faced with the question as to whether a maximum of effect can be achieved by a mere opposition of fact and fiction, as in *Cat's Cradle*, or whether other narrative structures are more suitable and more powerful.

The fantastic heteronomy of Vonnegut's futuristic world is always perceptible to the reader of SF. As *Cat's Cradle* shows, the illusionary world of San Lorenzo and Ice-Nine forms the interpretive opposite to Hiroshima and the atomic bomb. This fictitious universe is opposed to reality. *Cat's Cradle* shows the author's tendency to use SF-elements for the production of a mere modal discontinuity in regard to the empirical world. Through the use of such isolated SF-elements Vonnegut might have been able to create a new variety of narrative distance.[34]

Mother Night (1961)

> *Mother Night and God Bless you Mr. Rosewater* contain nothing that is impossible according to our present understanding of the limits of physical phenomena,

says Goldsmith (p. 32). He adds, "but they are just as much fantasies as the other four novels". Indeed it would be more precise to say that they were as much or as little fantasy as Vonnegut's other novels; for these two texts, especially *Mother Night*, make evident that Vonnegut here only sacrifices one narrative element - that is the physical discontinuity of the fictitious world with the real one - and that he can obviously dispose of this characteristic without giving up his themes which in these novels do not differ greatly from those of his other novels.

Mother Night exemplifies most clearly Vonnegut's "interest in the epistemological question of mankind's ability to distinguish between reality and illusion."[35] It would be more precise to speak in this connection of an "*in*ability" of mankind, which becomes obvious in the central character of *Mother Night*.

The title of the novel is a quotation from Goethe's *Faust II*, which in unabridged form recalls that *coincidentia oppositorum* which Vonnegut's novels exemplify. There the night is addressed as "The darkness that gave birth to light [...]" (p. XI).

This dichotomy and the paradoxical identity of illusion and reality, lies and truth, fact and fiction are the themes of *Mother Night* too, but in contrast to *Cat's Cradle* this novel does without the instruments of SF. The centre here is the narrator. Reed in his interpretation of *Mother Night* therefore calls it "A Portrait of the Artist" (p. 88). One might wish to add "as a person".

The editor of the fictitious diary which is *Mother Night*, describes the first-person narrator Campbell as "a writer as well as a person accused of extremely serious crimes [...]. To say that he was a writer is to say that the demands of art alone were enough to make him lie, and to lie without seeing any harm in it." (p. IX)

Mother Night is to a high degree a novel about language, not about its everyday use especially, but about language as means of communication, as work of art and instrument for exercising power. As the novel's topic it is the equivalent of its central character, the writer Campbell who is a poet, until he becomes a propagandist for the Nazis.[36]

Mother Night itself illustrates the various ways of using language in different types of texts: diary entries, letters, newspaper clippings, media broadcasts.

Howard W. Campbell, Jr. resembles in some respects Paul Proteus, in spite of their very different activities and roles in the world. Like Campbell he is deprived of his autonomy and integrity as an individual. Neither of them can successfully convince others of his identity; Campbell himself cannot believe in it any more. Campbell like Proteus becomes an instrument and a victim of the manipulation in which he himself wanted to be the active part, even the creator.[37] It is true that the process of recognition diverges: Proteus finds out late and only gradually that he is not the activist, but the victim of the rebellion. Howard Campbell, however, has to find out that he exercised an enormous power where he saw himself as passive: only on account of his propaganda speeches, containing coded news for the Allies, whose contents and purpose was unknown to himself, many of his audience became convinced Nazis. The reason for this ambiguity lies in the Protean nature of reality and man, which the artist incarnates in his person: he deals in confusing games of fact vs. fiction, lies vs. truth and illusion vs. reality. When Campbell meets his American contact after the end of WW II, he explains to Campbell the inextricable mingling of seeming contrasts. He tells Campbell that altogether only three people knew about his activity as an agent: he himself, President Roosevelt, and one general:

"Three people in all the world knew me for what I was -" I said.
"And all the rest -" I shrugged.
"They knew you for what you were, too," he said abruptly. (p. 138)

Here Campbell hears the bitter truth which as a moral is contained in the preface: "We are what we pretend to be, so we must be careful about what we pretend to be." (p. V)

The interdependence of an open and concealed identity, of appearance and reality completes the themes which *Player Piano* and *Cat's Cradle* were also concerned with. With the problem of identity Vonnegut connects his novels to the tradition of the American *mainstream* novel and to postmodernism: the manipulation of the individual by his social role takes from him his autonomy and, if he is not very cautious and alert, also his total moral integrity.

At the end of his confessions Howard Campbell decides to commit suicide, although his life has been saved once more. He wants to sentence himself to death "for crimes against himself". With his suicide he atones for his "innocence".

He is as innocent as Hoenikker, the father of the atom bomb, who withdrew from responsibility. Both entrench behind a fortification which leaves them physically and psychologically uncommitted and untainted. For Hoenikker it is science which like a wall surrounds and shelters his ego; for Campbell eroticism and art perform the same function. Schizophrenia, "that simple and widespread boon to mankind" (p. 133), secures Campbell's inner peace. The act of self-destruction thereby becomes a final and paradoxical attempt to find another identity beyond this schizophrenia. In consistent continuation of *Cat's Cradle*, *Mother Night* displays Vonnegut's tendency towards moralistic-didactic and poetological reflectiveness. In contrast to the earlier texts, however, the component of SF-motifs is missing here. That Vonnegut can discard it without essentially diminishing his message, leads to the conclusion that SF only functioned as an aid during a period of transition.

God Bless You, Mr. Rosewater (1965)

Although in this novel again there is no discontinuity with empirical reality it is probably most often mentioned in connection with Vonnegut's relation to SF. The reason lies in a passage which I want to quote as well:

Eliot Rosewater crashed a convention of science-fiction writers in a
motel in Milford, Pennsylvania. [...] The report contained Eliot's
speech to the writers word-for-word. [...]
"I love you sons of bitches [...]. You're all I read any more. You're
the only ones who'll talk about the *really* terrific changes going on,
the only ones crazy enough to know that life is a space voyage, and
not a short one, either, but one that'll last for billions of years.
You're the only ones with guts enough to *really* care about the
future, who *really* notice what machines do to us, what wars do to
us, what cities do to us, what big, simple ideas do to us, what
tremendous misunderstandings, mistakes, accidents and catastrophes
do to us. You're the only ones zany enough to agonize over time and
distances without limit, over mysteries that will never die, over the
fact that we are right now determining whether the space voyage for
the next billion years or so is going to be Heaven or Hell." (p. 18)

"Life is a space voyage", - space travel is a metaphor for life. SF is used
by Vonnegut as a connotative level, not as a separate genre functioning
according to rules of its own. This is the result of a development in the course
of which Vonnegut disconnects individual SF-elements from their system and
assigns to them new themes.

This instrumental use of SF also began to gradually reveal itself in the
earlier novels. In *Rosewater* another characteristic receives more weight: SF-
parody.

Significantly Vonnegut's satirical intention is not only directed against SF
as a literary genre, but chiefly against the SF-business.[38] The convention for
fans and authors mentioned in the passage quoted above, the appearance of the
protagonist Rosewater as speaker and the figure of Kilgore Trout are sufficient
occasion for Vonnegut to ironize the discrepancy between pretension and
reality, commercial purposes and salvation, common in the SF-business.[39]

Rosewater, the millionaire who gives away his money and wants to live
for the poor, is either insane or an idealist not to be changed by anything -
depending on the viewpoint taken up by the audience. He represents an
element of unreality in America's reality. Fundamentally he is a Christ figure -
like Billy Pilgrim in the subsequent novel - and a variation of the religious
founder Bokonon. All are "odd", unworldly saints and a foreign body in the
empirical world. Another variation of this type is Kilgore Trout, the
unacknowledged SF-author, whom Vonnegut from now on turns into a stock-
character of his novels. Like Rosewater himself Kilgore Trout is also a
grotesque Christ figure: "He looked like a frightened, aging Jesus, whose

sentence to crucifiction had been commuted to imprisonment for life." (p. 115) In *Slaughterhouse-Five* he is called "that cracked Messiah" (p. 167). Kilgore Trout more and more becomes the voice crying of the prophet who by means of SF wants to disclose the truth about the state of the world, and who functions as Vonnegut's *alter ego*.

The way in which SF is employed has changed in *Rosewater* and been extended by a further variation. In this novel SF as a cultural and literary phenomenon forms a level of allusion and a theme of its own, not a narrative medium. *Rosewater* contains statements *on* Science Fiction, without using or realizing SF or SF-motifs. Thus the distance from the genre becomes greater than before.

Slaughterhouse-Five (1969)

This novel was an immediate success with the American readership. Partly this was due to the political and sociocultural situation in the country[40]; on the other hand Vonnegut's combination of thematic and formal narrative techniques reaches a climax here.[41] The effect on the reader is achieved by an enhancement of its documentary character and by a complex fictional representation.

As in *Cat's Cradle* the author rejects conventional narration. The cause for his own skepticism in regard to narrative conventions is seen by him in the events to be described as well as in the nature of telling itself.

Vonnegut shares the distrust of the regulating and stylistic mechanisms of the narrative - he describes his own role as writer as "a trafficker in climaxes and thrills and characterization and wonderful dialogue and suspense and confrontations" (p. 5) - with a number of American authors of the sixties[42] and with the *Nouveaux Romanciers*, who maintained that *plot* and characters are anachronistic because they belong to an age which idealized the individual.[43] Vonnegut himself also cited quite similar causes for his distance from the traditional means of narrating:

> There are almost no characters in this story, and almost no dramatic confrontation, because most of the people in it are so sick and so much the listless playthings of enormous forces. One of the main effects of war, after all, is that people are discouraged from being characters. (p. 164)

Plot, characters and chronological sequence of events are, among others, the essential structural characteristics of realistic story-telling. But as this manner of presentation is inadequate to the topic of the book, the author looks for new means. When dealing with the topic of war, the conventional stylized art of narrative fiction seems almost dangerous to him.

The topic of the novel cannot be adequately presented by a "normal" narrative. One reason lies in the very nature of telling a story as it is traditionally understood; it structures reality where it was without structure, grants to it significance where it was felt to be without meaning, it differentiates and gives a profile where in reality there is chaos. But since in that part of reality represented in the novel - war[44] - chaos and meaninglessness are overwhelming, according to the author's opinion, the usual way of narrating would be in his eyes grotesque and unacceptable.[45]

Vonnegut's solution of this dilemma in itself seems very contradictory: in addition to autobiographical paragraphs there are the fantastic parts of the narration, which are of a truly ostentatious irreality, by which he can initiate and control the process of perception in his readers. Billy Pilgrim's fantasies in which he supposedly sees himself on the planet Tralfamadore, "where the flying saucers come from", are based on motifs that are known from SF. For readers and critics generally the autobiographical content of *Slaughterhouse-Five* is very important. This is not the case with fantastic alienation which transforms real events and figures into fictitious ones. They are easily ignored by the readers or dealt with as irrelevant, because their function is obviously intransigent in a text referring to current events and resembling at times a personal confession.

Vonnegut's earliest thorough critics, Reed and Schatt, offer different explanations for the question of the function of Tralfamadore passages in *Slaughterhouse-Five*. The first is based on Vonnegut's intentions explained on the title page of the novel, that the attitude of Tralfamadorians towards the events told is fatalistic and remote:

> a [...] philosophy of life which makes it painless for him to describe the fire-bombing of Dresden and Billy's suffering in a cold, detached, objective manner. Tralfamadorians, it should be remembered, are machines devoid of all human feelings of love and compassion. (Schatt, *Vonnegut*, p. 85)

Schatt himself, however, states that the reader might come to wrong conclusions on account of such an attitude in the narrator and that the perspective of Tralfamadorians could therefore at best appear as one aspect. Indeed the explanation quoted above is insufficient. The same author offers - in the form of a supposition - also another possible explanation:

> The Tralfamadorian sections of the novel may also serve another function since they provide a form of comic relief from the unbearable tension that builds as Billy approaches the day of the actual fire-bombing. (Schatt, p. 91.)

According to Vonnegut the SF-parts in *Slaughterhouse-Five* are humorous, parodistic reminiscences from the genre and therefore have the function of a comic relief.

To provide relief and refuge from the misfortunes of reality is also, according to a widespread opinion of critics, a purpose of serious SF, even though it is not necessarily the withdrawal into a better and happier world. Reed refers to this theory of the escapist function of SF with his explanation:

> There is another aspect of the science fiction, also pervasive in *The Sirens of Titan*, which calls attention to itself in *Slaughterhouse-Five*. That is the element of evasion and escape. For while the science fiction stresses grim aspects of existence - inevitability, meaninglessness, alienation and isolation, the absurd - it remains itself an escape into imagination and fancy. This ambivalence of science fiction contributes to the mixed tone common in Vonnegut [...]. (Reed, p. 196)

The last sentence seems to me to be the most important one. For if this contradicts the need of every critic to explain - apparently including the author in his role as an interpreter of his own work - there may be truly a number of very plausible interpretations for the SF-elements in *Slaughterhouse-Five*; but the impression of a rather strange mixture in the narrative tools of the novel and the question of the purpose of the Tralfamadore-parts in this context, remain valid. Each of the explanations mentioned is suitable for one aspect, but none of them can solve the whole problem. A widespread reading experience corresponds to this insight which I saw confirmed in my own courses on Vonnegut and which, for example, is also revealed by the movie *Slaughterhouse-Five*: the passages on Tralfamadore are found hardly worth mentioning and of minor importance. Of course that does not mean that they may be neglected in an interpretation, but compared to other elements they tend to be de-emphasized.

The statement is therefore justified that the dominant is changing in Vonnegut's fiction. Thus my interpretation will try to clarify the SF-elements from the perspective of change in contrast to earlier novels and focus on some aspects that had been neglected.

The elements borrowed from SF can be divided into two partly separate categories for *Slaughterhouse-Five*:

1. the transformation of SF-motifs as it is already well-known from *Sirens* and *Cat's Cradle*, and

2. the comments on the role of SF that we had found also in *Rosewater*.

In *Slaughterhouse-Five* familiar characters are revived, for example, Eliot Rosewater. In 1948 he is in a mental hospital, together with the protagonist Billy Pilgrim. Rosewater collects and reads SF novels by Kilgore Trout, an already familiar character from Vonnegut's literary universe. For Rosewater and Pilgrim SF fulfils a very important function as a stabilizing element in their disturbed ego.

> They had both found life meaningless, partly because of what they had seen in war. [...] So they were trying to re-invent themselves and their universe. Science Fiction was a big help. (p. 101)

This seems to confirm the suspicion that SF is escapist. But Vonnegut immediately undermines the thesis of SF as a refuge from reality. A number of fictitious SF novels by Kilgore Trout are listed and quoted. All of them are diametrically opposed to what an SF-reader may expect from the genre and they point out that Vonnegut has no use for what constitutes SF, its narrative structures and its concepts of man and the universe. The novels by Kilgore Trout, who as an SF-author only exists in fiction, are so radically different from the genre SF and its norms that it can verify the statements of one critic:

> The man-made, mechanized universe of science fiction is too presumptuous. Its technical realism, always on the side of the plausible, is founded on the basic tenet of progress and change, not necessarily positive, but involving a linear cause-and-effect concept of human existence. Vonnegut rejects both the idea of verifiable reality and man's control of his destiny.[46]

Vonnegut's fictitious SF novels by Kilgore Trout have other aims and purposes and use other narrative means than SF "proper". All of them - altogether five, which are more extensively described - lead into a world which is much better known and which has nothing to do with the future or with an alternate reality. In it Vonnegut creates an *objective correlative* (T.S. Eliot) to his concept of reality.[47]

The fictitious novel *The Gutless Wonder* by Kilgore Trout, which is quoted in *Slaughterhouse-Five*, makes this especially clear. This so-called SF-story is an interpretation of the bombardment of Dresden by Allied Forces in February 1945 as well as the bombardment of Vietnam by the US Air Force more than twenty years later:

> what made the story remarkable, since it was written in 1932, was that it predicted the widespread use of burning jellied gasoline on human beings.
> It was dropped on them from airplanes. Robots did the dropping. They had no conscience, and no circuits which would allow them to imagine what was happening to the people on the ground.
> Trout's leading robot looked like a human being, and could talk and dance and so on, and go out with girls. And nobody held it against him that he dropped jellied gasoline on people. But they found his halitosis unforgivable. But then he cleared that up, and he was welcomed to the human race. (p. 168)

The allegorization of SF - life as space travel, the soldier as robot, the physically and socially functioning man as a machine - suspends the parameters of SF. Instead "the various trappings of science fiction" serve the production of a "narrative distance"[48] from the Here and the Now - a distance, however, which only makes the confrontation with reality possible.

By creating a new and shocking perspective in inventing the Tralfamadorians - Billy Pilgrim calls this "prescribing corrective lenses for Earthling souls" (p. 29) - Vonnegut recreates in *Slaughterhouse-Five* the characteristics and qualities of Swift's satire.[49] Vonnegut's innovative impulses are not aimed at the genre SF but at the disclosure of new areas for an interpretative representation of reality. He borrows his metaphors partly from SF, which at the same time becomes the target of irony and parody.[50] Apart from SF the instrumentalizing of fiction in general is one of his characteristic narrative tools. He uses intertextual references for his fiction of reality. The numerous quotations from literary works[51] - from the Bible to Crane's *Red Badge of Courage* and *The Destruction of Dresden* to limericks - the reflection of fictitious books in his own books and finally the scope of variations prove this. Every text becomes a version of real events, the climax of which in Vonnegut's works is the destruction of Dresden.

Time travel, parallel times, space travel, aliens and alien planets are the chief motifs which Vonnegut borrows from SF for *Slaughterhouse-Five*. A special significance is ascribed to time-travel.[52] "Billy Pilgrim has come unstuck in time", is the opening of the novel.

The narrative swings back and forth between three levels of time, following its protagonist "Pilgrim", and the respective places: 1944 to '45 in Germany and Dresden in particular, then until 1967 in Ilium, N.Y., and from 1967 to 1968 simultaneously on Earth and on the planet Tralfamadore where the inhabitants display Billy as the object of illustration in a zoo.

Linear time sequence is replaced by a collage of fragments, interrupted by leaps in time and place. Dresden and Ilium, 1945 and 1967, are points in time and places from the real, objectively empirical biography of the protagonist:

> he was simultaneously on foot in Germany in 1944 and riding his Cadillac in 1967. Germany dropped away, and 1967 became bright and clear, free of interference from any other time. (p. 58)

This time-travel takes place in the protagonist's mind; it is a mixture of past and present, memories and current events:

> Billy drove through a scene of even greater desolation. It looked like Dresden after it was fire-bombed - like the surface of the moon. [...] This was urban renewal. (p. 59)

Simultaneity, contrastive juxtaposition, cross-references form a collage of Dresden and Ilium, past and present referring to each other. Not all of these relations are merely established in the protagonist's mind; the third-person narrator's point-of-view also has an influence on it. Fragments are arranged in a way that to the reader refractions and reflections are disclosed which remain concealed to the characters.[53]

Tralfamadore, however, is in contrast to Dresden and Ilium a place which remains a product of fantasy to the readers. Hallucinations are mixed with events and memories. The narrator himself distinguishes between "hallucination" and "time-travel":

> Billy Pilgrim was having a delightful hallucination. [...] This wasn't time-travel. It had never happened, never would happen. It was the craziness of a dying young man with his shoes full of snow. (p. 49)

His time-travels back to Dresden and World War II are flash-backs, intramental and intrasubjective processes, but with an actual biographical foundation. They have all the characteristics of the stream-of-consciousness technique.[54] The leap to the fantastic - instead of the recalled - world takes place, however, with the introduction of Tralfamadore to the novel.

The experienced and the recalled world glide into the imaginary world in the protagonist's mind. For Billy Pilgrim one is as real as the other, and even the narrator suggests that both exist on the same ontological level; he deals with Tralfamadore as if it had the same ontological status and characteristics as Dresden or Ilium. Only to the reader is it evident that there we are in a reality that is different from empirical reality.

Tralfamadore and the mechanical inhabitants of his strange planet helped Pilgrim and the readers to find new perspectives. The SF-motif then becomes a device and disguise for satirical and didactic purposes.

Vonnegut uses his following novel to uncover this "disguise". In *Breakfast of Champions* the author and narrator says about his double Kilgore Trout: "He advanced his theories disguised as science-fiction." (*Breakfast*, p. 15)

Breakfast of Champions (1973)

"I've finished my war book now. The next one I write is going to be fun", says the author in *Slaughterhouse-Five*. The next one is *Breakfast*, and indeed this novel is "fun", understood as a mixture of slapstick - the title of Vonnegut's novel published in 1976 - and cynicism.

Breakfast is a kind of *coda* to *Slaughterhouse-Five*. The two works "used to be one book [...] they just separated completely... they were not mixable", Vonnegut himself says about their relation, which is well characterized by this statement.[55] Some critics regard *Breakfast* as a dead end for the development of Vonnegut's novels.[56] In several respects *Slaughterhouse* was the result of tendencies developed in earlier fiction. *Breakfast* is a reflection of the preceding novels.

Parody plays a dominant role in this novel: parody of the American Way of Life, parody of literature, of art, of technology, of religion, and, last but not least, of language.

The figure of the author himself and his literary work, in particular the interpretative intentions of his critics, are also included; as in earlier works

Vonnegut uses his fictitious double Kilgore Trout to portray himself with ironical refractions:

> After Trout became famous, of course, one of the biggest mysteries about him was whether he was kidding or not. He told one persistent questioner that he always crossed his fingers when he was kidding.
> "And please note", he went on, "that when I gave you that priceless piece of information, my fingers were crossed." (p. 86)

In *Breakfast* the process of fictionalization is also reflected; it becomes meta-fiction. Especially the epilogue serves to destroy illusion; there the author meets his creature and self-caricature Kilgore Trout. The narrator regards himself as demiurge, whose creative abilities are the same as those of the Creator of the Universe, only on a small scale. As a consequence he dismisses Kilgore Trout from his service and at the same time marks the end of relevance of SF for his work. He has definitely completed a change of paradigm and genre at the end of this novel and joined postmodernism.

The dissolution of his ties to SF once more reflects its role in his earlier fiction. The metaphorical equation of man and machine extends to the author himself. This self-reflection, typical of postmodernism, has a cynical effect here:

> As for myself: I had come to the conclusion that there was nothing sacred about myself or about any human being, that we were all machines, doomed to collide and collide and collide. [...] Sometimes I wrote well about collisions, which meant I was a writing machine in good repair. [...] I no more harbored sacredness than did a pontiac, a mousetrap, or a South Bend Lathe. (p. 219f.)

Each of Vonnegut's protagonists in the course of a novel was led from a real into an unreal world. Kilgore Trout, who in *Breakfast of Champions* moves to the central position, meets with the same fate: even the reality which fiction had bestowed on him is taken away from him by the author and he is dismissed into an absolute "unreality".[57]

After *Breakfast* the possibilities for using SF are exhausted for Vonnegut. This novel reflects in ironical comments remnants from a development which at one time used the literary pattern of SF selectively and finally led to the melting of SF-motifs into the narrative techniques of postmodern American prose literature.

Breakfast in the context of this study is a comic after-piece, intermingled with Vonnegut's proverbial black humour, "By cutting his ties to Kilgore Trout", Vonnegut crosses the border.[58]

Vonnegut's relation to SF as it presents itself in his novels can be most precisely characterized by the concepts of distancing, instrumentality, and satire. While the satirical intention and the gradually growing distance to the genre SF are easily recognized, the instrumentalizing use of SF-elements is more complex and more concealed. The increasingly atypical use of SF-motifs is a result of a re-metaphorization of imaginary concepts whose materialization qualifies the genre SF. His aim is not an innovation of SF, but the opening up of new narrative means for the treatment of themes which to a large extent pervade the postmodern American novel. Vonnegut has loosened his ties to the literary conventions of SF; it is still present as a quarry for narrative details and as a social phenomenon of the American society which the author parodies.

4.2 William Burroughs

At the beginning of the sixties Burroughs was the target of violent controversies. Mary McCarthy, Jack Kerouac and Norman Mailer celebrated him enthusiastically as "the only American novelist living today who may conceivably be possessed of genius" (Mailer) and "the greatest satirical writer since Jonathan Swift" (Kerouac).[59] By other critics, however, he was vehemently opposed.

The waves of enthusiasm as well as fury in criticism are almost forgotten. In contrast to Vonnegut Burroughs never met with a wide acceptance, if one can take availability of a fictional text and number of reviewers as a sign of popularity. The emergence from the underground into the publicity of Popular Culture was only brief, although Burroughs like Kerouac and Allen Ginsberg is counted among the fathers of the counter-culture in the Beat Generation. The biography of the author often seemed more significant than his work and contributed much to its popularity.[60]

Critical studies of Burroughs' fiction remained rare; there is one book-length study on him.[61]

> He will for most readers remain an intellectually and verbally very uncomfortable, shocking, even disgusting novelist. Actually he

repeatedly provokes by his disclosure of sadistic rituals our moral sensitivity, he is tiring to a reader without homoerotic inclinations by his staccato of pederastic love, he creates nausea by his detailed visions of the terminal sewer, which is this world. (my translation)[62]

Primarily the unappealing character of Burroughs' novels described above may have caused the lack of response by readers and critics. They also wear on the nerves of the patient and receptive reader in two respects, as Poenicke thinks: first by the continuous and frequent violation of taboos existing still today by his obscene descriptions.

These, however, scarcely constitute the offence of pornographic writing according to the legislator's definition; for if there is one valid message to the reader it is the author's promise that instead of a "Garden of Delight" he will find a "terminal sewer" (*Nova Express*, p. 13).

Second, Burroughs is shocking because of his narrative technique, which is based upon a total rejection of the conventions of a linear narrative, so that his fiction also crosses the borderline of tolerance for most of his readers. Burroughs' fiction and his own explanations regarding the cut-up and fold-in methods arouse in the audience the impression that here we have a completely different understanding of language and narration than the one he knows. For the majority of the potential readers the ostentatious destruction of language, which is the author's self-proclaimed aim, bears the end of literature in itself.

"Nihilism" and "anarchy" are therefore the attitudes Burroughs is reproached for by the critics. Some of them, however, come to the conclusion that his role as a moralist, as a prophet predicting the end of American civilization, contradicts his being rejected as an eccentric or even psychotic figure from the fringe of the pop-art scene.[63]

In this study the relation between SF and Burroughs' works is at the centre of interest. The criticism on Burroughs shows once again the curious contrast between the frequent mentioning of SF in Burroughs and the well-known superficial use of the term SF without further explanation: "The central metaphor of his universe is science fiction"[64], - "[...] Burroughs' four novels controlled by strategies of SF"[65], "his unique brand of science fiction"[66], "basically [...] a science fiction fantasy"[67] - these are the expressions used in otherwise precise studies, and only Tanner goes beyond a vague and generalizing statement on Burroughs' use of SF.

Mottram, the author of a thorough study, restricts the term SF to innovative texts like those of the *New Wave*, in which the concept of the genre has partly been replaced by "inner space", hallucinatory imagination induced by drugs and mythological fantasies which constitute his idea of SF.[68]

Only rarely does the relation between this author and the genre SF become the thematic focus of a study, as, for example, in an article by Cordesse and, more recently, in the book by McHale on postmodernism. McHale's discussion of an SF-concept associated with "gadgetry" (p. 66) illustrates once more the difficulty of reconciling genre theory with descriptive poetics, since postmodernist writing, in which he includes Burroughs' novels, also employs "gadgetry", especially of the biological sciences, e.g. cloning, androids, overpopulation and biological warfare, and he is obsessed, like many other postmodern writers, by the notion of international conglomerates "taking over" the world.[69]

In order to define the relation between SF and Burroughs' novels it is necessary to first clarify the reasons for the supposition that such a relationship exists. They are included in the author's declared intention "to create a new mythology for the space age".[70] This intention meets with the attitude of some SF-critics.[71] Moreover, the motifs of SF have left traces in Burroughs' novels; their function is waiting for explanation and stimulates the critics to see a connection between SF and Burroughs' brand of postmodernism.

The SF-reader, nevertheless, will hardly find the familiar elements of SF: suspense, adventure, causality, a *plot* are absent from these novels; only fragments of a story or chronological time sequence are to be found, and nothing reminds of the central character described as individualistic, active, and powerful in SF.[72] Still more irritating is the permanent disorientation of the reader and the "abolition of language" to be discussed below. The parameters of SF as a definable literary genre are clearly missing, if - as this study does - it is assumed that the lasting structural characteristics constitute a literary genre in spite of individual innovations at certain points. For these reasons, to anticipate the results of the following analysis, it is not possible or meaningful for a critic to try and consider Burroughs as an SF-writer, not even as an experimental variety.

But the example of Burroughs throws a new light on the borders of SF; for Burroughs' novels point out overlappings and instrumentalizations of SF and postmodernism. These are analyzed in the following interpretations.

The Naked Lunch (1959) already exemplifies the most important themes and techniques of Burroughs' writing. It also illustrates a characteristic which later on will become more significant for the author's use of SF: the continuous metaphorical expansion of a drug consumer's experience to the interpretation of reality in general. Drug consumption becomes a symbol of every kind of dependence and thus of the controlling of human behaviour. Addiction for Burroughs is the human condition as such; it is the individual's soft spot because all kinds of manipulation can start from there. It is irrelevant what kind of addiction you have - and according to Burroughs every human being has some kind of addiction, because dependency is a part of man's physical nature and this dependency creates addiction, whether on heroin, alcohol, power, love, food or drink, - everybody will find "that's how you get caught, son - *If you have to have it well you've had it*".[73]

The example of *The Soft Machine* (1961) reveals more clearly to the reader how Burroughs' novels were related to SF by the critics. The chapter "The Mayan Caper" starts with an SF-cliché:

> A Russian Scientist has said: "We will travel not only in space but in time as well" - I have just returned from a thousand-year time trip and I am here to tell you what I saw - (p. 85)

In connection with the stereotype time-travel motif the narrator reveals that he only wants to "play" with the SF "gadgetry" and provides a stage direction for the correct understanding of the context: "You see it all on a subliminal level" (p. 86). The reader's subconscious is to be raised into consciousness by the narration. SF is only a demonstration of the unconscious. The aim of the text is for Burroughs to discover the Here and Now. To do this he uses all the hallucinations, historical segments and visions of the future, but especially the verbal and literary clichés that evoke fantasies and associations.

The central revelation about our reality is the insight that it does not truly exist in the sense of an ontologically autonomous world but that it is merely some kind of especially effective suggestion. This reality is fabricated by the media, primarily with words: "We don't report the news - We write it." (p. 152) Thus the borderline between fiction and nonfiction is abolished: "I am sent to this school in Washington to learn how this writing the news before it happens is done -" (p. 152).[74]

The "reality film" is produced in the "Reality Studio" (p. 155). As the "Prisoners of the Earth" are awakened they storm the studios, and the Reality Film burns with "the metal smell of interplanetary war" (p. 155f.).

Such phrases are associated almost compulsively with "Science Fiction" in the reader's consciousness. The only use, however, that Burroughs makes of SF, is this mechanism of associations that is little more than a conditioned reflex and which serves to prove once more the manipulative capacity of language by triggering a chain reaction. The terminology of SF discloses a supply of associations that the author can use for his communication with the readers.

He invites his audience with the phrase "Glad to have you aboard reader" (p. 167) for his parodistic variation of space travel which he documented at the end of the preceding chapter:

> Allusions to the science-fiction theme [...] keep floating up enigmatically and can only be stored away in a corner of the reader's mind in the hope that they will be decoded later on.[75]

This sentence characterizes well the vagueness and voidness of the SF-reminiscences in *The Soft Machine*. In contrast to the critic quoted above, however, I am of the opinion that even in the following novels the SF-pattern is never activated either and certainly nowhere in Burroughs' novels provides the dominant. There are only mere echoes of SF in his fiction, providing themes and ideas for postmodern writing.

In his subsequent novels, it is true, direct references to SF are more frequent: "I am reading a science fiction book called *The Ticket That Exploded*", (1962, p. 5). In spite of this declaration of the narrator the SF-reader is unable to meaningfully interpret this label, since it does not fit his previous reading experience. Again this novel uses "bits" from the verbal repertory and the catalogue of motifs common in SF, but without adapting any of its premises or forms of presentation. An example which is representative for a number of passages is this sentence: "Controls of their space craft had suddenly blanked out by the intervention of an invisible alien force" (p. 32). By this recourse to phrases typical of SF Burroughs only varies the theme of universal control which governs this one as well as his other novels. What seems to be a summary of an SF story is only a disguise for a "real" situation, which might also be described in different ways. A side-effect of such usage is that Burroughs' novels sometimes read like instructions for the handling of SF, but certainly not like SF itself.

The chapter about "Nova technique" in *The Ticket That Exploded* illustrates a less stereotype, more impressive, symbolic and consistent new application of an SF-motif. The narrator here describes how the annihilation of a planet in a nuclear explosion - a Nova - is brought about: by a systematic escalation of already existing conflicts and contrasting interests, in which the word is the main weapon (p. 54ff.). Here we are also confronted with the same observation that Burroughs wants to interpret and describe our own world exclusively and that the verbal SF-reminiscences only signal a limited game with inscrutable masks.

In *The Ticket That Exploded* the idea of entropy assumes an imagery which is characteristic of Burroughs to a great extent. The decline of the universe and the species *Homo Sapiens* expresses itself by a return through different metamorphoses of the individual to the most primitive organisms - bacteria, viruses, "Insect People", "Vegetable People" - and finally to an organic primeval slime. "The hopeless dead-end horror of being just who and where you are: Dying animals on a doomed planet." (p. 151)

This vision distinguishes itself significantly from the imaginative worlds of SF, even where these are equally concerned with a dying human race on a dying planet. The question "What if?" which stimulates our speculative fantasy and which is answered by the creation of a fictitious world in SF which is a possible rather than a future world seen from the reader's point-of-view - this question "What if?" does not interest Burroughs at all. He does not want an unreal or not-yet-real premise which then forms the basis of a fictitious world; but for him the "doomed planet" Earth is already reality. Not by possibly occurring events would man become a "dying animal", but he has always been one because of his nature, the only open question being whether he knows it or can find it out.

Nova Express (1964) does not add anything new to the use of SF. The idea that on the planet Earth an invasion takes place which brings total control with it and results in total self-alienation and depersonalization, has the same unreal-figurative meaning as in *The Soft Machine* and *The Ticket That Exploded*. Main motifs are once more war, invasion, destruction, and entropy as dead ends of evolution, which as before are transported by obsessively recurring images and rituals. Historical allusions are abundant: flash-backs into the Maya civilization and the kingdom of the Inkas, but also to the ovens of the Auschwitz extermination camp.

However, in *Nova Express* the narrator gives instructions for a possible liberation: under different masks (The Subliminal Kid, Mr. Bradley, Mr.

Martin, Uranian Willy) he recommends a "program of total austerity and total resistance" (p. 13) - a total denial especially in regard to the word. This is the end of the novel in a double sense: the *closure* and the destruction of narrative prose; the later proclaimed 'death of literature' (Jacques Ehrmann, 1971) is anticipated.

> My writing arm is paralyzed - No more junk scripts, no more word scripts, no more flesh scripts [...] Adios Meester William, Mr. Bradley, Mr. Martin - (p. 154).

The central and deeply ironic paradox in Burroughs - that someone with such a cynical contempt for the function of language uses fiction as a medium - completely undermines the novel. It is finished, its narrator commits verbal suicide.

There is nothing legitimate or acceptable as the author wants to make his readers believe, in the ability of language to create an illusion of reality that is consistent; yet the majority of SF-authors trust in these qualities. With nothing Burroughs, according to his fictional and non-fictional statements, shows such deep and hateful disgust as with this power of language, because only he can see the abuse of power. And yet he necessarily and inevitably uses it himself to expose its mechanisms.

Nova Express at first sight seems to be the text with the closest connection of all novels to SF. This impression, however, is deceptive, because it is obvious that all the fantasies and forms of presentation already occurred in the earlier novels, the solicitation to offer resistance excepted, which is stronger here. The topological similarities which connect the novel with SF appear ostentatiously inserted and do not go beyond the function of connotations.

Most often Burroughs' use of SF appears as mere nomenclature; at times it reaches the level of an allegorical filling of a word-shell that has lost its original matrix.

The Wild Boys: A Book of the Dead (1971), Burroughs' next novel, does not introduce decisive alterations in regard to the use of SF for postmodern fiction either.

Nevertheless, the opinion of the critic who writes that "*The Wild Boys* is science-fiction, *as the action takes place mainly in 1976, then 1989*",[76] is as typical as its causality is wrong. The mere statement in a text that it is about the future and time-travelling - only expressed by the years in the headings of the chapters - does not make the novel an SF text, even if the interpreter may try to find some more indications interspersed in the text. Much more to the point is another statement in the study by Cordesse in regard to Burroughs' concept of time: the fictitious world of his novels is "vaguely contemporary, in fact almost a-temporal" (loc.cit.). This state of indecision in regard to time is possibly a sign of fantastic or hallucinatory literature. Burroughs shares it with the later "Jerry-Cornelius-novels" by Moorcock, perhaps also with a few texts by Ballard. According to our understanding these works can also be counted among SF, if discontinuity in a literary genre is considered equal to innovation.

Burroughs' reference to SF as a literary genre is partly supported by the inversion of SF-conventions. The destruction of the system of the rules of language as well as every form of continuity in the description, in the structure of time, the *plot*, the *story*, the characters, is contrary to SF. In precisely these structural components we had recognized a considerable stability and a conservatism of SF which continue to exist, in spite of the opinion of some rebels like Moorcock that it has to come to an end. This, moreover, is a persistence which is missing from fiction that has dismissed "realistic" narrative conventions.

Suspense is a category altogether absent from Burroughs' works. That a dissociation of word and image, word and emotion, etc. is the goal of his dealing with language - is intended by him as an interruption of the verbally manipulated chain reaction, - all kind of expectation that is built up in the reader is wavered, suspense resulting from the *plot* as well as suspense resulting from the psychological development of the protagonist or from purely verbal units of suspense. According to the author's opinion all patterns ought to be destroyed - thus the reader finds it impossible to build up an expectation for specific possibilities of fulfilment. If this is done sporadically the creation of an illusion is destroyed from the beginning:

> there are too many breaks, jumps, unexplained shifts to different places, people, orderings of reality, etc., for us ever to feel so controlled by his vision that we forget we are reading a book. There is no consistent narrator, indeed no narrative principle.[77]

If in the texts by Burroughs all the characteristics specific to the SF-genre that determine the structure of a work, are missing, there are - in spite of the fact that Burroughs has remained a fringe figure of the literary scene -

connections with important characteristics of the postmodern American novel. This parallel is emphasized by Tanner, at certain points also by Mottram.

In spite of similarities with other authors of avantgarde fiction Burroughs' novels are extremely strenuous even to an audience experienced in reader irritation by fiction from Faulkner to Barth and Nabokov. Especially the themes - determination and external control, conspiracy, entropy - awaken in the reader the impression of a remarkable familiarity with other texts, e.g. by Ellison, Bellow, and Pynchon, in spite of all the shocking and irritating details of presentation:

> Most of the American heroes we have studied so far share one dread - of being 'taken over' by some *external force*, of being assimilated to an *alien pattern* not of their choosing, of being 'fixed' in someone else's 'reality-picture'.[78]

A protagonist in the sense of a central character, as mentioned by Tanner, is missing from Burroughs' novels, but partly it can be replaced by the first-person narrator. His narrative strategies communicate to the reader the attempt of individuals, well-known from numerous postmodern novels, to withdraw and to free themselves from the "external force", the "alien pattern", from roles and from masks. In Burroughs all these endeavours focus on the wish to free oneself from the constraints of language:

> To escape from words into silence and from mud and metal into space is Burroughs' version of a well-established American dream of freedom from conditioning forces.[79]

When Burroughs varies themes and narrative strategies that are rooted in the postmodern American novel and experimental fiction his variety is characterized by a special restriction, redundancy, and by a great monotony. His paranoid fixation on a limited number of ideas, images, and narrative attitudes violates the reader's autonomy. He is prevented from playing the game of fiction with reality, because the author refuses to play it.

Cordesse, who in spite of all his objections, wants to classify Burroughs as a representative of avantgarde SF, hypothetically says that Burroughs' specific role lies in his successful attempt to channel the emotional contents - menace, shock, surprise and amazement, disgust, defence - from the intellectual and cognitive abilities into the mythological and affective, whereas "SF proper" indulges in presenting itself in theory and practice as "literature of ideas", as rationally founded speculation. Thus Burroughs would be trying to reverse a process of repression and sublimation which SF has passed through and which it serves.[80]

This hypothesis is worth consideration, since in my opinion the discussion of symbol and metaphor is of special importance for SF, the characteristic tendency of SF being to "take conventional metaphors literally" and to grant them material reality.

Two points, however, in Cordesse's statements on Burroughs leave the readers doubtful; to me they are indefensible: first, that a theory by which SF is generally declared a fairy-tale for the space age, has ascribed to it the functions of myth and fairy-tale and which maintains that SF is purely mythology, is a simplification; for it does not cover vast areas of SF. Second, it contains an overestimation of the SF-element in Burroughs that was persistently maintained by the critics, including Leslie Fiedler, though only vaguely and without real cause. SF is only of marginal importance in Burroughs. It is employed for the author's attempt to reveal the illusionary character of reality - a typically postmodern objective - and to show the reader what our world really is like - not what it hypothetically might be like. The confrontation with our reality, the command to offer resistance according to the motto "Destroy what destroys you" are Burroughs' strongest didactic and moral interests pursued with a paranoid obsession.

Burroughs does not achieve, as some critics seem to believe, a convergence of the two literary areas SF and experimental fiction. Even if Cordesse admits that "Science fiction is accepted simply as a legitimate literary device among others" (p. 43), this still overestimates the role of SF. Apart from an ostentatious use of the SF-terminology betraying acquaintance with the most frequent SF-motifs, which appeals to the reader's knowledge of SF, there are no substantial reminiscences of the genre in Burroughs' works.

Burroughs is, even more than Vonnegut, an example of postmodern literature where it reflects other themes and types of literature, though he differs from it in his moral purpose. The gap is obviously narrowing. This phenomenon also leads to an overlapping of "serious" and "trivial" literature and pop-art, both in themes and narrative techniques: use of slang and vernacular, thematic focus on subjects formerly reserved for pornography and the "Blue Movie", techniques from film and comics. Genre borderlines are more and more difficult to define, and especially in the US the generation of hybrid forms is increasing in quantity and quality; there is also an enhancement of referential techniques and intertextuality between different genres.

4.3 Crossing of Borders and Change of Paradigms

In spite of the marked differences between the two oeuvres of Burroughs and Vonnegut, the use which they make of SF shows some similarities.

In 1968 Michel Butor described the novel as "the laboratory of narrative". In any case, whether postmodern or SF,

> the novel must suffice to create what it tells us. That is why it is the phenomenological realm par excellence, the best possible place to study how reality appears to us, or might appear.[81]

Both authors are representatives of the experimental novel that shows traces of SF, Burroughs being the author moving away from it much faster and with greater decision than Vonnegut, whose solution is more gradual. They use SF as raw material for its motifs and its images in another narrative system.[82] These compository elements assume new functions, which for both authors lie in SF-parody as well as in an instrumentalizing of SF for a satirical and didactic interpretation of postmodern reality. This instrumental use of SF-elements in a different context and function uses the allegorization of motifs, images, formulas and idioms which have their roots in SF.

At first sight, it seems paradoxical that SF often used a de-metaphorization of conventional imagery and that Vonnegut and Burroughs employ a number of motifs as representational means for themes that are widespread in postmodern American fiction as, e.g., fear of being determined and controlled by external and unknown forces, dissolution of time structure and manipulation of the individual. McHale in two chapter headlines calls this criss-crossing development "The science-fictionalization of postmodernism" (p. 65) and "The postmodernization of science fiction" (p. 68). Vonnegut's oeuvre shows a step-by-step development away from SF into postmodernism, mainly by a variety of new combinations of themes and motifs, while Burroughs employs an atomized raw material of motifs and *topoi* from SF which belong from the first novel onwards to the discourse of poststructuralist fiction. These borrowings from the SF-repertoire serve the projection of worlds created by telling, experimentally used in Butor's "laboratory of narrative".

Notes Chapter 4

[1] C.D.B. Bryan, "Kurt Vonnegut on Target", in: *The New Republik* (Oct. 8, 1966), p. 21-26; Scholes, "Kurt Vonnegut", in: *The Fabulators*. 1967, p. 35-55 (first published in October 1966 with the title "Mithridates, He died old" in *The Hollins Critic*).

[2] *City of Words*. Tanner's "The Uncertain Messenger: A Study of the Novels of Kurt Vonnegut" was first published in *Critical Quarterly* and reprinted with some changes.

[3] Peter J. Reed, *Kurt Vonnegut*, Jr., (1972). David H. Goldsmith, *Kurt Vonnegut. Fantasist of Fire and Ice* (1972).

[4] Jerome Klinkowitz / John Somer (edd.), *The Vonnegut Statement* (1973).

[5] Armin P. Frank, "Kurt Vonnegut". In: Martin Christadler (ed.), *Amerikanische Literatur* (1973), p. 408-424.
H. Breinig, "Kurt Vonnegut, Jr., "Tomorrow and tomorrow and tomorrow". In: Freese (ed.), *Die amerikanische short story* (1976), p. 151-159.
P. Freese, "Kurt Vonnegut, *The Sirens of Titan*. In: H. Heuermann (ed.), *Der Science-Fiction Roman in der angloamerikanischen Literatur* (1986), pp. 196-219.
F. Schulz, "*Slaughterhouse Five*". In Busch / Schmidt-von Bardeleben (edd.), *Amerikanische Erzählliteratur*, p. 155-169 (1975).
M. Pütz, "'Who am I this Time': Die Romane von Kurt Vonnegut". In: *JfA* 19/1974, p. 111-125.

[6] Stanley Schatt, *Kurt Vonnegut, Jr.* (1976).

[7] K. and C. Wood also conclude:
"Yet no full-scale examination of Vonnegut as a science fictionist has been made". They make the attempt to explain Vonnegut as an SF-author, but their concept of SF is scarcely precise and therefore questionable: SF for them is always sociological exploration on the ground of technology and sciences. This, however, only applies, if at all, to Vonnegut's first novel *Player Piano* (K. & C. Wood, "The Vonnegut Effect. Science Fiction and Beyond." In: Klinkowitz / Somer (edd.), op.cit., p. 133-157). In spite of existing deficiencies this contribution is one of the few serious attempts to debate the ambivalence of Vonnegut's novels. Reed's and Schatt's books also make valuable comments on this.

[8] Goldsmith, *Vonnegut*, p. 6.

[9] Wood, p. 134; Aldiss, *Billion Year*, p. 316; especially critical Moskowitz, *Seekers of Tomorrow* (1967), p. 420.

[10] Vonnegut himself shows surprise about the labelling as SF-author, thereby provoking the irritation and annoyance of the SF-prophets (cf. n. 7): "I learned from the reviewers that I was a science-fiction writer. I didn't know that. I supposed that I was writing a novel about life [...]." Kurt Vonnegut, "Science Fiction". In: Vonnegut, *Wampeters, Foma & Granfalloons* ([1]1965) 1974, p. 1-5, here p. 1).
Schatt states the dilemma of the critics when commenting on Vonnegut. "*Player Piano* was ignored by most literary critics because it was science fiction; unfortunately for Vonnegut, many science fiction-critics dismissed it as good satire but bad science fiction." (Schatt, *Vonnegut*, p. 17) In spite of this - or because of it - to become a bestselling author is an irony of literary history that fits this author who is also characterized as a representative of Black Humour.

[11] Thus, for example, Greiner, "Vonnegut's *Slaughterhouse-Five*". In: *Critique* 14/1973, p. 38-51; Reed, op.cit., p. 172-203.

[12] All quotes follow the Dell edition of Vonnegut's works.

[13] Cf. U. Broich, *Gattungen des modernen englischen Romans* (1975), p. 119ff. - Since the differences between SF and dystopia have already been defined several times and this is not of great importance for the analysis of Vonnegut's works it is sufficient to say that the antiutopian novel is a variation in the field of SF. Cf. also H.-U. Seeber, *Wandlungen der Form in der literarischen Utopie*, p. 256-260.

[14] In connection with Vonnegut also Wood, "The Vonnegut Effect", p. 136:

> Actually, science fiction is primarily social criticism, usually veiled in the remoteness of time and alien location [...] projecting current problems to their logical future conclusions. [...] Science Fiction [...] is an *extension* of current trends to logical and frequently horrible conclusions.

It is surprising in Wood's study that it applies this concept to all of Vonnegut's novels, because already *Player Piano* is only partially covered by it.

[15] "Vonnegut has admitted that he 'cheerfully ripped off the plot of *Brave New World*, whose plot had been cheerfully ripped off from Eugene Zamiatin's *We*'". (Schatt, *Vonnegut*, p. 18 and n.).

[16] There is a parallel for this in the field of the antiutopian satire in Part II and III of Burgess' novel *A Clockwork Orange*. There each party claims the protagonist for his purposes: one party wants to demonstrate the success of

their therapies in him, while for the other party he is a guinea-pig for undignified manipulations reducing him to a martyr and advertisement in the electoral campaign. This leads to a situation which finally makes the anti-social and brutal behaviour of the protagonist appear more humane than the conditioning methods directed towards social peace at all costs, but even more to scientific and political greed for power. Consequentially Alex is given back his identity as a criminal at the end of the novel.

[17] The character of the agent anticipates *Mother Night* where he becomes the central theme of his novel.

[18] Klinkowitz' opinion on the function of *Player Piano*, which is also quoted by Schatt, p. 28f., seems too early to me: "The object of Vonnegut's literary technique in the novel, similarly is the overthrow of the accepted literary conventions of visual imagery, continuous plotting, connected characterization, uniform point-of-view - all the mechanical aspects of pictorialism associated with Henry James and the mimetic novel." (Mellard, "'The Modes of Vonnegut's Fiction", p. 180). This is more appropriate for *Sirens of Titan*, *Cat's Cradle* or *Breakfast of Champions*.

[19] The parallel to the description of Total War in *Slaughterhouse-Five* is obvious; the sub-title used there, *The Children's Crusade*, is also true of the narration of the invaders from Mars in *Titan*.

[20] Goldsmith, *Vonnegut*, p. 6f. The author refers, however, to *Player Piano*. Cf. also P. Freese in his essay on *The Sirens of Titan* in: Heuermann (ed., 1986), p. 207.

[21] For this aspect cf. Tanner, "Uncertain Messenger", and Leff, "The Utopia Reconstructed", in: *Critique* 12 (1970/71), p. 29-37.

[22] This parallel was also pointed out by W. Schulz, "The Unconfirmed Thesis: Kurt Vonnegut, Black Humor, and Contemporary Art", in: *Critique* 12 (1970/71), here p. 25-27.

[23] Somer, "Geodesic Vonnegut", in: Klinkowitz / Somer (edd.), op.cit., p. 212; Somer thinks that this aspect is especially true of *Slaughterhouse-Five*, but he characterizes Vonnegut's novels increasingly, starting with *Sirens of Titan*.

[24] A.C. Clarke, "In Defense of Science Fiction", in: *UNESCO Courier* 15, p. 14-17 (cf. Clareson, *Science Fiction Criticism. An Annotated Checklist* (1972), p. 4).

[25] Cf. Scholes, *Fabulation*, p. 62. Freese says that he uses SF "props" as parodistically perverted vehicles of his message (p. 210).

[26] Precisely at this point the interpretation of Wood "The Vonnegut Effect" is inadequate (cf. n. 5 of this chapter). To call *Sirens of Titan* "the purest science-fiction novel Vonnegut has produced" (Wood, p. 148), if SF has previously been defined as the logical extrapolation of future possibilities, maintaining that "Science is the science fiction writer's technique of gaining credibility" (Wood, p. 137) is not logical. In this point I also differ from Freese who states that Vonnegut is not interested in new physics, but in old metaphysics, and nevertheless associates *Sirens of Titan* with SF (op.cit., p. 217).

[27] "Papa Doc" Duvalier (cf. Reed, *Vonnegut*, p. 121) forms an ironic parallel.

[28] For this cf. R. Borgmeier, "'Religion' in der Science Fiction" in: *Die Neueren Sprachen* N.F. H. 2/1975, p. 121-135; for *Cat's Cradle* cf. Borgmeier, p. 126f., also Schatt, p. 62-67.

[29] Christian religion is implicitly criticized by the author; this is not only true of *Cat's Cradle*, but even more of the other Vonnegut novels, especially *Slaughterhouse-Five*.

[30] The metaphorical contrast fire vs. ice recurs in *Slaughterhouse-Five*: the fire storm in Dresden is contrasted with the experience of Billy Pilgrim, whose most intensive perception during his time as a soldier and prisoner-of-war is the great cold.

[31] It would be worth investigating if this grip of fiction for reality - that is the fantastic narration as the only possible and adequate reproduction of a horrible reality - is a contrasting and complementary phenomenon to the non-fiction novel.

[32] The impossibility of making the events visible and reproducible by recording the "facts", is also described by the authorial narrator in chapter 1 of *Slaughterhouse-Five*:

> I thought it would be easy for me to write about the destruction of Dresden, since all I would have to do would be to report what I had seen. [...] But not many words about Dresden came from my mind (p. 2).

The report as narrative form is out of the question for Vonnegut.

[33] Reed, *Vonnegut*, p. 186.

[34] Cf. for this phrase n. 1 of chapter 3.

[35] Schatt, "The World of Kurt Vonnegut, Jr.", in: *Critique* 12 (1970/71), p. 54.

[36] Critics have pointed to the historical parallel of Ezra Pound (cf. Schatt, *Vonnegut*, p. 43f. who also mentions Tanner's hint). - The name Campbell also gave rise to speculations whether there is a connection intended with the SF-pioneer and editor of *Astounding Stories*, John W. Campbell.

[37] Niles Rumfoord in *Sirens of Titan* is also one of these victimizer-victim-characters who seem to be in control of earthly events, but is himself a victim of remote control from Tralfamadore.

[38] Vonnegut sarcastically expresses his opinion of this theme in an essay with the title "Science Fiction":

> Science-Fiction writers meet often, comfort and praise one another [...]. They are joiners. They are a lodge. If they didn't enjoy having a gang of their own so much, there would be no such category as science fiction. (p. 2)

Supposedly the author is totally right that this statement "will put them through the roof" (loc.cit.).

[39] Kilgore Trout is a fictitious character, although there is a real book by him. The at the time fictitious SF novel *Venus on the Half-Shell* (quoted by Vonnegut in *Rosewater*, p. 114f.) has existed since 1974. This book was written by the SF-author P.J. Farmer, known for his SF that includes sex as a topic, as a Vonnegut-parody and published by Dell in New York (cf. Jannone, "*Venus on the Half Shell* as Structuralist Activity", in: *Extrapolation* 17 (1976), p. 110-117).

[40] The connection between *Slaughterhouse-Five* and the contemporary reality of the United States is obvious, and is also mentioned in Reed's book, p. 199.

[41] Cf. Reed, op.cit., p. 172-203.

[42] Even the wording resembles the quotation concerning the situation described by Barth.

[43] Alain Robbe-Grillet, *Pour un Nouveau Roman* (1963); cf. Schatt, op.cit., p. 98.

[44] Reed claims boldly: "war becomes the general metaphor for Vonnegut's vision of the human condition, Dresden becomes the symbol, the quintessence. It acts as something concrete, a specific point of reference, to which all that is said about human behavior or the nature of man's existence can be related" (Reed, op.cit., p. 186f.).

[45] That Vonnegut's basic disposition has so often been called "existentialist" or "existential" (e.g. McGinnis, "The Arbitrary Cycle of *Slaughterhouse-Five*, in:

Critique 17 (1975, p. 55-68 and Burhans, "Hemingway and Vonnegut", in: *MFS* 21 (1975), p. 173-191) is not only based on philosophical views but is also in correspondence with J.P. Sartre's attitudes towards fiction, its role and its relation to reality:

> Quand on vit, il n'arrive rien. [...] Il n'y a jamais de commencements [...]. Il n'y a pas de fins non plus [...]. Ça, c'est vivre. Mais quand on raconte la vie, tout change; seulement c'est un changement que personne ne remarque: la preuve c'est qu'on parle d'histoires vraies. Comme s'il pouvait y avoir des histoires vraies; les événements se produisent dans un sens et nous les racontons en sens inverse [...]. En réalité c'est par la fin qu'on a commencé. Elle est là, invisible et présente, c'est elle qui donne à ces quelques mots la pompe et la valeur d'un commencement. [...]
> Mais il faut choisir: vivre ou raconter.
>
> (J.-P. Sartre, *La Nausée*, 1938, p. 61f.)

46 R. Pauly, "The Moral Stance of Kurt Vonnegut", in: *Extrapolation* 15 (1973), p. 66.

47 A. Robbe-Grillet, *Pour un Nouveau Roman* (1963); cf. Schatt, *Vonnegut*, p. 98.

48 Greiner, op.cit., p. 49.

49 Of course critics are often eager to claim without discrimination works like *Gulliver's Travels* for the history of the genre. Vonnegut himself sarcastically comments on this tendency:

> 'Boomers of science fiction might reply, "Ha! Orwell and Ellison and Flaubert and Kafka are science-fiction writers, too!" They often say things like that. Some are crazy enough to try to capture Tolstoy.'
>
> (Vonnegut, "Science Fiction", p. 4)

50 Goldsmith overlooks this breach when maintaining simplistically:

> 'Certainly he is fond of space ships, time travel and other gimmickry, but these phenomena, after all, represent the latter half of the twentieth century far better than would the riverboat journeys of Twain'.
>
> (Goldsmith, op.cit., p. 6)

The same is true of McNelly's statement in "Vonnegut's *Slaughterhouse-Five*: Science Fiction as Objective Correlative", in: W.E. McNelly / L.E. Stover (edd.), *Above the Human Landscape: A Social Science Fiction Anthology* (1972), p. 383-387).

[51] This characteristic of Vonnegut's novels is often ignored in criticism. Godshalk, "Vonnegut and Shakespeare" investigates only a small section.

[52] The significance of this motif is pointed at by some of the critics, e.g. (J. Klinkowitz, "The Literary Career of Kurt Vonnegut, Jr.", in: *MFS* 19 (1973), p. 57-67 and G. Meeter, "Vonnegut's Formal and Moral Otherworldliness: *Cat's Cradle* and *Slaughterhouse-Five*", in: Klinkowitz / Somer, op.cit., p. 204-220).

[53] Among them are especially identical perceptions, e.g. the colours orange and black that are used for the marking of the transport of prisoners-of-war as well as for the tent at the celebration of Pilgrim's daughter's wedding; these parallels are especially frequent in chapters 3 and 4 of the novel.

[54] This parallel is also recognized by McGinnis in "The arbitrary cycle of *Slaughterhouse-Five*. A relation of form to theme", in: *Critique* 17 (1975), here p. 62; however, it remains unclear what he means by "secondary use" of this narrative technique.

[55] Quoted from Schatt, *Vonnegut*, p. 97.

[56] Cf. P.B. Messent, "'Breakfast of Champions": The direction of Kurt Vonnegut's fiction", in: *JAS* 8 (1974), p. 101-114. - Originally Vonnegut had stated that he did not want to write another novel after *Slaughterhouse-Five* (according to Reed, op.cit., p. 218 and n. 5).

[57] P.J. Farmer later on gave him a new reality (cf. n. 39). We have reached absolute relativism, "mirrors reflecting mirrors" - a process that reminds the reader of the narratives by Borges (cf. Jannone, op.cit., p. 111). Cf. also McHale, *Postmodernist Fiction* (1986), p. 72.

[58] Schatt, *Vonnegut*, p. 115. Cf. M. Schulz, *Black Humor Fiction of the Sixties* (1973), which comprises the authors Borges, Pynchon and Vonnegut.

[59] Both quotations according to David Lodge "Objections to William Burroughs", in: *Critical Quarterly* 8 (1966), p. 203.

[60] For a long time Burroughs himself was a drug-addict; his first publication *Junkie* is autobiographical. Because of his offenses against drug-prohibiting laws he was persecuted by the police, imprisoned in Mexico City in 1950 and accused of having killed his wife. Whether this was an accident or murder was never clarified. Burroughs was diagnosed as a schizophrenic paranoid.

[61] E. Mottram's book *William Burroughs* (1970) is not very systematical and therefore dissatisfying.

[62] K. Poenicke, "William Burroughs", in: M. Christadler (ed.), *Amerikanische Literatur der Gegenwart in Einzeldarstellungen* (1973), p. 296f.
L. Fiedler (1984), in: Pütz / Freese (edd.), p. 159.

[63] Poenicke, op.cit., p. 297 and Tanner, *City of Words*, p. 110f. and 140.

[64] I. Hassan, "The Subtracting Machine: The Work of William Burroughs", in: *Critique* 6, Nr. 1 (1963/64), p. 6.

[65] Poenicke, op.cit., p. 268.

[66] Tanner, *City*, p. 131.

[67] Lodge, op.cit., p. 204.

[68] Mottram, op.cit., p. 65.

[69] G. Cordesse, "The science-fiction of William Burroughs", in: *Annales de l'Université de Toulouse*, Caliban XII, N.S. 11 (1975), H. 1, p. 33-43.
McHale (1987), p. 66f.; L. Fiedler (1984) is expecting W. Burroughs to cross the border to postmodern fiction completely (p. 159).

[70] Cf. Tanner, *City*, p. 110 and n. 1. - Burroughs calls himself "a cosmonaut of inner space" (cf. Mottram, op.cit., p. 9).

[71] E.g. M. Butor, "Die Krise der Science Fiction", in: Barmeyer (ed.), op.cit., p. 82ff.; U. Diederichs, op.cit., p. 127 and passim.

[72] Only Cordesse points at the absence of the structures of adventures as a typical characteristic of SF. He recognizes on the other hand the analogy between Burroughs' *Wild Boys* and Moorcock's counter-cultural hero Jerry Cornelius.
The lack of theoretical concepts and descriptive poetics for SF reveals itself in most of the critical studies on Vonnegut and particularly on Burroughs. Those readers and critics familiar with postmodern fiction are often not very familiar with SF, which renders competent criticism on authors who cross the border difficult and rare.

[73] *The Ticket That Exploded*, p. 143 (my emphasis). The edition of Burroughs' novels is that by Grove Press.

[74] These sentences show clear parallels to the simultaneously published social theories and theory of mass media from the field of social and political

sciences, especially those of Herbert Marcuse. At the time of publication the manipulative power of the media and the secret mechanisms of conditioning and repression were the centre of attention for many American readers. Cf. also R. Federman, "Surfiction", in: Pütz / Freese (edd.), *Postmodernism*, p. 149:

> It is obvious from the preceding propositions that the most striking aspects of the new fiction will be its semblance of disorder and its deliberate incoherency. Since, as stated earlier, no meaning pre-exists language, but meaning is produced in the process of writing (and reading), the new fiction will not attempt to be meaningful, truthful, or realistic, nor will it attempt to serve as the vehicle of a ready-made meaning.

[75] Cordesse, op.cit., p. 36.

[76] Cordesse, op.cit., p. 41; my emphasis.

[77] Tanner, *City of Words*, p. 122.

[78] Tanner, *City of Words*, p. 109; my emphasis. The passages in italics or in inverted commas could be from the vocabulary of SF. This is also Mottram's conclusion, op.cit., p. 63.

[79] Tanner, *City*, p. 134.

[80]

> In his works science-fiction is not an intellectual construction, it is rooted in obsessive metaphors. What is ironical is that science-fiction in order to repudiate its low-brow origins tends to pride itself on its conceptual, speculative character: it has taken an avantgarde artist to reactivate the affective charge of its motifs. (Cordesse, op.cit., p. 39)

This position comes close to Mottram's.

[81] Butor, "The Novel as Research", in: M. Bradbury (ed.), *The Novel Today* (1990), p. 45-50; here p. 46f. Noteworthy is the indeterminacy of this statement, as in much of the poststructuralist criticism.

[82] Cf. McHale, p. 65.

5. RESULTS AND CONCLUSIONS

This study was based on the concept of SF as a literary genre, which means that each single work participates in genre conventions and expectations characterizing the whole group of texts.

The most important of these conventions as interdependent components, against the background of a number of experimental and postmodern fictional texts, were pointed out in the second chapter. The structural pattern developed by methods of descriptive poetics contains the principal functions and characteristics and distinguishes this study methodologically from the definitions, apologetic discussions and the dogmatism that have been widespread in the literary criticism of SF for a considerable time. My contrastive and comparative analyses fulfil the purpose of representing a classical pattern of SF texts, whose further development, modification and transgression up to its dissolution was dealt with in chapters 3 and 4. This sequence of steps in the exploration not only fulfils a didactic purpose but is also an adequate instrument for the analysis of this particular field; for

> Literary forms like detective novel, robinsonade, utopian novel, picaresque novel, historical novel or SF can (*in contrast to deductive genre classifications*; my addition) only be empirically found out. They can only be defined as a series of characteristics which are not only of a material and thematic but also of a structural kind [...]. Moreover these fictional forms are of an empirical nature; as it turned out [...] their genre conventions were subjected to such an important historical change that frequently the question was asked whether later works still belonged to the same genre at all [...][1] (my translation)

Exactly this process has characterized SF for the past thirty or thirty-five years.

My catalogue of characteristics of a "classical" SF text contained - beside the action as dominant and the teleological purposeful directedness of the *plot* - the character of an active, rational and socially integrated hero, time as subject-matter (time-travel) and particularly the creation of an imaginary world constituted by the means of a realistic narrative. Only their interdependence and cooperation constitute the participation of a particular text in SF.

This basic pattern remained intact and has been copied innumerable times in short stories and novels. Besides, a series of variations and divergent developments including the dissolution of the system of conventions, its parodistic revival and the change of paradigm came into existence.

SF opens up to unusual literary forms and narrative techniques, and it also integrates new themes, on the other hand the representatives of experimental narrative prose use elements that they have borrowed from SF. Roman Jakobson said as early as 1935 in one of his lectures:

> The hierarchy of artistic devices changes within the framework of a given poetic genre; the change, moreover, affects the hierarchy of poetic genres, and, simultaneously, the distribution of artistic devices among the individual genres. Genres which were originally secondary paths, subsidiary variants, now come to the fore, whereas the canonical genres are pushed toward the rear.[2]

Thus considerable overlappings and flowing transitions are created, which complicate a clear coordination with a specific genre or make it appear impossible; this is true of authors like Ballard, Moorcock, Disch, but also of the last novels by Brunner. As representatives of the *New Wave* they destroy the pattern of SF, still reflecting it, thereby approaching authors like Pynchon with "Entropy" and *Gravity's Rainbow*, like Borges and Burroughs. These are inspired by fantastic literature, the latter by cultural phenomena like the beat, hippie and drug scene as well as by trivial mass literature like comics and by other media like radio play, film and TV.

Metaphor and allegory play a key role in the transgression and dissolution of borders. We recognized in classical SF a "materialization" of matters usually represented by imagery or intrasubjective representation in narrative fiction as typical procedures.

The relation of fictitious world and verbal representation is reversed and complementary in SF proper (cf. diagram, p. 92).

This relation is often violated in experimental *New Wave* SF. If it is possible to describe classical SF as a mimetic representation of scientific research and experiment - where the Newtonian understanding of science appears as a substrate of our interpretation of the universe - where, however, this act of representation itself is not reflected but has to be disclosed by the interpreter some representatives of the *New Wave*, e.g. Aldiss, Bester, Zelazny, refer explicitly, or, like the postmodern authors Pynchon and Burroughs, implicitly to theories from the sciences and the humanities, so that the texts themselves become interpretations and explanations of science.

A classification of text into genres is becoming more and more problematic. SF as a genre has certainly not died out, but it is becoming more diversified, resulting in overlappings and new varieties. Postmodernism rejects genre concepts altogether.

Broich's statement on detective fiction can also be applied analogously to SF, namely that several phases of development exist simultaneously.

The description of SF as a "closed genre"[3] and a genre that is sophisticated but less contemporary than "mainstream fiction"[4] has to be rejected at the end and as a result of this study; it is opposed by the innovations in recent SF, its "postmodernization". Classification becomes more difficult, borders are crossed, gaps closed; nevertheless it would be a mistake to see this movement simply as a process of convergence between the genres.[5] A more intricate and diversified picture of the mutual influence between experimental fiction and SF presents itself, compared to thirty years ago.

A problem-oriented questioning of the genre concepts is closely connected to the dubious classification into "trivial" and "non-trivial" genres, as they are labelled in German, "serious" and "popular" literature in the US. German literary criticism led the more violent debates on this dichotomy, as we were already able to conclude from the report on German SF-criticism in chapter 1. More than in the US the value of a certain work of fiction is judged according to its belonging to a certain genre. The term "Popular Literature" is the equivalent of the German mass literature whereas the term "trivial" is already a negative evaluation that renders an unbiased artistic appreciation difficult.[6]

As chapter 2 revealed, however, the components that are often explained as "trivial", namely an obsolete world view, the type of the protagonist, the sometimes anachronistic ideas about science and the conservative narrative techniques of SF "proper", which all serve the purpose of producing the illusion of reality, partly result from structural necessities of SF and can therefore not merely be based on ideological or commercial motivation.

Instead SF assumes functions formerly fulfilled by the "realistic" novel and enhances its objectives: "the representation of an orderly and explicable universe [...], enlightenment by insight into the nature of reality."[7] (my translation). "Innocent realism", as Stephan Kohl calls it, has become alienated to postmodern fiction. In spite of innovative tendencies which are fully grown into *New Wave* SF I come to the conclusion that there is a specific affinity between SF - the literature of change - and the skills and crafts of writing a "good story", with characters, *plot*, and *closure*. The postmodern "surfiction" or "metafiction" is still separated by a gap from SF, but this gap is narrowing, as we have seen. The more demanding and intricate products of SF are postmodernizing, so that it is certainly unjustified to call the whole genre "trivial". On the other hand the conventional way of narrating a story, which still characterizes the bulk of SF is not a sign of "triviality", it is more a sign of lack of those innovative inclinations that often lead to auto-destructive fictional texts.

"Innocent realism", according to John Barth, belongs to the past:

> Once upon a time I told tales straight out, alternating summary and dramatization, developing characters and relationships, laying on bright detail and rhetorical flourish, et cetera. I'm not that amateur at the Lion's Gate; I know my trade. But I fear we're too far gone now for such luxury.[8]

Yet it is not possible that the straightforward story with mimetic intentions and representational qualities is obsolete or simplistic. It is characteristic of many of those "fictions of the future" which we have explored here. The pattern of the continuous story and a structured *plot*, unequivocal and based on causality has been surpassed by postmodern fiction, which pronounced the death of the novel and the death of the author.[9] Self-reflexivity and exploration of the nature of fiction become the central concern of W. Burroughs, Borges, Barth and Nabokov. As Ahrends writes about Barth's and Borges' short fiction:

> Contemporary postmodern short fictions are based on the idea that reality is not an objective measure, but a projection of subjective experience. The definable place, the chronologically ordered time-sequence, the character that exists independently of the author's experience and the plot based on causality are abandoned as categories of a perception of reality. (op.cit., p. 212; my translation)

Although the prevalence of so-called simple structures often serves to explain the "trivial" nature of a given text, this argument alone is insufficient to explain the often-displayed "straightforwardness" of such a great number of SF texts as well as the fact that the genre offers resistance to postmodernization without "crossing the border" and becoming a postmodern work, with only a few faint reminiscences of SF. SF can to a great extent do without auto-reflexion, as well as metaphorization, intrasubjective perspective, allegorical meaning because the "willing maintenance of disbelief" is an unuttered precondition of the genre. It lies before the beginning of the narrative process and is part of an unquestioned consensus between the author and his reader. It is therefore more characteristic of SF than of other genres of narrative fiction that it covers a wide range of levels and expectations in the readership and in its experimental texts reaches innovative and elitist developments of mainstream fiction.

The different positions in regard to the dichotomy of *belles-lettres* or "high" and trivial or "low-brow" literature can best be exemplified by the German critics Kaes / Zimmermann and Schulte-Sasse[10], and for American criticism by Leslie Fiedler[11]. Although these publications were very thought-provoking the debate has not yet reached definite conclusions, nor has postmodern fiction proved to be capable of closing the gap. Evaluation of literary works has remained a problem that is parodied in postmodern fiction, which has proved irreverent towards taboos and conventions, and extremely playful. This last characteristic it shares, of course, with SF. Change and innovation connect them both, and obviously the desire for play is prevalent regardless of the genre.

Notes Chapter 5

[1] Broich, *Gattungen*, p. 185.

[2] R. Jakobson, "The Dominant", p. 85.

[3] Suerbaum, "Text und Gattung", p. 112.

[4] Suerbaum, Brunner, "The Windows of Heaven", op.cit., p. 347.

[5] Cf. T.L. Ebert, "The Convergence of Postmodern Innovative Fiction and Science Fiction", in: *Poetics Today* 1 (1979), p. 91-104.

[6] A. Kaes / B. Zimmermann (edd.), *Literatur für viele 1* (1975), preface, p. 7.

[7] S. Kohl, *Realismus*, p. 181.

[8] J. Barth, *Lost in the Funhouse*, p. 171f.

[9] R. Sukenick, *The Death of the Novel and Other Stories* ([1]1960) and "The New Tradition in Fiction", p. 35ff. Cf. J. Ehrmann, "The Death of Literature", in: R. Federman (ed.), *Surfiction*, p. 229-253.

[10] Kaes / Zimmermann, op.cit., especially the preface and the contribution by J. Schulte-Sasse; cf. also the latter's book *Trivialliteraturkritik seit der Aufklärung* (1971).

[11] Leslie Fiedler, "Cross the Border - Close that Gap: Postmodernism", in: Pütz/Freese, *Postmodernism in American Literature. A Critical Anthology* (1984), p. 151-166.

BIBLIOGRAPHY

I. Texts

1. Science Fiction

a) Novels

ALDISS, Brian. Frankenstein Unbound. London 1973.

ALDISS, Brian. Report on Probability A. London ([1]1968) 1973 (repr.).

BALLARD, J.G. The Drowned World. Harmondsworth 1965.

BALLARD, J.G. The Crystal World. New York 1966.

BALLARD, J.G. The Wind From Nowhere. New York 1962.

BRADBURY, Ray. The Martian Chronicles. New York 1967 (1946).

BRADBURY, Ray. Fahrenheit 451. (1953) New York 1968.

BRUNNER, John. The Productions of Time. Harmondsworth 1970 (1967).

BRUNNER, John. The Sheep Look Up. New York 1972.

BRUNNER, John. Stand On Zanzibar. (1969) London 1971.

BRUNNER, John. Times Without Number. New York 1969.

BURGESS, Anthony. A Clockwork Orange. (1962) New York 1972.

CLARKE, Arthur C. Childhood's End. (1953) New York 1974.

CLARKE, Arthur C. 2001 - A Space Odyssey. New York 1968.

CLARKE, Arthur C. Rendezvous With Rama. (1973) New York 1974.

DELANY, Samuel R. Babel-17. New York 1966.

DELANY, Samuel R. The Einstein Intersection. New York 1967.

DICK, Philip K. The Crack In Space. New York 1966.

DICK, Philip K. Do Androids Dream of Electric Sheep? New York (1968) 1969.

DICK, Philip K. The Man In The High Castle. (1962) New York 1974.

GALOUYE, Daniel F. Simulacron-3. New York 1964.

HARRISON, Harry. Captive Universe. New York 1969.

HARRISON, Harry. Make Room! Make Room! (1966) New York 1973.

HEINLEIN, Robert A. The Day After Tomorrow. New York 1949.

HEINLEIN, Robert A. Methuselah's Children. New York 1958.

HEINLEIN, Robert A. Stranger In A Strange Land. (1961) New York 1968.

HOYLE, Fred. October the First is Too Late. (1966) Harmondsworth 1974.

HUXLEY, Aldous. Brave New World. (1932) Harmondsworth 1970.

LeGUIN, Ursula. The Left Hand Of Darkness. (1969) New York 1974.

LEM, Stanislaw. Solaris. (1968) Düsseldorf 1972.

LEM, Stanislaw. Transfer. (1961) Düsseldorf 1974.

MILLER, Walter M. jr. A Canticle For Leibowitz. (1959) New York 1972.

MOORCOCK, Michael. An Alien Heat. London 1972.

MOORCOCK, Michael. Behold The Man. (1966) New York 1972.

MOORCOCK, Michael. Breakfast In The Ruins. (1971) London 1975.

MOORCOCK, Michael. A Cure For Cancer. (1971) Harmondsworth 1974 (repr.).

MOORCOCK, Michael. The Warlord Of The Air. New York 1971.

ORWELL, George. 1984. (1949) Harmondsworth 1966 (repr.).

POHL, Frederik. Drunkard's Walk. (1960) New York [3]1973.

POHL, Frederik/KORNBLUTH, C.M. The Space Merchants. (1952) New York 1953.

POHL, Frederik/WILLIAMSON, Jack. Starchild. New York 1965.

SAMJATIN, Jewgenij. Wir. München 1975.

SILVERBERG, Robert. The World Inside. (1970) New York 1972.

SIMAK, Clifford D. City. (1952) New York ^{4}1973.

SIODMAK, Curt. Hauser's Memory. London 1968.

TROUT, Kilgore. Venus on the Half Shell. New York 1974.

WELLS, H.G. The Invisible Man. London (1953) 1965.

WYNDHAM, John. The Chrysalids. (1955) Harmondsworth 1973 (repr.).

b) short story-Anthologies

ALDISS, Brian (ed.). The Penguin SF Omnibus. (1961) Harmondsworth
    1973.

ALDISS, Brian/HARRISON, Harry (edd.). The Year's Best SF No. 6.
    London 1972.

BALLARD, J.G. The Day Of Forever. London 1967.

BALLARD, J.G. The Four-Dimensional Nightmare. Harmondsworth 1965.

BALLARD, J.G. The Overloaded Man. London (1967) 1971 (repr.).

BALLARD, J.G. Terminal Beach. New York 1964.

BALLARD, J.G. Terminal Beach. Harmondsworth 1966.

BRADBURY, Ray. The Illustrated Man. (1951) New York 1972.

CRISPIN, Edmund (ed.). Best SF Four. London (1960) 1970 (repr.).

FERMAN, Edward L./MALZBERG, Barry N. (edd.). Final Stage. The
    Ultimate Science Fiction Anthology. New York (1974) 1975.

HEINTZ, Bonnie L./HERBERT, Frank/JOOS, Donald A./McGEE, Jane
    Agorn (edd.). Tomorrow, And Tomorrow, And Tomorrow... New York
    1974.

KNIGHT, Damon (ed.). Nebula Award Stories. New York 1966.

MOORCOCK, Michael (ed.). The Best SF Stories From New Worlds (1965-66). New York 1967.

PEAKE, Mervyn/BALLARD, J.G./ALDISS, Brian W. The Inner Landscape. New York 1971.

SILVERBERG, Robert (ed.). The Mirror Of Infinity. A Critics' Anthology of Science Fiction. New York 1970.

SURVIVAL PRINTOUT (ed. by Total Effect). New York 1973.

WOLF, Jack C./GERALD, Gregory Fitz (edd.). Past, Present, & Future Perfect. A Text Anthology of Speculative & Science Fiction. Greenwich, Conn., 1973.

WOLLHEIM, D.A./CARR, T. (edd.). World's Best SF 1. New York 1965.

WYNDHAM, John. The Seeds of Time (1956). Harmondsworth 1972 (repr.).

ZELAZNY, Roger. Four For Tomorrow. New York (1967) 1974.

c) short stories

ASIMOV, Isaac. "Jokester", in: ALDISS (ed.). SF Omnibus, p. 377-390.

BALLARD, J.G. "Billenium", in: The Terminal Beach (1966), p. 177-193.

BALLARD, J.G. "The Day Of Forever", in: The Day of Forever, p. 9-26.

BALLARD, J.G. "The Cage Of Sand", in: The Four-Dimensional Nightmare, p. 143-167.

BALLARD, J.G. "Chronopolis", in: The Four-Dimensional Nightmare. p. 198-223.

BALLARD, J.G. "The Delta At Sunset", in: The Terminal Beach (1966), p. 119-135.

BALLARD, J.G. "The Drowned Giant", in: The Terminal Beach (1966), p. 40-51.

BALLARD, J.G. "The Last World of Mr. Goddard", in: Terminal Beach (1964), p. 45-60.

BALLARD, J.G. "The Lost Leonardo", in: The Terminal Beach (1966), p. 204-224.

BALLARD, J.G. "Now Wakes The Sea", in: Terminal Beach (1964), p. 75-85.

BALLARD, J.G. "The Overloaded Man", in: The Overloaded Man, p. 146-158.

BALLARD, J.G. "A Question of Re-Entry", in: The Terminal Beach (1966), p. 7-39.

BALLARD, J.G. "Subliminal Man", in: Terminal Beach (1964), p. 27-45.

BALLARD, J.G. "Terminal Beach", in: Terminal Beach (1964), p. 140-160.

BALLARD, J.G. "The Venus Hunters", in: Terminal Beach (1964), p. 85-115.

BALLARD, J.G. "The Voices Of Time", in: PEAKE/BALLARD/ALDISS, The Inner Landscape, p. 67-103.

BESTER, Alfred. "Fondly Fahrenheit", in: SURVIVAL PRINTOUT, p. 45-67.

BLISH, James. "Common Time", in: ALDISS (ed.). SF Omnibus, p. 566-587.

BRUNNER, John. "The Last Lonely Man", in: WOLLHEIM/CARR (edd.). World's Best SF 1, p. 142-159.

DICK, Philip K. "Oh, to be a Blobel!", in: WOLLHEIM/CARR (edd.). World's Best SF 1, p. 178-198.

DISCH, Thomas. "Now is Forever", in: WOLLHEIM/CARR (edd.). World's Best SF 1, p. 235-251.

DISCH, Thomas. "The Squirrel Cage", in: MOORCOCK (ed.). The Best SF Stories From New Worlds, p. 143-158.

HEINLEIN, Robert A. "'All you Zombies'", in: SURVIVAL PRINTOUT, p. 295-308.

KORNBLUTH, C.M. "MS Found in a Chinese Fortune Cookie", in: ALDISS (ed.). SF Omnibus, p. 511-522.

MASSON, David. "A Two-Timer", in MOORCOCK (ed.). The Best SF Stories From New Worlds, p. 94-132.

McINTOSH, J.T. "The Bliss of Solitude", in: CRISPIN (ed.). Best SF 4, p. 152-172.

MILLER, Walter M. jr. "Command Performance", in: ALDISS (ed.). SF Omnibus, p. 107-125.

POHL, Frederik. "The Tunnel Under The World", in: ALDISS (ed.). SF Omnibus, p. 337-369.

PORGES, A. "The Rescuer", in: ALDISS (ed.). SF Omnibus, p. 478-484.

TENN, William. "Eastward Ho!", in: ALDISS (ed.). SF Omnibus, p. 536-552.

WYNDHAM, John. "Chronoclasm", in: The Seeds of Time, p. 9-31.

WYNDHAM, John. "Opposite Number", in: The Seeds of Time, p. 121-139.

WYNDHAM, John. "Pawley's Peepholes", in: The Seeds of Time, p. 96-120.

ZELAZNY, Roger. "He Who Shapes", in: KNIGHT (ed.). Nebula Award Stories, p. 65-150.

2. Mainstream Fiction

BARTH, John. Lost in the Funhouse. Fiction for Print, Tape, Live Voice. (1963) New York 1969.

BELLOW, Saul. Herzog. (1961) New York 1964.

BORGES, Jorge Luis. Ficciones. New York 1962 (Span. Buenos Aires 1956).

BURROUGHS, William S. Naked Lunch. New York 1959.

BURROUGHS, William S. The Soft Machine. New York (1961) 1967.

BURROUGHS, William S. The Ticket That Exploded. New York (1962) 1967.

BURROUGHS, William S. Nova Express. New York (1964) 1965.

BURROUGHS, William S. The Wild Boys. New York (1969) 1973.

ELLISON, Ralph. Invisible Man. (1952) Harmondsworth 1970 (repr.).

NABOKOV, Vladimir. Pale Fire. New York 1962.

NABOKOV, Vladimir. Ada, Or Ardor. A Family Chronicle. New York 1969.

PYNCHON, Thomas. The Crying of Lot 49. (1966) Philadelphia 1972.

ROBBE-GRILLET, Alain. Le Voyeur. Paris 1955.

ROBBE-GRILLET, Alain. La Jalousie. Paris 1957.

SARTRE, Jean-Paul. La Nausée. Paris 1938.

VONNEGUT, Kurt. Player Piano. (1952) New York 1974.

VONNEGUT, Kurt. The Sirens of Titan. (1959) New York 1970.

VONNEGUT, Kurt. Mother Night. (1961) New York 1974.

VONNEGUT, Kurt. God Bless You Mr. Rosewater. (1965) New York 1970.

VONNEGUT, Kurt. Slaughterhouse-Five. (1969) New York 1971.

VONNEGUT, Kurt. Breakfast of Champions. (1973) New York 1974.

II. Criticism

ABERNETHY, Peter L. "Entropy in Pynchon's 'The Crying of Lot 49'", in: Critique 14/2 (1972/73), p. 18-33.

AHRENDS, Günter. Die amerikanische Kurzgeschichte. Theorie und Entwicklung. Stuttgart 1980.

ALDISS, Brian. Billion Year Spree: The True History of Science Fiction. New York 1973.

ALLAN, L. David. The Ballantine Teacher's Guide to Science Fiction. New York 1975.

ALPERS, H.J. (ed.). SF Times Nr. 126. Bremerhaven 1972.

ALPERS, H.J./W. FUCHS /R.M. HAHN/W. JESCHKE. Lexikon der Science Fiction Literatur (Bd. I). München 1980.

AMIS, Kingsley. New Maps of Hell: A Survey of Science Fiction. New York 1960.

APPEL, Benjamin. The Fantastic Mirror. Science Fiction Across the Ages. New York 1969.

ARMYTAGE, W.H.G. Yesterday's Tomorrows. A Historical Survey of Future Societies. Toronto 1968.

ASH, Brian. Faces of the Future: The lessons of science fiction. Pemberton / London 1975.

ATHELING, Wm. (alias James Blish). The Issue at Hand. Chicago 1964.

ATHELING, Wm. (alias James Blish). More Issues at Hand. Chicago 1970.

BAILEY, J.O. Pilgrims through Space and Time. New York 1947.

BALLARD, J.G. "The Coming of the Unconscious", in: The Overloaded Man. London 1967, p. 140-145.

BALLARD, J.G. "Notizen vom Nullpunkt", in: SCHECK, Frank Rainer (ed.). Koitus '80. Neue Science Fiction. Köln 1970, p. 40-44 (engl. "Notes from Nowhere", in: New Worlds 167).

BARJAVEL, René. "La science-fiction - c'est le vrai 'nouveau roman'", in: Les nouvelles littéraires. Paris, 11 octobre 1962, p. 1f.

BARMEYER, Eike (ed.). Science Fiction. Theorie und Geschichte. München 1972.

BARMEYER, Eike. "Kommunikationen", in: BARMEYER (ed.). Science Fiction. p. 203-218.

BARTHELL, J. "Science Fiction: A Literature of Ideas", in: Extrapolation 13 (dec., 1971), p. 56-63.

BELLER, Manfred. "Von der Stoffgeschichte zur Thematologie. Ein Beitrag zur komparatistischen Methodenlehre", in: Arcadia 5 (1970), p. 1-38.

BERTHEL, Werner (ed.). Insel-Almanach auf das Jahr 1976: Stanislaw Lem. Der dialektische Weise aus Krakow. Frankfurt 1976.

BESTER, Alfred. "Science Fiction and the Renaissance Man", in: DAVENPORT (ed.). The Science Fiction Novel, p. 77-96.

BETTELHEIM, Bruno. Kinder brauchen Märchen. Stuttgart 1977 (Engl. The Uses of Enchantment. New York 1975).

BLISH, James. "Nachruf auf die Prophetie", in: BARMEYER (ed.). Science Fiction, p. 118-127.

BLOCH, Robert. "Imagination and Modern Social Criticism", in: DAVENPORT (ed.). The Science Fiction Novel, p. 97-121.

BODGANOFF, Igor & Grichka. La Science-fiction. Paris 1976.

BORGMEIER, Raimund. "'Religion' in der Science Fiction", in: Die Neueren Sprachen 1975, p. 121-135.

BRADBURY, Malcolm (ed.). The Novel Today. Contemporary Writers on Modern Fiction. London 1990.

BRADBURY, Ray. "Ohne Phantasie keine Zukunft", in: Der Spiegel, Nr. 6 (1978), p. 162.

BREINIG, Helmbrecht. "Kurt Vonnegut, Jr., Tomorrow and Tomorrow and Tomorrow' (1954)", in: FREESE, Peter (ed.). Die amerikanische Short Story der Gegenwart, p. 151-159.

BRETNOR, Reginald (ed.). Modern SF: Its Meaning and Its Future. New York 1953.

BRETNOR, Reginald (ed.). Science Fiction today and tomorrow. (1974) Baltimore 1975.

BRETNOR, Reginald (ed.). The Craft of Science Fiction. New York 1976.

BRINEY, Robert/WOOD, Edward. SF Bibliographies: An Annotated Bibliography of Bibliographical Works on SF and Fantasy Fiction. Chicago 1972.

BROICH, Ulrich. "Die Annäherung von Mainstream Literature und Science Fiction im Zeitalter der Postmoderne", in: D. PETZOLD/E. SPÄTH (edd.). Unterhaltungsliteratur. Ziele und Methoden ihrer Erforschung. Erlangen 1990, p. 71-86.

BROICH, Ulrich. Gattungen des modernen englischen Romans. Wiesbaden 1975.

BROICH, Ulrich. "Robinsonade und Science Fiction", in: Anglia 94/2 (1976), p. 40-62.

BRYAN, C.D.B. "Kurt Vonnegut on Target", in: The New Republic (Oct. 8, 1966), p. 21-26.

BUCK, Lynn. "Vonnegut's World of Comic Futility", in: Studies in American Fiction 3 (1975), p. 181-198.

BUNGERT, Hans (ed.). Die amerikanische Literatur der Gegenwart. Aspekte und Tendenzen. Stuttgart 1977.

BURGER, H.O. (ed.). Studien zur Trivialliteratur. Frankfurt 1968.

BURGHANS, Jr./CLINTON, S. "Hemingway and Vonnegut: Diminishing Vision in a Dying Age", in: MFS 21 (1975), p. 173-191.

BUSCH, Frieder/SCHMIDT-v. BARDELEBEN, Renate (edd.). Amerikanische Erzählliteratur 1950-1970. München 1975.

BUTOR, Michel. "Die Krise der Science Fiction", in: ROTTENSTEINER (ed.). Insel Almanach auf das Jahr '72, p. 76-85 (repr. in: BARMEYER (ed.). Science Fiction).

BUTOR, Michel. "The Novel as Research" (1968), in: BRADBURY, Malcolm (ed.). The Novel Today. Contemporary Writers on Modern Fiction. London 1990, p. 45-50.

CARTER, Paul A. The Creation of Tomorrow. Fifty Years of Magazine Science Fiction. New York 1977.

CHRISTADLER, Martin (ed.). Amerikanische Literatur der Gegenwart in Einzeldarstellungen. Stuttgart 1973.

CLARESON, Thomas D. (ed.). Many futures - many worlds: theme and form in science fiction. Kent, Ohio, 1977.

CLARESON, Thomas D. (ed.). Science Fiction: The other Side of Realism. Bowling Green 1971.

CLARESON, Thomas D. (ed.). A Spectrum of Worlds. Garden City, New York 1972.

CLARKE, Arthur C., "In Defense of Science Fiction", in: UNESCO Courier 15 (Nov. 1962), p. 14-17.

CLARKE, Arthur C., Time Probe: The sciences in Science Fiction. 1966.

CLARKE, J.G., The Pattern of Expectation: 1644-2001. London 1979.

CONQUEST, Robert. "Science Fiction and Literature", in: Critical Quarterly 5 (1963), p. 355-367 (repr. in: ROSE (ed.). Science Fiction).

CORDESSE, Gérard. "Fantastique et science-fiction", in: Du fantastique à la science-fiction americaine. Paris 1973, p. 39-62 (Etudes Anglaises 50).

CORDESSE, Gérard. "The science-fiction of William Burroughs", in: Annales de l'Université de Toulouse. Caliban XII, N.S. 11 (1975), p. 33-43.

DAVENPORT, Basil. Inquiry into Science Fiction. New York 1955.

DAVENPORT, Basil (ed.). The Science Fiction Novel. Imagination and Social Criticism. Chicago 1959.

DE CAMP, L. Sprague. Science Fiction Handbook. New York 1953.

DELANY, Samuel R. "About five thousand one hundred and seventy-five words", in: Extrapolation 10 (May, 1969), p. 52-66 (repr. in: CLARESON (ed.). The Other Side of Realism, p. 130-146).

DE MOTT, Benjamin. "Vonnegut's Otherwordly Laughter", in: Saturday Review 54 (May 1, 1971), p. 29-32.

DICKSON, Gordon R. "Plausibility in Science Fiction", in: BRETNOR (ed.). Science Fiction Today and Tomorrow, p. 295-308.

DIEDERICHS, Ulf. "Zeitgemäßes - Unzeitgemäßes", in: SCHMIDT-HENKEL et al. Trivialliteratur, p. 111-141.

EBERT, Teresa L. "The Convergence of Postmodern Innovative Fiction and Science Fiction. An Encounter with Samuel R. Delany's Technotopia", in: Poetics Today 1 (1979), p. 91-104.

EDDINS, Dwight. The Gnostic Pynchon. Bloomington 1990.

EHRMANN, Jacques. "The Death of Literature", in: FEDERMAN, R. (ed.). Surfiction, p. 229-254.

ELLIOTT, Robert C. The Shape of Utopia: Studies in a Literary Genre. Chicago 1970.

ENZENSBERGER, Hans M. (ed.). Kursbuch 14 (August 1968).

ESHBACH, Lloyd A. Of Worlds Beyond: The Science of Science Fiction Writing. Chicago 1964.

ETUDES ANGLAISES 50 (no ed.). Du fantastique à la science-fiction américaine. Paris 1973.

FABIAN, Bernhard (ed.). Ein anglistischer Grundkurs. Frankfurt [1]1971.

FEDERMAN, Raymond (ed.). Surfiction. Chicago 1975.

FIEDLER, Leslie A. "Cross the Border - Close that Gap: Post-Modernism", in: PÜTZ, Manfred/FREESE, Peter (edd.). Postmodernism in American Literature. A Critical Anthology. Darmstadt 1984, pp. 151-166.

FIEDLER, Leslie A. "The Divine Stupidity of Kurt Vonnegut", in: Esquire (September, 1970), p. 195-203.

FIEDLER, Leslie A. Waiting for the End. Harmondsworth 1967.

FINER, S.E. "Profile of Science Fiction", in: Sociological Review, N.S. 2 (December, 1964), p. 239-246.

FIORE, Robert L. "Critical Studies in Jorge Luis Borges", in: MFS 19 (1973/74), p. 475-480.

FLEISCHMANN, Wolfgang B. "Die 'Beat Generation' und ihre Nachwirkung", in: BUNGERT (ed.). Die amerikanische Literatur der Gegenwart, p. 80-89.

FOSTER, David William. "Borges and Structuralism: Toward an Implied Poetics", in: MFS 19 (1973/74), p. 341-351.

FRANK, Armin P. "Kurt Vonnegut", in: CHRISTADLER (ed.). Amerikanische Literatur der Gegenwart, p. 408-424.

FRANKLIN, H. Bruce. "Fictions of Science", in: Southern Review 3 (1967), p. 1036-1049.

FREEDMAN, William. "The Literary Motif: A Definition and Evaluation", in: Novel 4 (1971), N. 2, p. 123-131.

FREESE, Peter (ed.). Die amerikanische short story der Gegenwart. Interpretationen. Berlin 1976.

FREESE, Peter. "Kurt Vonnegut, The Sirens of Titan", in: HEUERMANN, Hartmut (ed.). Der Science-Fiction-Roman in der angloamerikanischen Literatur. Interpretationen. Düsseldorf 1986, pp. 196-219.

GERBER, Richard. Utopian Fantasy. New York 1973.

GODSHALK, William L. "Vonnegut and Shakespeare: Rosewater at Elsinore", in: Critique 15/2 (1973), p. 37-48.

GÖLLER, Karl Heinz/HOFFMANN, Gerhard. Die englische Kurzgeschichte. Düsseldorf 1973.

GOLDSMITH, David H. Kurt Vonnegut. Fantasist of Fire and Ice. Bowling Green 1972.

GRAAF, Vera. Homo Futurus. Eine Analyse der modernen Science Fiction. Hamburg 1971.

GREINER, Donald J. "Vonnegut's 'Slaughterhouse-Five' and the Fiction of Atrocity", in: Critique 14/3 (1973), p. 38-51.

GRIFFITHS, John. Three Tomorrows. American, British and Soviet Science Fiction. London 1980.

GUNN, James. "Science Fiction and the Mainstream", in: BRETNOR (ed.). Science Fiction today and tomorrow, p. 183-216.

HARRIS, Charles B. Contemporary American Novelists of the Absurd. New Haven 1971.

HASSAN, Ihab. The Postmodern Turn. Essays on Postmodern Theory and Culture. Columbus 1987.

HASSAN, Ihab. "The Subtracting Machine: The Work of William Burroughs", in: Critique 6/1 (1963/64), p. 4-23.

HASSELBLATT, Dieter. Grüne Männchen vom Mars. Science Fiction für Leser und Macher. Düsseldorf 1974.

HAY, George (ed.). The Disappearing Future. A Symposium of Speculation. London 1970.

HEINLEIN, Robert A. "Science Fiction: Its Nature, Faults and Virtues", in: DAVENPORT, (ed.). The Science Fiction Novel, p. 14-48.

HEUERMANN, Hartmut (ed.). Der Science-Fiction-Roman in der anglo-amerikanischen Literatur. Interpretationen. Düsseldorf 1986.

HIENGER, Jörg. Literarische Zukunftsphantastik: Eine Studie über Science Fiction. Göttingen 1972.

HIENGER, Jörg. "Abenteuer und Gedankenspiel. Gesichter der Science Fiction", in: RUCKTÄSCHEL/ZIMMERMANN (edd.). Trivialliteratur, p. 339-356.

HILLEGAS, Mark. The Future as Nightmare. H.G. Wells and the Anti-Utopians. New York 1967.

HILLEGAS, Mark. "The Course in Science Fiction: a hope deferred", in: Extrapolation, Dec., 1967.

HIRSCH, E.E. Validity in Interpretation. New Haven (1967) 1969.

HUME, David. "Enquiry concerning Human Understanding", in: HUME. Enquiries Concerning the Human Understanding and Concerning the Principles of Morals (ed. L.A. Selby-Bigge). Oxford (^{2}1901) 1963 (repr.).

ISER, Wolfgang. Der Akt des Lesens. Theorie ästhetischer Wirkung. München 1976.

ISER, Wolfgang. Der implizite Leser. Kommunikationsformen des Romans von Bunyan bis Beckett. München 1972.

JAKOBSON, Roman. "The Dominant", in: L. MATEJKA/K. POMORSKA (edd.). Readings in Russian Poetics, pp. 82-87.

JANNONE, Claudia. "Venus on the Half-Shell as Structuralist Activity", in: Extrapolation 17 (1976), p. 110-117.

JEHMLICH, Reimer/LÜCK, Hartmut (edd.). Die deformierte Zukunft. Untersuchungen zur Science Fiction. München 1974.

KAES, Anton/ZIMMERMANN, Bernhard (edd.). Literatur für viele 1+2. Beiheft zu LiLi. Göttingen 1975.

KAYSER, Wolfgang. Das Sprachliche Kunstwerk. Eine Einführung in die Literaturwissenschaft. Bern (^{1}1948) ^{10}1964.

KETTERER, David. New Worlds for Old. The Apocalyptic Imagination, Science Fiction and American Literature. New York 1974.

KETTERER, David. "Science Fiction and Allied Literature", in: SFS 3 (1976), p. 64-74.

KLEIN, Klaus-Peter. Zukunft zwischen Trauma und Mythos: Science-fiction. Zur Wirkungsästhetik, Sozialpsychologie und Didaktik eines literarischen Massenphänomens. Stuttgart 1976.

KLINKOWITZ, Jerome. "The Literary Career of Kurt Vonnegut, Jr.", in: MFS 19 (1973), p. 57-67.

KLINKOWITZ, Jerome. "Kurt Vonnegut, Jr., and the Crime of his Times", in: Critique 12/3 (1970/71), p. 38-53.

KLINKOWITZ, Jerome/SOMER, John (edd.). The Vonnegut Statement: Original Essays on the Life and Work of Kurt Vonnegut, Jr. New York 1973.

KNIGHT, Damon. In Search of Wonder: Essay on Modern Science Fiction. Chicago 1967.

KOHL, Stephan. Realismus: Theorie und Geschichte. München 1977.

KOLODNY, Anette/PETERS, Daniel James. "Pynchon's 'The Crying of Lot 49': The Novel as Subversive Experience", in: MFS 19 (1973/74), p. 79-81.

KORNBLUTH, C.M. "Failure of the Science Fiction Novel as Social Criticism", in: DAVENPORT (ed.). The Science Fiction Novel, p. 49-76.

KREUZER, Helmut (ed.). Literarische und naturwissenschaftliche Intelligenz. Dialog über die "zwei Kulturen". Stuttgart 1969.

KREUZER, Helmut (ed.). Literatur für viele (2 vols.). Studien zur Trivialliteratur und Massenkommunikation im 19. und 20. Jh. Göttingen 1976.

KREUZER, Helmut. "Trivialliteratur als Forschungsproblem". in: DVJS 41 (1967), p. 173-191.

KRUEGER, John R. "Language and Techniques of Communication as Theme and Tool in Science Fiction", in: Linguistics 39 (May 1968), p. 68-86.

LÄMMERT, Eberhard. Bauformen des Erzählens. Stuttgart ([1]1955) [2]1967.

LEFF, Leonard J. "Utopia Reconstructed: Alienation in Vonnegut's 'God Bless You Mr. Rosewater'", in: Critique 12/3 (1970-71), p. 29-37.

LEINER, Friedrich/GUTSCH, Jürgen. Science-fiction. Materialien und Hinweise. Frankfurt (1972) [2]1973 (Texte und Materialien zum Literaturunterricht).

LELAND, John P. "Pynchon's Linguistic Demon: 'The Crying of Lot 49'", in: Critique 16 (1974/75), p. 45-53.

LEM, Stanislaw. "Erotik und Sexualität in der Science Fiction", in: ROTTENSTEINER (ed.). Insel-Almanach auf das Jahr '72. p. 23-60.

LEM, Stanislaw. "On the Structural Analysis of Science Fiction", in: SFS 1 (1973/74), p. 26-33.

LEM, Stanislaw. "Roboter in der Science Fiction", in: BARMEYER (ed.). Science Fiction, p. 163-185.

LEM, Stanislaw. "Science Fiction: Ein hoffnungsloser Fall - mit Ausnahmen", in: ROTTENSTEINER (ed.). Polaris 1. Ein Science Fiction Almanach, p. 11-59.

LEM, Stanislaw. "The Time-Travel Story and Related Matters of SF Structuring", in: SFS 1 (1973/74), p. 143-154.

LEM, Stanislaw. "Todorov's Fantastic Theory of Literature", in: SFS 1 (1973/74), p. 227-237.

LEVINE, George/LEVERENZ, David (edd.). Mindful Pleasures. Essays on Thomas Pynchon. Boston 1976.

LE VOT, André. "The rocket and the pig: Thomas Pynchon and Science Fiction", in: Annales de l'Université de Toulouse. Caliban XII, N.S. 11 (1975), p. 111-118.

LEWIS, C.S. Of Other Worlds. Essays & Stories (ed. Walter HOOPER). New York 1966.

LEWIS, C.S./AMIS, Kingsley/ALDISS, Brian. "Unreal Estates. On Science Fiction", in: Encounter 24 (March, 1965), p. 61-65.

LOCKEMANN, Wolfgang. Lyrik-Epik-Dramatik - oder die totgesagte Trinität. Meisenheim 1973.

LODGE, David. "Objections to William Burroughs", in: Critical Quarterly 8 (1966), p. 203-212.

LORENZ, Konrad. Die Rückseite des Spiegels (1973). München 1977.

LOTMAN, Jurij M. Die Struktur literarischer Texte. München 1972.

LÜCK, Hartmut. Fantastik - Science Fiction - Utopie. Das Realismusproblem der utopisch-fantastischen Literatur. Gießen 1977.

LUNDWALL, Sam. SF: What it's all about. New York 1971.

LYON, Thomas E. "Borges and the (somewhat) Personal Narrator", in: MFS 19 (1973/74), p. 363- 372.

MANGEL, Anne. "Maxwell's Demon, Entropy, Information: 'The Crying of Lot 49'", in: LEVINE/LEVERENZ (edd.). Mindful Pleasures. Essays on Thomas Pynchon, p. 87-100.

MARCUSE, Herbert. "Aggressiveness in Advanced Industrial Society", in: Negations, p. 248-268.

MARCUSE, Herbert. Negations. Essays in Critical History. Boston 1968.

MARCUSE, Herbert. "Repressive Tolerance", in: WOLFF / MOORE / MARCUSE, A Critique of Pure Tolerance, p. 81-123.

MATEJKA, Ladislav/POMORSKA, Krystyna (edd.). Readings in Russian Poetics. Formalist and Structuralist Views. Michigan 1978.

MAURER, Karl. "Formen des Lesens", in: Poetica 9 (1977), p. 472-498.

MAY, John R. Toward a New World: Apocalypse in the American Novel. Notre Dame 1972.

MAY, John R. "Vonnegut's humor and the limits of hope", in: Twentieth Century Literature 18 (1972), p. 25-36.

McCLINTOCK, Michael William. Utopias and Dystopias. Cornell University 1970.

McGINNIS, Wane D. "The arbitrary cycle of 'Slaughterhouse-Five'. A relation of form to theme", in: Critique 17/1 (1975), p. 55-68.

McHALE, Brian. Postmodernist Fiction. New York 1987.

McLUHAN, Marshall. The Medium is the Message. New York 1967.

McNELLY, Willis E. "Vonnegut's 'Slaughterhouse-Five': Science Fiction as Objective Correlative", in: McNELLY / STOVER (edd.). Above the Human Landscape, p. 383-387.

McNELLY, Willis E./STOVER, Leon E. (edd.). Above the Human Landscape. A Social Science Fiction Anthology. Pacific Palisades 1972.

MEETER, Glenn. "Vonnegut's Formal and Moral Otherworldliness: 'Cat's Cradle' and 'Slaughterhouse-Five'" in: KLINKOWITZ / SOMER (edd.). The Vonnegut Statement, p. 204-220.

MESSENT, Peter B. "Breakfast of Champions: The direction of Kurt Vonnegut's fiction", in: Journal of American Studies 8 (1974), p. 101-114.

MITCHELL, Stephen O. "Alien Vision. The Technique of Science Fiction", in: NFS 4 (1958), p. 346-356.

MOORCOCK, Michael. "Eine neue Literatur", in: SCHECK (ed.). Koitus '80, p. 7-11.

MOSKOWITZ, Sam. Seekers of Tomorrow. New York 1967.

MOTTRAM, Eric. William Burroughs: the algebra of need. New York 1970.

MYERS, David. "Kurt Vonnegut, Jr.: Morality myth in the antinovel", in: The international fiction review 3 (1976), p. 52-56.

NAGL, Manfred. Science Fiction in Deutschland: Untersuchungen zur Genese, Soziographie und Ideologie der phantastischen Massenliteratur. Tübingen 1972.

NEWMAN, Robert. Understanding Thomas Pynchon. Columbia 1986.

NICHOLLS, Peter. "Science Fiction and the Mainstream: part 2. The Great Tradition of Proto Science Fiction", in: Foundation 5 (1976), p. 150-157.

NICOL, Charles. "Ballard and the Limits of Mainstream SF", in: SFS 3 (1976), p. 150-157.

NOLTING-HAUFF, Ilse. "Märchen und Märchenroman. Zur Beziehung zwischen einfachen Formen und narrativer Großform in der Literatur", in: Poetica 6 H. 2 (1974), p. 129-178 and H. 4 (1974), p. 417-455.

NUTZ, Walter. Der Trivialroman. Seine Formen und seine Hersteller. Ein Beitrag zur Literatursoziologie. Köln ([1]1962) [2]1966.

ODIER, Daniel. The Job. Interviews with William S. Burroughs. New York (1969) 1974.

OLDERMANN, Raymond M. Beyond the Waste Land. A Study of the American Novel in the Nineteen-Sixties. New Haven 1972.

PACKARD, Vance. Die große Versuchung. Eingriff in Körper und Seele. Düsseldorf 1978.

PANSHIN, Alexej & Cory. "Science Fiction - New Trends and Old", in: BRETNOR (ed.). Science Fiction Today and Tomorrow, p. 217-234.

PARRINDER, Patrick (ed.). Science Fiction. A Critical Guide. London 1979.

PAULY, Rebecca M. "The Moral Stance of Kurt Vonnegut", in: Extrapolation 15 (1973), p. 66-71.

PAWLING, Christopher (ed.). Popular Fiction and Social Change. New York 1984.

PEHLKE, Michael/LINGFELD, Norbert. Roboter und Gartenlaube: Ideologie und Unterhaltung in der Science Fiction-Literatur. München 1970.

PENZOLDT, Peter. The Supernatural in Fiction. New York 1965.

PETZOLD, D./SPÄTH, E. (edd.). Unterhaltungsliteratur. Ziele und Methoden ihrer Erforschung. Erlangen 1990.

PLANK, Robert. "Aliens in der Science Fiction", in: ETC. 11/1 (Autumn, 1953), p. 16-20.

PLANK, Robert. The Emotional Significance of Imaginary Beings. A Study of the Interaction Between Psychotherapy, Literature, and Reality in the Modern World. Springfield, Ill., 1968.

POE, Edgar Allan. Poems and Essays. London 1982 (repr.).

POENICKE, Klaus. "William Burroughs", in: CHRISTADLER (ed.). Amerikanische Literatur der Gegenwart, p. 268-298.

PROPP, Vladimir. Morphologie des Märchens (transl. by K. Eimermacher). München 1972.

PÜTZ, Manfred. "Who am I this time: Die Romane von Kurt Vonnegut", in: Jahrbuch für Amerikastudien 19 (1974), p. 111-125.

PÜTZ, Manfred/FREESE, Peter (edd.). Postmodernism in American Literature. A Critical Anthology. Darmstadt 1984.

REED, Peter J. Kurt Vonnegut, Jr., New York (1972) 1974.

RINGGUTH, Rudolf. "Wissenschaft ohne Wirklichkeit?", in: Der Spiegel, Nr. 8 (1978), p. 186-190.

ROBBE-GRILLET, Alain. Pour un Nouveau Roman. Paris 1963.

ROSE, Mark (ed.). Science Fiction. A Collection of Critical Essays. Englewood Cliffs 1976. (Twentieth Century Views).

ROTTENSTEINER, Franz. "Erneuerung und Beharrung in der Science Fiction", in: BARMEYER (ed.). Science Fiction, p. 340-364.

ROTTENSTEINER, Franz (ed.). Pfade ins Unendliche. Insel-Almanach auf das Jahr 1972. Frankfurt 1971.

ROTTENSTEINER, Franz (ed.). Polaris 1. Ein Science Fiction Almanach. Frankfurt 1973.

ROTTENSTEINER, Franz. "Science Fiction - eine Einführung", in: ROTTENSTEINER (ed.). Pfade ins Unendliche, p. 5-21.

ROTTENSTEINER, Franz. The Science Fiction Book: An Illustrated History. London 1975.

ROTTENSTEINER, Franz/BLISH, James/LeGUIN, Ursula/FRANKLIN, H. Bruce/DAVIS, Charles. "Change, Science Fiction, and Marxism: Open or Closed Universes?", in: SFS 1, p. 84-94.

RUCKTÄSCHEL, Annamaria/ZIMMERMANN, Hans-Dieter (edd.). Trivialliteratur. München 1976.

RUSS, Joanna. "Towards an Aesthetic of Science Fiction", in: SFS 2, p. 112-119.

RUTTKOWSKI, Wolfgang Victor. Die Literarischen Gattungen. Reflexionen über eine modifizierte Fundamentalpoetik. Bern 1968.

SCORTIA, Thomas N. "Science Fiction as the Imaginary Experiment", in: BRETNOR (ed.). Science Fiction Today and Tomorrow, p. 135-149.

SEEBER, Hans-Ulrich. Wandlungen der Form in der literarischen Utopie. Studien zur Entfaltung des utopischen Romans in England. Göppingen 1970.

SILVERBERG, Robert (ed.). The Mirror of Infinity: A critic's anthology of science fiction. Dayton, Ohio, 1972.

SKINNER, B.F. Futurum zwei. "Walden Two". Die Vision einer aggressionsfreien Gesellschaft. Hamburg 1972. (engl. New York 1948).

ŠKLOVSKIJ, Viktor. "Der parodistische Roman. Sternes "Tristram Shandy", in: STRIEDTER, Jurij (ed.). Russischer Formalismus, p. 245-299.

ŠKLOVSKIJ, Viktor. Theorie der Prosa (transl. by Gisela Drohla). Frankfurt 1966.

ŠKLOVSKIJ, Viktor. "Der Zusammenhang zwischen den Verfahren der Sujet-fügung und den allgemeinen Stilverfahren, in: J. STRIEDTER (ed.). Russischer Formalismus. München 1969, p. 37-121.

SLADE, Joseph W. Thomas Pynchon. New York 1974.

SMUDA, Manfred. "Variation und Innovation. Modelle literarischer Möglich-keiten in der Nachfolge Edgar Allan Poes", in: Poetica 3 (1970), p. 165-187.

SNOW, C.P. The Two Cultures and A Second Look. Cambridge (1965) 1967.

SOMER, John. "Geodesic Vonnegut; or, If Buckminster Fuller Wrote Novels", in: KLINKOWITZ/SOMER (edd.). The Vonnegut Statement, p. 221-254.

DER SPIEGEL, Nr. 6 (1978). "Science Fiction - Flucht ins Weltall", p. 158-171.

SPRIEL, Stéphane/VIAN, Boris. "Un nouveau genre littéraire: La science fic-tion", in: Les Temps Modernes 7 (1951/52), p. 618-627.

STRELKA, Joseph P. (ed.). Theories of Literary Genre. London 1978.

SUERBAUM, Ulrich. Krimi. Eine Analyse der Gattung. Stuttgart 1984.

SUERBAUM, Ulrich. "Der gefesselte Detektivroman. Ein gattungstheoreti-scher Versuch", in: Poetica 1 H. 3 (1967), p. 360-374.

SUERBAUM, Ulrich. "Text und Gattung", in: B. FABIAN (ed.). Ein anglisti-scher Grundkurs. Frankfurt 1971, p. 104-132.

SUERBAUM, Ulrich. "Brunner. The Windows of Heaven", in: GÖLLER, K.H./ HOFFMANN B. (edd.). Die englische Kurzgeschichte. Düsseldorf 1973, p. 337-348.

SUERBAUM, Ulrich. Science Fiction. Studienbrief. Deutsches Institut für Fernstudien an der Universität Tübingen. Tübingen 1978.

SUERBAUM, Ulrich. in: SUERBAUM, Ulrich/BROICH, Ulrich/ BORGMEIER, Raimund. Science Fiction. Theorie und Geschichte, Themen und Typen, Form und Weltbild. Stuttgart 1981.

SUKENICK, Ronald. The Death of the Novel and Other Stories (1960). New York 1969.

SUVIN, Darko. Metamorphoses of Science Fiction. On the Poetics and History of a Literary Genre. New Haven 1979.

SUVIN, Darko. "On the Poetics of the Science Fiction Genre", in: College English 34 (1973), p. 372-382.

SUVIN, Darko. "Stanislaw Lem und das mitteleuropäische soziale Bewußtsein der Science-fiction", in: BERTHEL (ed.). Insel-Almanach auf das Jahr 1976, p. 157-171.

SUVIN, Darko. "Zur Poetik des literarischen Genres Science Fiction", in: BARMEYER (ed.). Science Fiction, p. 86-104.

SZPAKOWSKA, Malgorzata. "Die Flucht Stanislaw Lems", in: BARMEYER (ed.). Science Fiction, p. 293-303.

SZPAKOWSKA, Malgorzata. "Vom Weissagen aus dem Kaffeesatz und der moralischen Verantwortung", in: ROTTENSTEINER (ed.). Polaris 1, p. 89-96.

SCHÄFER, Martin. Science Fiction als Ideologiekritik? Utopische Spuren in der amerikanischen Science Fiction-Literatur 1940-1955. Stuttgart 1977.

SCHATT, Stanley. "The World of Kurt Vonnegut, Jr.", in: Critique 12/3 (1970/71), p. 54-69.

SCHATT, Stanley. Kurt Vonnegut, Jr., Boston 1976.

SCHECK, Frank Rainer (ed.). Koitus 80. Neue Science Fiction. Köln 1970.

SCHIFFER, Reinhold. "Modern Writers: Saul Bellow", in: Praxis des Neusprachlichen Unterrichts 19 (no. 1, 1972), p. 58-62.

SCHLEUSSNER, Bruno. "'Science Fiction' als Gegenstand der Literaturwissenschaft - 'Science Fiction' im Fremdsprachenunterricht", in: LWU 8/2 (1975), p. 72-83.

SCHMIDT-HENKEL, Gerhard u.a. (edd.). Trivialliteratur. Literarisches Colloquium. Berlin 1964.

SCHOLES, Robert. The Fabulators. New York 1967.

SCHOLES, Robert. Structural Fabulation. An Essay on the Fiction of the Future. Notre Dame 1975.

SCHOLES, Robert. Structuralism in Literature. An Introduction. New Haven [2]1974.

SCHOLES, Robert/RABKIN, Eric S. Science Fiction - History, Science, Vision. London 1977.

SCHRÖDER, Horst. Science Fiction Literatur in den USA. Vorstudien für eine materialistische Paraliteraturwissenschaft. Gießen 1978.

SCHULTE-HERBRÜGGEN, Hubertus. Utopie und Anti-Utopie. Von der Strukturanalyse zur Strukturtypologie. Bochum 1960.

SCHULTE-SASSE, Jochen. Trivialliteratur-Kritik seit der Aufklärung. Stuttgart 1971.

SCHULTE-SASSE, Jochen. "Karl Mays Amerika-Exotik und deutsche Wirklichkeit", in: KAES, Anton/ZIMMERMANN, Bernhard (edd.). Literatur für viele 1+2. Beiheft zu LiLi. Göttingen 1975.

SCHULZ, Franz. "'Slaughterhouse-Five'", in: BUSCH, Frieder / SCHMITT-V.-BARDELEBEN, Renate (edd.). Amerikanische Erzählliteratur 1950-70, p. 155-169.

SCHULZ, Max F. Black Humor Fiction of the Sixties. Athens, Ohio, 1980 ([1]1973).

SCHULZ, Max F. "The Unconfirmed Thesis: Kurt Vonnegut, Black Humor, and Contemporary Art", in: Critique 12/3 (1970/71), p. 5-28.

SCHWARTZ, Sheila. "Science Fiction: Bridge Between the Two Cultures", in: English Journal 60/1971 H. 8, p. 1043-1051.

SCHWONKE, Martin. "Naturwissenschaft und Technik im utopischen Denken der Neuzeit", in: BARMEYER (ed.). Science Fiction, p. 57-75.

SCHWONKE, Martin. Vom Staatsroman zur Science Fiction: Eine Untersuchung über Geschichte und Funktion der naturwissenschaftlich-technischen Utopie. Stuttgart 1957.

STRIEDTER, Jurij (ed.). Russischer Formalismus. München ([1]1969) 1971.

TANNER, Tony. Saul Bellow. Edinburgh 1965 (Writers and Critics).

TANNER, Tony. City of Words. American Fiction 1950-1970. New York 1971.

TODD, Richard. "The Masks of Kurt Vonnegut, Jr.", in: New York Times Magazine (January, 24, 1971), p. 16-30.

TODOROV, Tzvetan. Einführung in die fantastische Literatur. München 1972 (French 1970).

TODOROV, Tzvetan. Genres in Discourse. Cambridge 1990 (French 1978).

TUCK, Donald H. The Encyclopedia of Science Fiction and Fantasy (through 1968), vol. I, "Who's Who", A-L. Chicago 1974.

TYNJANOV, Jurij. "Das literarische Faktum", in: STRIEDTER (ed.). Russischer Formalismus. München ([1]1969) 1971, p. 393-431.

TYNJANOV, Jurij. "Über die literarische Evolution", in: STRIEDTER (ed.). Russischer Formalismus. München (1969) [1]1971, p. 434-461.

VERNIER, Jean-Pierre. "La science-fiction. Problèmes de définition", in: Du fantastique à la science-fiction. Etudes Anglaises 50, p. 53-60.

VOM SCHEIDT, Jürgen. "Tiefenpsychologische Aspekte der Science Fiction", in: BARMEYER (ed.). Science Fiction, p. 133-162.

VOLEK, Emil. "Die Begriffe 'Fabel' und 'Sujet' in der modernen Literaturwissenschaft. Zur Struktur der 'Erzählstruktur'", in: Poetica 9 (1977), p. 141-166.

VONNEGUT, Kurt. "Science Fiction", in: VONNEGUT, Wampeters, Foma & Granfalloons, p. 1-5.

VONNEGUT, Kurt. Wampeters, Foma & Granfalloons: Opinions of Kurt Vonnegut, Jr. New York 1974.

WALDMANN, Günter. Theorie und Didaktik der Trivialliteratur. Modellanalysen - Didaktikdiskussion- literarische Wertung. München 1973.

WARRICK, Patricia S. The Cybernetic Imagination in Science Fiction. Cambridge, Mass., 1980.

WEINBERG, Steven. Die ersten drei Minuten. Der Ursprung des Universums. München ([1]1979) 1980 (Engl.: The First Three Minutes: A Modern view of the Origin of the Universe. 1976).

WELLECK, René/WARREN, A. Theory of Literature. ([1]1949) 1963.

WESSELS, Dieter. Welt im Chaos. Struktur und Funktion des Weltkatastrophenmotivs in der neueren Science Fiction. Frankfurt 1974.

Von WILPERT, Gero. Sachwörterbuch der Literatur. Stuttgart [4]1964.

255

WOLFE, Gary K. "The Limits of Science Fiction", in: Extrapolation 14 (1972), p. 30-38.

WOLFF, R.P./MOORE, B. Jr./MARCUSE, H. A Critique of Pure Tolerance. Boston 1965.

WOLLHEIM, Donald A. The Universe Makers: Science Fiction Today. New York 1971.

WOOD, Karen & Charles. "The Vonnegut Effect: Science Fiction and beyond", in: KLINKOWITZ/SOMER (edd.). The Vonnegut Statement, p. 133-157.

INDEX

W
Warrick, 23, 24, 93
Wells, 24, 33, 92, 105
Woolf, 106

Wyndham, 104

Z
Zelazny, 25, 146, 224